Just A Child

BRITAIN'S BIGGEST CHILD ABUSE SCANDAL EXPOSED

The Rotherham whistleblower tells
her shocking true story

SAMMY WOODHOUSE

WITH RACHEL MURPHY

BLINK

bringing you closer

Published by Blink Publishing
2.25, The Plaza,
535 Kings Road,
Chelsea Harbour,
London, SW10 0SZ

www.blinkpublishing.co.uk

facebook.com/blinkpublishing
twitter.com/blinkpublishing

Paperback – 978-1-788-700-07-8
Ebook – 978-1-788-700-08-5

A CIP catalogue of this book is available from the British Library.

Typeset by seagulls.net
Printed and bound by Clays Ltd, St. Ives Plc

1 3 5 7 9 10 8 6 4 2

Sammy Woodh[...] [...]or of this
Work in a[...] [...]88.

This book is a [...] [...]llections
of Sammy [...] [...]laces
and da[...]

Every [...] [...]f
materia[...] [...]y
ove[...]

Blink [...]

In loving memory of Brooker

'Our lives begin to end the day we become silent about things that matter.'

Martin Luther King, Jr.

Contents

Prologue

It has been very hard to put myself back into the shoes of the trusting child I once was, but that's what I have tried to do in order to tell my story. I want to describe events as I lived through them as a girl, when I was too young to spot the dangers or see through the lies, and when I had none of the adult wisdom and insight I possess now.

You may be shocked, incredulous even, at just how easy I was to exploit. I can scarcely believe it myself, and there have been many times during the writing of this book when I have thought *this doesn't make any sense – how could I have been so gullible?*

The answer is simple: I wasn't an adult then; I was a very vulnerable and impressionable child.

Most of us forget exactly how we thought and felt as a child, and don't understand how our developing minds worked, but unfortunately those who groom children do not. They are masters at getting inside a child's head and finding out what makes them tick, and they know exactly how to abuse that knowledge for their own gratification, stealing childhoods and wrecking lives as they go.

I know all this now, but it took me many years to grasp the truth, and to even begin to recognise I was groomed.

I exposed the child sexual exploitation scandal in Rotherham by talking to *The Times* newspaper in 2013, when I felt nobody else would listen. This triggered the opening of every so-called 'historic' case of child sexual exploitation (CSE) in South Yorkshire and prompted the Jay Report, which identified at least 1,400 victims in the town and shone a spotlight on the appalling scale of child grooming across the UK.

In February 2016 I saw my abuser, Arshid Hussain, jailed for 35 years. He was the ringleader of a gang who groomed and sexually abused me and many other underage girls over a 16-year period. I told the court my life was shattered into a million pieces and that I felt I was held together by sticky tape.

It's too late to recapture my childhood and my twenties – I am 32 now – but today I work with the police, schools, the NHS and many other key agencies to help prevent more children from becoming victims, and to help other survivors move on.

I have suffered not only sexual abuse, but psychological abuse too. If I seem dispassionate about some of my recollections that's because I was groomed to believe that feeling perpetually frightened and unhappy was normal. I suppressed my emotions as a method of surviving, and to this day I am still learning how to express myself in the way most people take for granted. Some of the things that happened to me were so terrifying that professionals believe my brain stopped processing them. I pulled the mental shutters down when it became too much for my young mind to take, and many of my memories are buried deep, or lost.

At the trial, I was referred to as Girl J, and in the past I have used the pseudonym Jessica in the media, but it's time to leave that child in the past. My new life started on the day my abuser went to jail.

I am Sammy Woodhouse, and this is my story.

Chapter 1
'I told you that you were beautiful!'

'And the winner of our Little Miss Princess competition 1991 is … Samantha Woodhouse!'

Mum cheered and started shouting loudly from the audience: 'That's my babby! Well done, our Sammy! I'm right proud of you!'

I beamed as two grinning compères placed a silver tiara on top of my blonde curls, a satin sash across my white and pink dress and presented me with a handmade sign that said '1st' in thick black felt tip pen.

I had just turned six years old and had beaten off competition from scores of other little girls at the caravan park in Cleethorpes we stayed at every summer.

'I told you that you were beautiful!' Mum exclaimed, buzzing with happiness. 'Come here, my princess, let me give you a great big hug and a kiss.'

My mum Julie and dad Melvin always made me feel special, and from as far back as I can remember Mum told me I was a little star and that I could achieve anything I wanted.

My parents were childhood sweethearts, born and bred in Rotherham, and they both worked hard and doted on my two older sisters and me. Our Kate was 11 years older than me, but there was just 15 months between me and our Lisa. The age gaps meant I was a lot closer to Lisa than I was to Kate, and even in my earliest childhood memories Kate is already a very grown-up teenager, doing her own thing. I can't remember ever having much in common with our Kate, but it was different with Lisa. We both loved to dance, and we'd make up routines together and practise our dances at every opportunity.

'Sammy, your tea's ready, love,' Mum would call.

'Can I eat it in here? I'm practising.'

Mum would roll her eyes but always let me have my tea wherever it suited me, and I'd often end up doing the splits and eating my fish fingers and chips at the same time.

'What's going on?' Dad would say if he saw me eating food in the front room, music blaring. My dad's nickname for my mum was Brooker, while everybody called my dad Peck. 'What's happening, Brooker?' he'd say. 'Sammy should be sitting at the kitchen table!'

Mum would defend me, as she always did. 'She's all right, Peck, she's practising!'

Dad would grumble that Mum was too soft with us. Mum hardly ever told Lisa or me off and left all the disciplining to Dad, who was strict but generally very fair. I adored them both equally.

Dad had a painting and decorating business before I came along, which was named after Kate and Lisa. I was jealous of this, apparently, and had a face on me when I found out about it.

'We've got a surprise for you, Sammy,' Mum and Dad announced one day. 'Come and see.'

I was four years old but I remember the day clearly. Dad had bought a 'pool' club, they said, explaining that pool was a game you played on a table with cues and balls.

As we pulled up outside in Dad's car, they made me close my eyes. I got out of the car and stood on the pavement, scrunching my eyes tight shut. Then Dad took me in his arms and said, 'Look up, Sammy!' I opened my eyes and squealed in delight. My name was lit up in bright yellow squiggly lights. He'd named the club after me! I was beyond thrilled – this was the most exciting thing that had ever happened to me! I gave my mum and dad a great big hug each and told them I loved it.

Mum and Dad both worked in the club every Saturday night and they'd ask Kate to babysit me and Lisa at home.

'Here's a tenner,' Mum would say, giving instructions for Kate to order a takeaway. Being a typical teenager, Kate didn't always do as she was told, and one time I can remember me and Lisa eating cold sprouts out of the fridge while Kate partied in the house with her mates. She wanted to be out instead of babysitting her two little sisters, but Kate's attitude was that if she couldn't go to the party, the party would come to her. In the end, our parents started taking me and our Lisa to the club with them on a Saturday night instead, which everybody was happy about.

I absolutely loved being at the club. Dad ran it as a lively bar and entertainment venue as well as a pool club and most of the people who came in were friends, family or neighbours. I'd get up on the stage and do my latest dance routine, and then go round the audience with an empty pint pot, collecting tips. Everyone was really nice and I'd always get a glass full of pennies and be absolutely thrilled to bits. Often the night ended with Uncle Gary and me on stage.

'Will you come on the stage and sing, Uncle Gary?' I'd ask him, because I was never any good at singing.

'Course I will,' he'd smile.

'My Girl' by the Temptations was always the song he chose, and I'd sit on the stage swaying to the music as he sang, lapping up the attention of the audience. The mic was huge in my little hand but I loved holding it and dreaming of being a big star on a famous stage one day. I'd dance to Bob Marley too, because Dad loved his music and I thought it was cool.

We lived in a small three-bedroom, terraced house, which was on a close-knit estate. It was a council estate but a lot of people owned their homes, as we did. Dad made a Wendy house for me and Lisa in the garden, and I'd spend hours out there, often prancing around in a shiny, green bridesmaid dress I'd worn for a relative's wedding. It made me feel like I was a princess, and the Wendy house was my castle.

Our estate was full of kids and it was a lively and fun community to grow up in. When the weather was nice all the mums sat at the back of the houses keeping an eye on the big field, where all the kids played. I loved it best when we all had a game of rounders. We'd use two trees as first and second bases and then put a jumper or a shoe down to make bases three and four. When it was our Lisa's turn, Mum would shout: 'Go on, babby! Slog it! You can do it!'

Lisa would smack the ball with the bat as hard as she could and set off running, but she would only ever get as far as third base before the ball came back from a fielder and she had to stop. Then she'd throw a tantrum, chuck the bat on the floor and storm off into the house.

'I wanted a rounder!' she'd wail, pulling a miserable face.

Five minutes later she'd be back, and when it was her next turn she'd usually repeat the whole performance.

The playing field belonged to my primary school. I started there when I was four and I couldn't wait, because I always wanted to do whatever Lisa was doing. I was as proud as anything when I finally got to be dropped off in my classroom in the morning by Mum, just like our Lisa.

On my very first morning I sat next to a girl called Sophie. I liked the look of her and so I asked her outright: 'Will you be my best friend?' Sophie asked me the same question, at exactly the same time. We both started giggling.

'Yes, forever,' we pledged in unison.

From that day on we were inseparable.

I wasn't particularly interested in most things I was being taught at school because even at that young age all I wanted to do was dance, not do sums and writing. I liked PE and drama, and if there was a school play I always got a part and loved it, but mostly I lived for playtime. I'd be in my element, dancing around the playground, or making up silly games and having fun with the other girls, and especially Sophie.

My parents and Sophie's soon became good friends and they took it in turns to do stuff with us after school and in the holidays. My mum in particular had a reputation for laying on great entertainment. Our house was like a youth club in the holidays, with loads of kids running in and out and Mum dishing out drinks and snacks. Despite working various jobs, including hairdressing, shifts in a factory and helping my dad run the club, she always made time for us. The school holidays were packed with trips out to the park or ice-skating, bowling and the cinema.

Camping in the garden was one of my favourite things about the summer. Mum and Dad would let me and Lisa put a tent up when the weather was good and sleep out with our friends. They'd leave the back door open so we could come in and use the toilet, and when it went dark we'd take turns to shine the torch under our chin and tell scary stories. We'd try to stay awake for as long as we could, so we could have a midnight feast. We were allowed loads of sleepovers too, and me and our Lisa would invite our best friends from school and the neighbourhood. I had loads of friends. I took after my mum like that, and I always liked to be busy, and not on my own.

'I'm joining in with you!' Mum would say at the sleepover parties. 'What video are you watching, girls? Ooh, I love that one! Is that the *Spice Girls*? Is this how it goes?' She'd be up dancing. I'd groan and roll my eyes, telling her she was embarrassing, but really, I was very proud of her and thought she was a right laugh. She was the life and soul of the party, and in a lot of ways she was more like my best friend than my mum.

Dad was a massive Man United fan and he'd take me and our Lisa to the match, kitted out in scarves and red football shirts. He wanted us to share his passion, and he was always buzzing and telling us stories about the team and how he had supported them through thick and thin. We had posters of lots of the players on our bedroom walls at home, and it made me happy to know how much this meant to Dad. He was a family man through and through, and Mum, me, Lisa and our Kate were his world. I adored him.

Chapter 2

'I'm going to be a famous dancer one day'

'Come and have a look at my new dance routine!'

Me and our Lisa went to a youth club every Friday night and I nagged the youth worker there something rotten.

'Just give me a minute, love,' she'd say.

I was about eight or nine years old by now and absolutely obsessed with dancing. I'd been to all kinds of classes in church halls and community centres throughout my primary school years and loved every dance going, whether it was ballet and tap, modern or disco.

'I'm going to be a famous dancer one day,' I'd tell anyone who'd listen. I'd be glued to all the dancers I saw on Saturday night telly, or on *Top of the Pops* or Nickelodeon. I was fascinated not only by their steps and moves but also their clothes and hair and make-up. Dancers were the most amazing people in the world as far as I was concerned, and I couldn't think of anything more exciting than being in the spotlight, all eyes on me. I was very dainty, bouncing around with boundless energy, and people remarked how small I was for my age. I couldn't wait to be all grown up.

The whole time I was at the youth club I never stopped doing the splits, pirouetting or showing off my best disco moves. It was exhausting to watch, apparently, but I never wanted to stop.

When I was about ten my dad's club went bankrupt. I didn't know the club had been in financial difficulties until it was being shut down. I was too young to understand, and in any case my dad was a very private person who wasn't one to ever share personal information or talk about his feelings. He was the polar opposite of my mum, and he kept himself very much in check at all times. Dad was teetotal, unlike my mum. She loved a drink, and she always let her hair down at a party. Dad didn't mind at all; he was very proud of her and they loved each other to bits.

While he had the club, Dad had kept his painting and decorating firm going on the side – the one that was named after our Kate and Lisa – and now the plan was that he was going to revamp the business and take on some contract work in Germany, where the money was good. This meant he'd be away from home for weeks or even months at a time. I don't remember this bothering me, or feeling it was even an issue. There was no question of my mum feeling she'd been left on her own to cope either. She had a good support network with all her friends, and we had my grandmother living nearby, who I was close to and called 'Nanan', as well as lots of aunties and uncles and other family members.

I loved Nanan so much. She is my dad's mum and has a heart of gold. She often took me and our Lisa to the caravan park at Cleethorpes for a little break, along with our cousins. The site had tennis courts and a swimming pool. Lisa and I absolutely loved swimming and would spend all day in the water, and then we'd get changed, have our tea, drink lemonade in the clubhouse and dance all night.

The first Christmas after the club was shut down, Mum warned us that money was tighter than normal and we were not to expect a lot. I was gutted. Lisa and I had both desperately wanted a Cabbage Patch Doll, which were all the rage at the time, but also very expensive. We had no chance now, but what could we do? Mum and Dad didn't have the money, and that was the end of it.

When Christmas morning came, we ripped open our presents, only to find that our main gift was a set of bed sheets each. Worse still, they were green and purple striped and absolutely awful.

'Hang on,' Dad said eventually, once all our presents were open. 'Didn't we have something else for these two … ?'

I looked up to see that Mum and Dad had the same expressions on their faces they'd had on the night they took me to see my name up in lights at the club.

'Ta-dah!' Mum said as they pulled out a couple of carefully wrapped parcels. Lisa and I tore into them. We'd each got a Cabbage Patch Doll after all, and we jumped up and down and squealed our heads off. Dad had managed to buy them in Germany as they were very hard to get hold of in the UK.

The following year I started at secondary school, where practically all of my friends went too – including my best friend Sophie, so I couldn't wait to get started.

We never had a uniform at primary school and I can remember being right happy with my new blue skirt, white polo shirt and blue jumper. Mum took a photo of me on my first day, standing in our living room, smiling. I was 11 years old and full of hope and expectation. It felt like I was growing up and catching up with our Lisa, and I was chuffed to bits.

I still wasn't particularly interested in learning. I'd done really well at primary school and the teachers would tell my mum I was bright and had lots of potential, but academic work never interested me. I was still focused on the big prize: dancing. That was what I was going to do when I left school. I continued to put a lot of effort into PE and drama, and I was quite keen on art, but not much else caught my imagination in the classroom.

I hadn't been at school for long when Sophie asked if I fancied auditioning for a local dance team that her cousin was in. The team was called Diamonds and was part of Diane Benny's British Aerobic Championship Squad, which was very successful and well known in dancing circles.

'I'd love to do that!' I exclaimed. 'Oh my God, that would be so amazing!'

We both went along for auditions and I got into the team, while Sophie was placed on the reserve list.

My mum jumped in the air when she heard the news. 'You did it! My babby did it! I'm right proud of you!'

We did some form of training every single night after school, whether it was step aerobics, Callanetics, fitness training or practising a routine for a show or competition. I absolutely loved it. Diane was a fantastic teacher and coach and she thought outside the box when it came to choreography and choosing the music. One of the tracks we often used to dance to in competitions was Céline Dion's 'River Deep, Mountain High', and another was the Contours' 'Do You Love Me?' from *Dirty Dancing*. We'd practise like mad to make sure our routines were absolutely flawless, and ensured we looked immaculate every time we stepped on the dance floor or stage.

I loved competing. Before a big contest we'd all meet at Diane's house really early in the morning. We had to have a full slap of make-up applied by a professional make-up artist, complete with red lipstick, thick mascara and pink blusher, and then we'd have our hair scraped back into the tightest buns ever, tied in nets and set with what seemed like a full tin of hairspray each. The whole team would be dressed in matching grey sweatshirts and jogging bottoms emblazoned with the squad's logo, and we had our own coach and driver to take us to venues all around the country.

As soon as we got on the coach the excitement would be racked up another notch. We'd all be singing songs and chanting, even if it was only 6 a.m., and on the way, we'd eat bananas or Mars Bars, as they were the only foods permitted before competitions. The moment we arrived at a venue we'd be in 'competition mode', which meant we'd size up the other teams and wouldn't talk to anybody but each other. Our outfits were really extravagant and had to be absolutely perfect, every single time. They cost my parents an absolute fortune, but Mum and Dad always found the money.

Our best competition outfit was a yellow and green high-necked leotard that Diane had designed, complete with a flesh-coloured, see-through diamond section cut out in the middle and loads of diamanté and silver sequins. To complete our look, we wore shimmer tights that were so dark they made your skin look orange, layered with bright white socks, scrunched down on top of our special dance trainers.

We won gold nearly every time, and being presented with medals was the best feeling in the world. Everything was so exciting, and I loved the adrenaline rush I felt when the music started and all eyes were on me and my teammates.

Mum, Lisa and Nanan nearly always came to support me, following in the car while I was on the coach, even if we'd be out all day, travelling for hours on end. 'Do I need my passport?'

Mum once joked when we went to Cardiff, as she'd never been to Wales before.

I was excited even if we competed somewhere closer to home, like the Pink Coconut Nightclub in Derby. Being only 11, it was always a thrill to go into an exciting, grown-up venue like that, and I felt like I was getting closer to my dream of being a professional dancer one day. My ambition was fired up even more when we performed at a nightclub called Zone in Rotherham, and a presenter from Nickelodeon came to interview us. Our photo was in the local paper and I was so proud of myself and all the team. Then we were invited to Tokyo to take part in a big dance competition, where we would be representing Britain. We didn't actually get there, as the invitation came through at short notice and several of the girls didn't have passports. I was gutted, but once I'd got over the disappointment I told myself I'd have so many other opportunities to travel the world, so it didn't matter.

I was living and breathing dancing. I didn't care about anything else, and I was going to make it to the very top.

Chapter 3

'We'll see who's around, see what happens'

'Sammy, we need to have a talk,' Dad said, with a serious look on his face.

I thought he was going to tell me off about my behaviour in school, as I'd become slightly mischievous. I don't know if it was because I was doing so well with my dancing and thought I had my future all mapped out, but I'd become a bit too full of myself.

Mum would never hear a bad word about me, and when the teachers mentioned this at parents' evening she defended me fiercely, claiming I was just a 'confident girl' who was 'bubbly' and 'naturally lively'. Dad wasn't so soft. The A grades I normally got were slipping because I wasn't paying enough attention in certain subjects, and he wasn't going to sit back and let this happen.

'What do we need to talk about?' I asked Dad nervously.

'Me and your mum have decided to pull you from the dance squad. You can still go training, but you're not taking part in any more competitions until your grades improve.'

He explained that it would only be a temporary measure, provided I pulled my socks up at school.

Gutted isn't the word; I was absolutely devastated. Dancing was my life. My parents knew this and thought that taking away my favourite thing of all – the competitions – would be the biggest incentive to do well at school they could possibly give me.

'You can't do that!' I protested. 'It's not fair at all. Dancing is all I'm interested in!'

'That's the problem, Sammy. You're 11 years old and in your first year of secondary school. You have to work hard and you have to take school seriously.'

'But why? I'm not interested in hardly any of the subjects. The only lesson I really like is PE.'

'Well, a GCSE in PE is not going to get you a job, is it?'

'I don't want a boring old job. I don't want to work in an office or a bank. I just want to dance! Pleeeease! How can you do this to me?'

'Look, Sammy love, I'm not saying this is forever. You need to get yourself back on track and we'll talk again.'

I ran to my bedroom, slammed the door and burst into tears. This was so unfair. Even Mum didn't jump to my defence this time. When I confronted her later that day she sided with Dad. 'He's right, love. We don't want to stop you dancing altogether, but you've got to get the balance right.'

I felt like screaming. My whole world had come tumbling down.

Worse news soon followed. Shortly after I stopped competing, Diane, our dance manager, had to stop teaching for a while, due to ill health. The Diamonds had scooped every gold medal and winners' trophy going, and before long Diane decided to quit while she was ahead, and the team folded.

There wasn't another team like ours locally, and so even when my grades improved I didn't go back to dancing. It slipped away, just like that. By the time I was 12, I wasn't dancing at all, not even at home.

Finding myself with nothing to do in the evenings and weekends wasn't easy. For so long all my spare time outside of school had been filled with intense exercise, dance training and competitions. I didn't just miss the dancing itself, but also the camaraderie I shared with the other girls, dressing up, the fun of having my hair and make-up done, and the excitement of travelling on the coach. My parents had my best interests at heart, but their decision to pull me from competitions had backfired. I was lost and miserable and didn't know what to do with myself.

'Come on, Sammy, pick yourself up,' Mum said when she found me moping around the house. 'Why don't you go out for a bit?'

'Where? There's nowt to do.'

'Why don't you see some of your friends from school?'

I was at that awkward stage when I was too old to be playing out or having friends over for tea, but too young to go out and do something by myself. There was nothing to do within walking distance of our house, the buses were rubbish, and so it was down to me to make my own entertainment, but how?

Eventually, my best friend Sophie solved the problem when she asked if I fancied meeting her one night, after we'd been home from school and had our tea.

'OK then. Where shall we go?'

'We could sit on the bench across from the shop.'

'All right. Er, then what?'

'We'll see who's around, see what happens. We'll have a laugh.'

I knew a lot of the kids from school and from our estate – including my sister Lisa – hung around this little supermarket at the bottom of our hill. A small parade of shops was another local haunt.

Now it was my turn to be one of the big girls, and I felt quite excited. I got changed out of my school uniform and put on a pair of jeans Sophie had lent me, some big wedge shoes, a blue cotton Ben Sherman shirt I pinched from my sister's wardrobe, and a puffy Kappa jacket. Me and Sophie walked down to the bench and sat ourselves down together. We'd been best friends for eight years by this time and were so close we often talked about how we'd stay friends forever, and maybe even live together when we left home. Once, we got a big cardboard box and designed the house we'd share, working out the layout and what would go where. I loved Mel B – Scary Spice – from the Spice Girls, and was obsessed with the animal prints she wore. I sketched out zebra print fabrics that me and Sophie would have for the curtains in our dream house.

There were loads of kids we knew from school and the neighbourhood hanging around, some the same age as us and some older. A lot of them were smoking and drinking cider. I'd experimented with alcohol and fags before this, as it made me feel grown up and cool. It was only on the odd occasion though, when I'd been allowed to go out with my sister and her friends, and I'd also sneaked swigs of alcohol at family occasions when I thought no one was watching.

As time went on we got to know a lot of the crowd who gathered there, and we also started knocking about with a big group of teenagers who hung around at the park, which wasn't far away. Before long I felt confident enough to go out on my own and see who was about, even if Sophie wasn't out.

I was having fun, but very quickly I was doing all kinds of things my mum and dad would have gone mental about.

Friday night was my favourite night because a few of us would club together to buy cheap cider like White Lightning, which came in cans or a big plastic bottle. I'd have about half a bottle, and I'd be well on my way. I was smoking now too, and we'd all put money in to buy ten fags. Everyone smoked weed, and I did that too. It made me feel relaxed and always gave me the giggles and the munchies. Me and my friends would sit around for hours, laughing and joking and having the best time ever. I never saw it as doing anything wrong. It was just me and my mates having a laugh, experimenting and growing up.

We were too young to go into the shops and buy cigarettes and alcohol ourselves, and we didn't have a clue where to get hold of weed, but fortunately there were quite a few older boys, aged around 18, who were always knocking about and were very willing to get stuff for us. It was great.

Mum and Dad didn't suspect a thing, even though me and our Lisa used to always joke that Dad was like the FBI. I suppose the fact he was strict made me hyper-careful. I always went home at 10 p.m. on the dot and I wasn't drinking or smoking excessively, so I never fell in the door or gave Mum or Dad any reason to suspect what I was up to. If I felt I'd had a bit too much to drink I'd say the bare minimum to my parents and scoot up to bed as quickly as possible.

By the summer I was hanging around the streets all the time and was well in with the group who hung around the park. I started getting invited to parties in friends' houses, usually held when parents were away or older siblings were meant to be in charge, but instead joined in or went out. It was great to be part of the 'Park Crew' as we were known; it was the best crew in town.

I started dating a boy who was the same age as me and was in the same crew, and not long afterwards I lost my virginity to him. We were at a house party, I'd been drinking White Lightning, and we went in one of the bedrooms and did it. I didn't have a clue what I was doing, but I liked him and he was my boyfriend, and that's what boyfriends and girlfriends did. Everyone around me seemed to be having sex, or at least they were saying they'd done it, and I felt I would have been called a nerd if I'd said no. The experience wasn't pleasant at all. It hurt and it was over almost before it began. I'm sure it wasn't pleasant for him either. We were two very young teenagers having sex, because we thought what was what you did.

I'd had sex education at school, which amounted to a biological description of how the sperm reaches the egg. We were shown how to put a condom on, and of course we all blew them up like balloons and fell about laughing. There was no discussion about healthy relationships, sexual feelings, self-respect or peer pressure, and certainly no mention of abuse. Nevertheless, I knew what a paedophile was: a fat old man who pervs on kids out the window, or pulls up in his van and offers you sweets then grabs you off the street.

Me and my boyfriend did use a condom, and I felt a little bit more grown up once I'd had sex for the first time. I felt a bit embarrassed too, as I knew my boyfriend would tell all his mates, but at the same time I couldn't wait to tell Sophie. I wasn't a little child any more, and I liked that feeling. It was very cool to be growing up.

Chapter 4
'You all right, love? D'you want a lift?'

It was confusing and frustrating being 13. I couldn't wait to be an adult and I was pushing boundaries all the time. Some of the other kids were allowed out later than me and I started nagging Mum and Dad to be more lenient and give me more freedom. They said absolutely not: 10 p.m. was late enough. I thought they were mean and treating me like a baby.

I was with my boyfriend for a few months before we split up, and then a boy called Phillip started showing interest in me. He was about 18, which made me feel even more grown up. It was exciting to have attention from an older boy, and even when I found out that he sold drugs I wasn't put off. It was the opposite: I felt flattered that someone so grown up was interested in me. Apart from smoking weed, I wasn't interested in drugs and I didn't want to know about hard drugs at all, which is what Phillip was dealing. I liked the fact he was a bit of a bad boy though; that appealed to me.

Heroin was a huge problem in the area at that time. Out of the 50 or so people who were part of the same groups as me and hung around the neighbourhood, I'd say there were only about nine or ten of us who refused to touch it. The first time I was offered heroin was by a girl called Jill. She was pregnant and was smoking it through a pipe.

'Do you want some?' she asked.

I looked at her in horror. Apparently, what she was doing was called 'tooting' heroin. I'd only ever heard of people injecting heroin so I was confused.

I knew heroin was called the 'dirty drug' and I was asking questions all the time about why they took it. Phillip himself was a user. 'Don't ever touch it, Sammy,' he told me. 'You'll be hooked and never get off it.'

I never wanted to. I couldn't see the attraction at all.

* * *

My parents would have been absolutely horrified to know I was involved with Phillip, but I'd become very good at telling them tales about what I'd been up to. I'd talk about what I'd done with my friends and describe how we walked to the park or up to the chip shop. I didn't feel guilty about keeping secrets. What teenager ever tells their parents exactly what they've been up to? As I continued to go home at 10 p.m. on the dot every night they didn't see any cause to worry.

I started to develop feelings for Phillip and wanted to spend more time with him. He was my first big crush. He was always right nice to me and looked out for me. He had a car, albeit a clapped-out old thing, and he'd pick me up from school so I didn't have to catch the bus or walk.

It wasn't long before we slept together. I didn't think about his age at all. Lots of my friends had older boyfriends so it was the norm. After the first time I was staying the night at Sophie's house and I told her I'd had sex with Phillip. 'Are you OK?' she asked, because I was sitting on the toilet and was bleeding and sore.

I reassured her that Phillip hadn't done anything to hurt me, at least not deliberately. 'It right hurts. He was massive. I didn't think it could be that big!'

I sorted myself out and we laughed about it in the end and went to sleep.

Unfortunately, it wasn't long before Phillip was unfaithful, with a girl who was about a year older than me, called Ruth. When I found out he'd cheated on me I was absolutely devastated and heartbroken, but I still wanted to go out with him. My feelings for him ran really deep, and I couldn't stand the thought of splitting up from him.

One day Phillip took me for a drive and said we needed to talk. I can remember being in an old derelict building with him, and Phillip saying, 'Look, Sammy, I need to finish with you. If you continue to go out with me you'll go down a really bad path. You're too good for that.'

I reluctantly agreed to split up after that, but I didn't really know what Phillip was on about. I wasn't interested in hard drugs and I knew I would never take them, so what exactly was this 'bad path' he was talking about?

I found it very hard to deal with the rejection I felt when Phillip finished with me. It made me think there must be something wrong with me. The pain of the rejection was so intense I started to feel very low, and I wasn't myself at all.

One night I felt so bad I took a razor blade from the bathroom at home, sat in darkness on my bed and cut myself. I'm not sure what made me even think about doing this. I sliced the blade really fast across both wrists. It was so painful and I was bleeding, but for some reason the physical pain helped release the emotional pain I was feeling.

I regret doing this now as I have scars across and up my wrist. I should have spoken to someone about the way I was feeling, but as a child I found it difficult to speak to anyone about emotions and relationships. There was no way I could talk to my parents because they didn't even know about Phillip.

Straight after Phillip I started dating another boy called Richard, who I already knew quite well. Richard was one of Phillip's friends and he also hung around with our crew. I didn't particularly fancy Richard but he'd always been kind to me, had a good personality and was funny and cool. I think what appealed to me most was that Richard acted in a much more mature way than the boys my age. Like Phillip, he was 18, so it wasn't that surprising he seemed more grown up and sure of himself.

I knew Richard was also involved in drugs. He used hard drugs, and he dealt heroin for a friend of his called Bash. This didn't shock me as I'd been down this road before with Phillip. Dealing drugs was what so many teenagers did in this part of Rotherham. They couldn't find a proper job when they left school and so they did what they could to get some money. It was so commonplace it was barely even mentioned, and if you were bothered about it you were seen to be on the outside; someone who wasn't part of the gang.

I never questioned how wrong it was to deal drugs. I had the attitude that I wasn't stupid enough to take hard drugs and never would, so whatever they were dealing in had nothing to do with me.

Not long after I'd started dating Richard I met his friend Bash for the first time, by the parade of shops. Bash was Asian, in his early twenties and drove a dark-coloured sports car. He came over and said hello.

'Nice to meet you,' I said politely.

Bash smiled at me and I thought he seemed quite nice. He had a bit of a swagger about him and, although I didn't think he was good-looking, he impressed me. He had a reputation for being a 'Mr Big', and I thought he was cool.

I can't remember how the conversation came to focus on my looks, but Bash made a comment that I had a 'piggy nose'. I don't think he was being nasty and trying to hurt me, but it right stung me and made me feel self-conscious. I'd always been confident about my looks.

'You could be a model, babby!' Mum said to me all the time. 'No wonder you won all them pageants and beauty contests! You'll never have to worry about a job. People will snap you up, they will.'

I believed her.

I wasn't interested in Bash as a potential boyfriend – the thought never entered my head – but his personal remark bothered me, a lot. I didn't want him or any other boy to think I had a piggy nose or was just some ugly little girl. My confidence was knocked, which wasn't good at all, as I was still feeling insecure after Phillip's rejection.

The next night was a Friday and I'd been drinking cider with my friends. It was about quarter to ten and I was a bit tipsy, standing at the bus stop and desperately hoping I'd be in by 10 p.m. The next thing I knew, Bash pulled up in his sports car and wound down the window.

'You all right, love? D'you want a lift?'

'Erm … no. I'm OK, my bus will be here in a minute.'

'Don't be daft! I'll drop you off!' He gave a little laugh as he said this, as if it was funny of me not to accept the lift.

'Are you sure you don't mind?'

'No, course not. Jump in.'

I got in. His car was well flashy and had black leather seats. It was completely the opposite to the old wreck Phillip used to drive me around in, plus Bash had dance music blaring out of a really good stereo system. I was well impressed.

'Where d'you live?' he asked.

'Quite close. You can drop me at the top of the road.'

'Oh, we'll have you home in no time.'

We made small talk and then Bash said: 'You're all right, you, aren't ye?'

I wasn't sure what to say.

'You're pretty, you know that?' he went on. 'You're all right. I think we're gonna be friends.'

We had reached the top of my street by this point. Bash pulled over, and then he leaned over, snogged me and said he wanted to be with me.

I was completely caught off guard.

'I've got to go,' I stuttered, getting out of the car and feeling flustered. 'Thanks for the lift.'

'Not a problem, love, anytime! I'll see you soon, yeah?'

I wanted to get in the house and get to bed as quickly as possible, without my dad sussing out that I'd been drinking. Dad appeared and asked me where I'd been and who with. I said as little as possible in case I slurred my words. I was still Sophie's friend but we'd both made new sets of friends too. By now I was in with a gang of girls who all went to my school. Holly, Tina, Alison and me had become quite a foursome. I think I told Dad I'd been out with Holly and maybe one or two other girls. He accepted this.

I got myself into bed and thought about what had happened with Bash. I tried to tell myself at least one good thing had come out of this turn of events. *My piggy nose couldn't be that bad, could it? He wouldn't have kissed me if he thought I was bad-looking, would he?* That's what I thought as I sank into a deep sleep.

The next morning I woke up with a start and thought: *Shit! What did I do that for?* I shut my eyes, and all over again I could see Bash's face moving closer to mine as I sat in the passenger seat of his car. I could smell his aftershave and the air freshener in his car, and I could hear his breathing. 'Oh God, that was a big mistake!' I said to myself. 'I don't even fancy him. What was I doing?' I vowed not to let that happen again; it really wasn't what I wanted at all and I had no interest whatsoever in being Bash's girlfriend.

Not long after that I slept with Richard for the first time. He took me to his house, where he lived with his mum and dad, and we had sex in the front bedroom while they were out. As with Phillip, I still had no clue what I was doing. It was a simple case of 'Right, take your trousers down, Sammy. Lay down and open your legs while I put a condom on.' I lay there while he moved his skinny body up and down, grunting in my ear for the whole of probably two minutes.

The next weekend I went out with Holly. We bought some White Lightning and drank a bit too much, and then we ended up walking past some garages by a pub not far from where I lived.

Bash and Richard drove past in Bash's car and offered us a lift. We got in and went to Pizza Hut, where Bash bought us all a takeaway pizza, which I thought was right nice of him. After that we drove round for a bit and then ended up in the car park at the big shopping centre in town. While we were there Bash asked me and Holly to give him a back and shoulder massage, saying he was tensed up. It seemed a bit weird, but Richard was there and didn't seem bothered, so I reluctantly rubbed Bash's shoulders.

'You're not strong enough!' Bash laughed. 'You're no good at this.'

He got Holly to have a go and he said she was better than me. I could tell she was pleased, and I realised then that she quite fancied Bash.

Later that evening me and Richard had sex in his mum and dad's house again. When we'd finished – again, after two minutes with him laid on top of me, grunting in my ear – I heard a noise outside.

'Who's that?' I asked.

'I don't know,' Richard replied, but somehow I didn't believe him.

Then I heard a voice outside. It was a man's voice saying: 'Have you done it yet?'

'What's going on?' I asked in alarm. 'Why is there somebody outside, asking that?'

'Honest to God, I don't know.'

'I'm going,' I said. 'There's something weird going on here.'

Chapter 5

'If he asks how old you are, say you're sixteen'

'You two go off and enjoy yourselves,' Mum said. 'I'm happy here, catching me tan.'

It was the autumn of 1999 and I was on holiday in Kos with Mum and Dad and our Lisa: Kate didn't come as she was so much older and had her own life by then. I'd been really looking forward to going away. I was still kind of dating Richard but I wasn't really bothered about him either way. I'd found out, through Holly, that it was Bash creeping around outside the house when me and Richard were having sex. I thought that was right strange, and it made me feel a bit wary and uncomfortable. I wasn't going to miss Richard while I was in Kos and I didn't give him a second thought when I headed to Manchester Airport with my family.

Mum really hated flying and had done what she always did, every single time we went on holiday. She started stressing out even before we checked in, had a few drinks to try to calm her nerves on the flight but then got tipsy and totally freaked out. Me and our Lisa took the mickey out of her something rotten, which irritated my dad and made him stress out too.

Once we arrived at our resort everybody relaxed. The weather was fantastic, we had a lovely little bungalow right by the pool and we slotted into a familiar routine. Dad hired a bike and took himself off on long rides around the island. Meanwhile, Mum planted herself by the pool straight after breakfast each morning and stayed there all day long, catching her tan, reading magazines and having a few drinks. Lisa and I spent hours in the swimming pool, made some new friends, chilled out and had a lot of fun.

Every night the four us would find a restaurant and have a nice family meal together. After that we'd look for some entertainment, whether it was a show or a cabaret or a lively bar we could sit in and listen to some music, or have a dance. Mum absolutely loved to be out enjoying herself. This wasn't Dad's scene at all, but as we were on holiday he made an effort and we all stuck together.

One night we went to a variety show in the resort and a drag queen approached Dad and started chatting him up. Lisa and I thought it was very funny and took the mickey, which Dad wasn't happy about at all. To his credit, he took it quite well, even though he really wasn't amused. He was always a bit more laid-back when he was on holiday, and we took advantage of this and enjoyed the chance to be a bit cheeky with him.

We would never have got away with that back home. Dad was always very strict, although he only laid down the law when he had good reason and was putting something important like our health, safety or education first. I respected him for that.

Dad would have had a fit if he knew some of the things I got up to in Rotherham. He never even wanted me to have a boyfriend, let alone an older boyfriend who wasn't exactly law-abiding. Both he and my mum worked really hard, but that didn't mean they weren't hands-on at home. Mum was working shifts for a kitchen supplier at this time, packing parts in a factory. She did either 6 a.m. – 2 p.m. or 8 a.m. – 4 p.m. so she could be in for me coming home from school, and home in the evenings. Dad was forever making sure I came home at 10 p.m. prompt, and there was no breaking that rule.

Whatever I was up to with my friends and with Richard, I was still always home on time. If I did have a drink of cider or a puff on a cigarette I tried to get straight up to bed as soon as I got in. I was never in a bad way, so Dad didn't suss me out.

I'm sure Mum had her suspicions about me being with boys, but she was of the opinion that I was a teenager and was going to have boyfriends and push the boundaries, just like she had. Mum thought bad stuff only happened on the news, in other parts of the world.

To my parents, I was the perfect daughter. I was bubbly, confident, intelligent and ambitious – the beautiful child whose dreams would come true; the lucky girl who would live happily ever after.

* * *

When I got back from Kos I couldn't wait to see my friends. I'd caught a tan and my hair, which was mousy brown by then, had some natural golden highlights running through it. I pulled it up into a twisted ponytail that fanned out on top of my head, leaving one carefully placed strand hanging down the side of my face. This was the fashion and I thought it looked really cool. I also plucked my eyebrows so they were in neat, thin arches, and put on some blue eyeshadow and mascara.

I arranged to meet up with Holly, Tina and Alison outside a pub on the first night I was back.

'What have I missed?' I smiled.

There were quite a few other people sitting on the wall and hanging around on the street, and one girl suddenly blurted out: 'Haven't you heard?'

'Heard what?'

A few people started laughing and then somebody told me that Alison had given Richard oral sex while I'd been on holiday.

'You what?' I said, flabbergasted. 'I've only been on holiday for a week and you've been at it with my boyfriend?'

Alison paused and looked scared of what my reaction would be.

'I didn't even wanna fucking do it, I don't even like him,' she spat. She looked really embarrassed in front of the group.

'All right then, Alison,' I said. 'Chill out. Jesus Christ!'

Everybody laughed. I totally believed Alison when she said she didn't want to do it, although at the time I didn't recognise how wrong this situation was.

'Well, you can all fuck off,' Alison shouted.

'Listen, Alison, I'm not bothered anyway. I'm cool about it. Don't worry.'

In the end, we both started laughing about it. Richard might have been 18, but he had turned out to be a lot more immature than I'd thought he was. I didn't have strong feelings for him so what he did with Alison didn't upset me, and when I saw him next we just kind of picked up where we'd left off before my holiday.

A few nights later I met up with Holly. It was a school night, but even so I was looking forward to having some fun with my mates.

I still had a healthy tan and felt really good about myself. I remember I felt excited as I walked out of my house. It was about 6 p.m., which was my favourite time of day. School was done, I'd had my tea and now I had a few hours of freedom until I had to be home at 10 p.m.

It was October and the weather was quite chilly, so I put on some dark blue jeans that fitted really well and my sister's light-blue Ben Sherman shirt. I had my hair down this time and I also wore a blue bomber jacket, to keep warm.

Lisa hung around with a totally separate gang to me, in another part of town, and had made it clear many times that she didn't want her little sister following her around. This suited me down to the ground. She was allowed out a bit later than me and so I could 'borrow' her clothes and put them back in her wardrobe before she even knew they'd gone. If I ever did spot her or her mates when I was out and about I would dodge them so she couldn't see what I was wearing. I'd tell my sister I was simply doing as she asked and keeping out of her way, which worked like a dream, especially as I didn't want her to know all my other business either.

Holly was sat on the wall that faced the kebab shop and a take-away pizza place. You got to this little parade of shops by walking up some wide concrete steps that took you away from the main road and slightly above pavement level. I think this was why it was such a popular place for kids like us to hang out, as it was a little bit hidden from the main road that ran alongside.

That night there was another girl there we knew, called Pamela. She was also sat on the wall, and she had a big bag on her lap.

'What's in the bag?' Holly asked.

'Some clothes, I'm sleeping out,' Pamela replied quietly.

'Let's have a look what you've got.'

Pamela showed Holly a pair of Levi jeans she had in the bag, and Holly grabbed them jokingly.

'I'm having them!' Holly teased. 'Here, Sammy, shove them up your coat.'

I caught the jeans as Holly threw them at me and stuffed them under my jacket.

'Give 'em back right now!' Pamela said.

At that moment, I heard a car revving up the street and looked over to see a smart silver Astra being driven by a right good-looking guy. He was Asian, with a shaved head and big brown eyes, and I fancied him the moment I saw him. I watched as he parked up in front of the white bus stop close by and stepped out of his car.

This guy looked very different to all the other boys I was used to hanging about with. He was dressed immaculately in a pair of blue cord jeans, Ben Sherman boots and a sleeveless, gold-coloured body warmer. Around his neck was a massive gold chain.

'It's Bash's big brother, Ash,' Holly hissed as he looked over. 'If he asks how old you are, say you're 16. He might take us for a drive. Come on.'

I said nothing, which was very unusual for me. Instead I stared, unable to take my eyes off this guy. *He's right fit.* I couldn't think of anything else as I stood up and followed Holly over to the car to say hello. She and Ash started talking, but I felt very shy in his company and didn't say a word.

'Who's your mate?' Ash asked Holly, nodding his head in my direction.

'Sammy.'

Ash looked at me and smiled. 'How old are you?'

'Sixteen.'

The word came out in a little whisper instead of in my usual loud and confident voice. I looked young for my age anyway, and I didn't think I'd done a very good job of lying. I'd never lied before about my age; it had never been an issue.

Ash grinned. 'Do you want to go for a spin?'

Seconds later Holly and I were getting in the back of his car. I can't remember if Ash had a friend with him in the front seat, which says a lot about the effect he had on me. I only had eyes for Ash; I was spellbound right from the start.

As I sat down I realised I still had Pamela's jeans shoved up my jacket, which made me laugh. I was enjoying myself even though I felt so shy, and I certainly didn't think twice about whether or not it was a sensible idea to get in the car. The fact I knew Ash's brother Bash, and Holly knew Ash, meant he wasn't a stranger. I wasn't worried about where he might be taking us. That was the last thing on my mind. It was exciting and fun to be in Ash's car, and that's all I could think about as we sped off, going way over the speed limit as Ash slammed his foot on the accelerator.

Ash's car was right flash inside, with a posh black interior and a top-of-the-range stereo. I looked at Holly and giggled. *How good is this?* I thought. *Aren't we the lucky ones?* I never thought for one second that this night would change my life forever.

Chapter 6

'Come and meet some of my friends'

Ash took us for a spin around the neighbourhood, just as he'd promised. He was chatty and friendly, asking us about what we'd been doing and if we liked the dance music he had on. I let Holly do the talking because I still felt right shy. Ash had a really lively personality and was full of energy. It was entertaining just listening to him talk. He was driving really fast, which I found exciting, and I sat there quietly, soaking it all in.

Ash drove a mile or so up the road, then pulled on to a paved driveway in front of a flat in a terraced row of properties on Clough Road. I vaguely knew this road. It was closer to the town centre than my house, and very near to where my parents' club used to be. The area was known locally as 'Paki land' because of the predominantly Pakistani community living and working there. Obviously this is not a polite or politically correct way of describing it, but it's what a lot of white people called this particular part of Rotherham, and still do. The Pakistani population had expanded as I grew up, and in fact I'd learned that one of the reasons my dad's club went bust was because so many Muslims who didn't drink moved into this particular area, which wasn't good for a business dependant on the sale of alcohol.

I peered out of the window of Ash's car, excited to see what was going to happen next. The driveway went right up to the front window as there was no front garden. The paving stones had grass and weeds growing through the cracks while the flat itself looked old and tatty, with a dirty, brown-painted front door, unwashed windows and peeling window frames. I didn't like the look of it. My house was always very neat and tidy and well kept. I wasn't used to anything shabby-looking like this, but I never said a word. I was too taken with Ash to worry about peeling paint, and this was an adventure I wanted to be involved in. It was way more fun than hanging around outside a kebab shop.

'Come and meet some of my friends,' Ash smiled. Me and Holly got out of the car and followed him to the front door. Everything about Ash was immaculate, and he smelled right nice too as he was wearing expensive aftershave. I was in awe of him.

As soon as we stepped inside the flat a different smell hit me. There was a stink of dirty rubber, like you'd smell in an old garage. Straight ahead there was a narrow, rectangular kitchen that had tyres stacked up all around. It was cold, and didn't look like a place you could live in at all.

I suddenly felt nervous. The door to the living room was on the left-hand side. It was open and I peeped inside. It was very dark, but I could see there were about five or six Pakistani men all sat around on the floor and on chairs, laughing, smoking and drinking. I didn't know any of them. It must have been obvious I wasn't at ease in this situation. Whenever I feel uneasy I clench my hands in towards my chest and go all quiet, and that's exactly what I was doing.

'Come in, love,' one man said, beckoning me into the room. 'Don't be shy.'

Ash introduced me to the man, who was another of his brothers, Bono. He looked to be a few years younger than Ash and Bash, who I guessed were both in their early twenties. The men all seemed friendly and so I went in. I sat down nervously on an old red chair, still tensing myself and saying nothing. I had never been around men like this before, and I wasn't sure what to make of it all.

There was a bottle of vodka in the room, and I think it was Ash who gave me a drink and encouraged me to 'chill'. I started to relax quite quickly. Ash smiled at me and I felt butterflies in my stomach, and like my heart skipped a beat.

I was also offered a fag and a drag on a spliff. Everyone was smoking and drinking and so I joined in. I didn't have very much at all, because I was feeling nervous, plus it was a school night and I never normally drank or touched weed when I had school the next day.

All the men were joking and swearing and taking the piss out of each other. The atmosphere was very relaxed but I still felt out of place and right unsure of myself. I watched and listened, wondering if there was any chance at all that Ash might be interested in me. I doubted it. He was really fit, and he wouldn't be interested in a kid like me, would he? I watched him laughing and chatting, making his friends laugh. He seemed right popular. The other men were treating him like he was some kind of a god. I wasn't surprised. He was the coolest of them all – the one to watch.

We'd been in the flat for less than an hour when Holly said we needed to go or we'd be late home. I stood up to leave straight away. Ash came out to the car with me and I sat in the passenger seat beside him, waiting for Holly to come out.

'You're not really 16, are you?' Ash said softly.

As he spoke he looked me in the eye and stroked my face. His touch felt so electric it was like I'd been struck by lightning. I'd had feelings for my boyfriends before, but nothing like this. It felt like love at first sight.

'No, I'm 15,' I replied. My heart was beating really fast now and I was thinking non-stop, *oh my God, he touched me, oh my God he touched me.*

Ash smiled at the lie. 'No, you're not.'

'OK, I'm 14, but I'm 15 on my next birthday.'

'I knew you weren't 16,' he said, smiling. 'You look way too young.'

Holly came out of the flat moments later and got in the back of the car. Ash drove off and dropped her just up the road from where she lived, which was only a few minutes' away.

'Are you hungry?' he asked me.

'I'm starving,' I told him, even though I knew if we went to get food I wouldn't be home by 10 p.m. I couldn't believe Ash was being so nice and attentive to me. He really did seem interested in me, and I didn't want to spoil any chance I might have with him by going home now.

'Right, let's get some food then,' he smiled.

We drove to a takeaway just up from the petrol station. People were pipping their horns or waving to Ash as we pulled in. Everyone knew who he was and he was obviously very popular.

'I'll pick your food,' he said. 'Trust me, Sammy, it's the best chicken and chips in town.'

He was right. We ate the food in the car and it was really good.

'Nice chips, aren't they, Sammy?'

'They're right nice, thanks,' I said, smiling as I tucked in.

Ash played some R&B music in the car while we ate and he chatted to me about what music I liked, and what I was into generally. I told him I liked Usher and Craig David, and he said he did too, and had loads of their stuff. I didn't feel quite so intimidated by him now it was just the two of us, but even so I only spoke when I was spoken to. I was afraid of saying the wrong thing, because I wanted to impress Ash and make him like me.

When we'd finished eating we went and parked up in some woods at the back of Clough Road. This was Ash's idea, and I was happy to go along with it. You had to drive round the houses to reach the woods and find a quiet spot, but it only took a few minutes to get there. When the car stopped and the engine cut out I could feel my heart beating in my chest. It was thrilling to be with Ash. I couldn't stop thinking about how good-looking he was, how much I liked the way he smelt, and how mature and thoughtful he was. He had big muscles too. *He can have any girl he wants*, I thought, *and here he is, sat here with me*.

I had never met anybody like Ash, ever. He was different. He captivated me, and right from that first night I felt spellbound in his company.

Ash started telling me stories about when he was eight or nine years old and got up to all sorts of mischief, like jumping out of windows at home and even stealing cars. I laughed, because I knew that's what he wanted me to do, and he also knew how to tell a story in a funny way. He enjoyed painting himself as a 'bad boy', but the way he spoke was right gentle. I couldn't imagine him doing anything really bad, even though he went on to tell me he had recently spent some time in prison because of his 'mischief'.

This didn't put me off him at all; in fact, I think it was quite the opposite. Ash seemed proud at having served time, like it was a badge of honour. I was excited by the fact he had a crazy, wild side and it made him even more attractive to me. I didn't ask what he'd been in jail for; I was far more interested in the fact he was sharing this information with me, and whether that meant he liked me. I guess I thought his prison term was for stealing a car or something, as that was the kind of mischief he'd told me about.

Ash talked about making his money through property, which his family owned. They had a string of other businesses too, like a café, a car spray shop and a window company. I hung on to his every word.

'I think you're very pretty,' Ash told me more than once.

'Thanks,' I blushed every time.

'You're intelligent too, I can tell. You're clever, aren't you, Sammy?'

I was embarrassed and I think I just laughed.

'You're amazing.'

I'd never had compliments paid to me like that before. He made me feel really good about myself and I was falling deeper under his spell with every word he spoke.

* * *

Eventually, I told Ash I had to go home. I didn't want to leave but I knew I'd be in loads of trouble for being late. I could have stayed there all night talking to him. Everything he said made me think how exciting he was, how charming, or how kind and sensitive. There wasn't one single thing that put me off him. We seemed to have things in common too, which I was surprised and very happy about. Ash liked to listen to Usher and he loved Ben Sherman clothes, just like I did. He and his brothers were friends with lots of my friends, which was another good thing. In fact, I was surprised we'd never met before. It seemed I was destined to meet Ash. That is how I felt, right from that first night.

'I'll drive you back, make sure you're safe,' Ash said, as soon as I said I had to go.

'Thank you,' I smiled. 'That's good of you.'

On the short drive home I started trying to think up excuses to give my mum and dad. It was well past 10 p.m. and I was prepared for them to go absolutely mental. Ash dropped me off, out of sight of our house, and when we said goodbye and I stepped out of his car I felt like I was floating on air. He didn't ask if he could see me again, and he didn't even kiss me, but I could tell this wasn't going to end here. As he waved me off Ash smiled and told me: 'I don't want to get you into trouble.'

I can't recall what excuse I gave my parents for being late but it must have been a good one because, after giving me a right good telling off, Dad didn't ground me. I had a grin on my face from ear to ear, and I thought to myself, *I'm not going to forget this night for the rest of my life*. I went to bed dreaming of seeing Ash again. I could hardly sleep, I was that excited.

Every time I closed my eyes I saw Ash's big brown eyes looking into mine. I thought back over bits and pieces of the conversation. 'You're right pretty,' I heard him say again and again. 'You're clever. I can tell you're intelligent. You're amazing.' His image was burnt on my mind. I could see his smile. I could hear his laugh, smell his gorgeous aftershave and picture his gold chain, his leather boots, his body warmer and his shaven head. He was funny and he was kind and gentle. Everything about him was perfect.

Chapter 7
'Where the hell have you been?'

'See you at Dawn's,' Holly said as we left school.

It was the day after I'd met Ash and I had my head in the clouds. 'What for?'

'We said we'd babysit for a couple of hours, didn't we?'

Dawn was Richard's sister, and he turned up to babysit with us too. Then, when Dawn came home, me, Holly and Richard ended up meeting some other friends.

Richard knew Bash and Bono so I reckoned he must know Ash too. It was as if he read my mind, because as I was thinking about this Richard said something about the fact he went to the gym with Ash. I got goosebumps at the mention of Ash's name, and then moments later I saw him driving down the road towards us.

Oh my God, it's him. My heart was racing as he pulled up next to us.

I couldn't believe how lucky this was, to have bumped into Ash like this just when I was thinking about him. He put the car window down, and asked all three of us if we wanted to get in and go for a spin. We didn't hesitate in saying yes and Richard got in the front while me and Holly climbed in the back.

We sped off, because Ash never drove anywhere slowly, and I felt really excited to be in his car again. He had one of my favourite

Usher tracks playing and I looked at him as he drove, thinking again how well dressed and good-looking he was.

The car skidded to a halt. Ash jumped out and went up to a guy who was standing on the street corner. I recognised the man as a well-known drug addict called Bobby.

Ash started shouting in his face. 'Where's me money, ya motherfucker?'

'I haven't got it, mate,' Bobby was stuttering and trying to find an excuse.

Out of nowhere, Ash smacked Bobby really hard in the face. He fell to the ground, groaning and holding his nose.

'You best get my fucking money. You're taking the piss!'

Ash dusted off his knuckles and got back in the car, behaving as though he'd just eaten his tea. Me and Holly were in complete shock but Richard started laughing. 'Fucking hell, he's knocked my man out!' Then we sped off to continue our drive, as if nothing had happened.

It was obvious Ash was involved with drugs but this didn't put me off him. I still didn't understand how bad this was. I was so naïve I saw it as a way of earning money, and who could possibly get hurt by selling drugs? I couldn't see further than the fact that Ash had power and knew how to handle himself. This added to his appeal; now I was even more in awe of him.

'Did you grow up around here?' Ash asked me as we drove.

'Ye, my dad used to have a club not far from here.'

Ash shot round to look at me in the back of the car. 'Are you Peck's daughter?'

I said yes and asked him how he knew my dad.

Ash started laughing and told a story about how he'd stolen my dad's car from outside the club one night and taken it for a spin.

I knew straight away that the story was true, as I'd heard it before from my family, not realising Ash was the culprit. The car was a white Sierra Cosworth with a big spoiler on the back. Dad was right proud of it and took great care of it. Ash fetched it back with no damage done, but nevertheless my dad was absolutely fuming.

'Your dad really hated me,' Ash laughed. 'He barred me from the club. I was only a kid though and we soon sorted it. I can't believe you're Peck's daughter! That's right funny!'

Ash offered to drop Holly off at the top of her road, and Richard said he could get out there too.

'I'll drop you two off first then, as it's closer. Sammy, I'll drop you off last if that's OK, love?'

'Ye, that's great, thanks.'

Once Holly and Richard had gone Ash asked me if I was hungry, and I said I was.

'Shall we get some chicken and chips again?'

I nodded and said OK.

'Come on, then. Come and sit next to me.'

I felt the same shyness I'd experienced the night before. I didn't want to say the wrong thing, and so I smiled and climbed in the passenger seat next to Ash. He put Usher's 'Nice & Slow' on and grinned.

'I like this,' I said.

'I've got some wicked tunes, Sammy, proper love-making songs,' he replied. Then he lifted his eyebrows up and down in a suggestive but jokey way. It made me smile, and the butterflies were back in my stomach.

I had some money to pay for the food but Ash made it clear he was paying. 'I like looking after you,' he said. 'When you're with me, Sammy, you don't ever need to pay for a thing.'

I couldn't believe how nice he was. He was like my Prince Charming, and I felt like the luckiest girl in Rotherham.

Once again it was past 10 p.m. by the time we'd eaten the food. Just like the night before, I knew that I'd get into trouble, but it was worth it, to spend time alone with Ash.

Dad was pacing the hall and went mental when I got in. I wasn't as late as I had been the night before, but I didn't have a mobile phone, and so he had no way of contacting me to make sure I was safe. He'd been getting very annoyed and anxious.

'Where the hell have you been, Sammy?' he asked. 'I've been worried sick.'

'Out.'

'Who with, at this time of night?'

It was a fair question, as most of my friends from school also had to be home by 10 p.m.

'Just out, with friends. Sorry, I lost track of time. I won't do it again.'

'I'll give you sorry!' Dad bellowed, eyes blazing.

Mum intervened as she could see how angry Dad was. He was definitely in the mood to ground me, but Mum being Mum, she wanted to smooth things over and make my life as easy as possible.

'She's said sorry, Peck,' Mum soothed. 'Just make sure you're back at ten from now on, OK, love? We worry about you, that's all. We don't want to spoil your fun but you're too young to be out so late. It's not safe.'

'Sorry,' I said, not really meaning it. I was only sorry that I'd been caught, and all I could think about was seeing Ash again. I'd risk my dad's temper any day if it meant spending time with Ash.

Chapter 8

'You need to take her home right now'

There was a frantic knock on the window.

'Ash, are you in there? It's me, Richard.'

I nearly jumped out of my skin. I was in the living room of the Clough Road flat again, but this time it was very quiet, as it was just me and Ash in there.

He'd picked me up in his car earlier in the evening, after I'd begged my mum to let me out, and promised faithfully I wouldn't be late again. As I was making the promise I knew I might break it, but I didn't care. All I cared about was getting out of the house, so I would have the chance of seeing Ash again. We hadn't arranged a time or a place to meet, but he knew all the usual haunts where I hung out with my friends and I knew he'd have a drive around to look for me.

Sure enough, Ash pulled up when I was walking along the street. I got in his car, trying to look as cool as I could, even though my heart was fluttering with excitement, and we went for a drive.

Ash drove even faster than normal, which I thought was daring and crazy. This time he was in a different car, a dark-coloured one that had sporty wheels and was even more flash than his Astra. After our spin he'd suggested we could go back to Clough Road, where we'd be able to chat and chill out together.

'OK,' I'd said shyly.

I didn't really want to go back to the flat as it was so tatty and horrible, but I did want to spend time with Ash, so I agreed. When we arrived the smell of rubber and tyres hit me again as I walked in the door, and the flat was cold and damp-smelling, just like it was before.

'We'll go in here and put the fire on,' Ash said, leading me into the living room. Nothing was how I remembered it from last time, when the room was full of men. There had been chairs, a table and a settee in this front room before. Now there was nothing but a right dirty old mattress on the floor and some stained bed covers. The walls and paintwork were mucky and the whole place looked like it needed a good scrub.

I sat down on the mattress while Ash put the fire on. It was an old-fashioned gas fire like the one Nanan had, with a mirrored section around the gas bars in the middle, a safety grill over the front and a dial on top that you clicked round to turn the gas on and off and control the temperature.

While the room was warming up Ash put the bed cover around us both. We were huddled up together, and he was telling me again how pretty I was and how it was nice to spend time with me. I couldn't take my eyes off him. He was looking at me intently, like he was really interested in me.

The scruffiness of the room, the fusty smell and the grubby mattress on the floor were very soon the last things on my mind, even though this was a world away from what I was used to.

I didn't question why the room I was in with Ash was set up like this. He had told me the flat was owned by his family but I don't think anyone actually lived there. He explained again that the family was into property, and said something about the fact this place was waiting to be done up.

I wasn't bothered. All I cared about was that I was here with Ash and we were spending time alone together. He could have taken me to a derelict building and I'd have been happy.

Our arms and legs touched as we sat side by side. It felt like he was giving me electric shocks, even though I was dressed in jeans and a jacket and he was too. I was so excited to be this close to him. Then he leaned in and kissed me. My heart was beating out of my chest and I was buzzing inside, but I felt so shy and nervous I kept very quiet, and I barely kissed him back. He was in charge, and I was soaking it all in, tingling and wondering how a kiss could make me feel so electrified.

Ash said he wanted to find out more about me, because I was so interesting and clever and pretty. I told him a little bit more about my family, and that I had two big sisters, but I think he already knew that, from knowing my dad through the club.

Ash told me he had a nickname, which was Mad Ash, and he seemed right proud of it. I liked the nickname. It suited him, because he was a real bad boy. I liked being with a bad boy; it was exciting, and it made me feel more grown up than ever.

When Richard banged on the window so frantically, not only did it give me a shock, but it also pissed me off. I didn't know if he'd got wind I was in there alone with Ash, or what he was playing at. Nevertheless, my instinct was to stay very quiet and let Ash deal with him. Ash had that effect on me. He was the leader and I was happy to be led, even though this wasn't my typical style at all. In my eyes, Ash could call any shots he wanted, because I was so mesmerised by him.

'Ash, Ash, can you hear me?' Richard shouted again.

'Sssshhhh,' Ash said with his finger on his lips and a grin on his face. I giggled childishly with my hand over my mouth, trying to be quiet.

I think he was hoping Richard would go away and leave us alone, but then there was another almighty bang on the window.

'ASH! I know you're in there with Sammy. Listen, you need to take her home right now. The police are looking for her!'

Ash's eyes widened. 'Shit,' he muttered, getting to his feet and going outside to speak to Richard.

I'd completely lost track of time and had no idea how late it was. My guess was that it was well past 11, so it was hardly surprising my mum and dad had got this worried. What were they doing ringing the police though? Surely that was well over the top?

Ash returned to the living room and gave me a reassuring smile. 'Come on, Sammy. I'll drop you off at the top of your road. It'll be fine.'

I trusted Ash and didn't say a word as I followed him to the car. Richard had gone by the time I left the flat but I thought to myself that it was a good job he had known where we were. I wasn't sure how Richard knew about the police, but he was one of those people who was always hanging around the streets at all hours and getting involved in whatever was happening. It was a blessing he had his ear to the ground, and he'd done us a favour. Imagine if the police had found me with Ash? My dad would never have let me out of the house again.

When I got home it was well past midnight. 'Here's me babby!' Mum sobbed, giving me a big hug. 'Thank heavens you're home, Sammy, love. I've been out of my mind with worry.'

Dad was absolutely furious. 'Have you got any idea the trouble you've caused? Well? Have you? We've called the police we were so worried! I've even asked them to get the helicopter and sniffer dogs out to help look for you. What the bloody hell are you playing at?'

'Sorry,' I muttered.

'SORRY!' Dad shouted. 'Who have you been with? Where have you been?'

'Just out with my friends.'

'You're lying, Sammy. There's something going on, you're not telling the truth.'

'Dad, there's nowt going on. I lost track of time, that's all.'

'Right, that's it! I've heard enough. Now get to bed, fast. You're grounded, do you hear me? GROUNDED! You're on a TOTAL LOCKDOWN.'

I ran up to bed, relieved to get away from my parents. I didn't care about the trouble I'd caused them. All I was bothered about was how I was going to see Ash again after this.

The next day I found out that my dad, the police and our Lisa had been round to Holly's, demanding to know where I was. My dad had also been driving round in a police car looking for me.

Even though Lisa hung out with a completely different crowd to me she knew most of my friends, and she knew full well that some were knocking about with older lads and drinking and smoking. Holly had told Lisa she didn't know where I was that night, which was true, but my sister was so worried and upset that she lost the plot, accusing Holly of lying, calling her names and screaming at her and her mother on their doorstep.

I was normally really bothered about what Lisa thought of me. Something changed that day, though, because all I could think about was how angry I was that Lisa had stuck her nose in like this, and what an absolute nerve she had going round to Holly's like that. I was fuming and I wanted to kill my sister, I really did.

I also found out that Dad knew more than he had let on to me. He was sharp and streetwise and he'd been doing a lot of talking and asking around, trying to find out why I was suddenly coming in late, as I'd never done that before.

Someone had mentioned to Dad that they had seen me going into the Clough Road flat the very first time Ash took me there, and when he'd called the police to report me missing, Dad had told them he was very concerned about the people I was associating with. The fact Ash and his friends were Pakistanis wasn't what worried him. He'd heard rumours that the guys I was hanging around with were older than me, and involved in drugs and crime. Dad wrote out details of every bit of information he'd picked up locally, and he gave the police everything.

The police told Dad that in order for them to get involved further I would have to make a complaint myself about the people or person I was involved with. As it stood, this was just a family dispute between an errant teenage girl and her parents, and there was no evidence of any wrong-doing. My dad was spitting tacks and couldn't understand how the onus was on me, a naïve and impressionable 14-year-old schoolgirl, to complain about the company I was keeping. His gut was telling him something wasn't right and I was in danger, but a father's instinct and some hearsay evidence wasn't enough for the police. They left us to sort out our family dispute among ourselves.

The next day I was sitting at home sulking because I was grounded, watching one of the soaps on TV while Mum cooked tea. Dad was keeping an eye on me.

'You stay away from that flat, and from those Asians,' he warned me, because by now I'd got up to speed with everything Dad knew.

The phone rang and he sprang to answer it.

'Hey up! How are you? I haven't seen you for years!'

It sounded like an old friend, someone Dad was really happy to hear from. Then suddenly his tone of voice changed.

'Samantha, have you taken someone's jeans?' he shouted.

My eyes widened and my mouth dropped to the floor.

Oh shit, I'm in deep trouble here.

I'd forgotten all about nicking Pamela's jeans on the first night I met Ash, and worse still, I'd left them in the Clough Road flat. Dad looked furious and embarrassed all at the same time.

'It wasn't me, it was my mate,' I stuttered. 'But then she gave them me. I haven't got them. They're in—'

'In that bloody flat?'

I nodded, feeling really bad about Pamela's jeans. It was a stupid thing to do to take them off her like we did, and to lose them was terrible. Dad was absolutely fuming but he held himself together and returned to the phone call.

'I can't apologise enough. How much were they? Fifty quid? Right. I'll give you the money to buy new ones, of course.'

When the call was over Dad began really ranting.

'How can you steal things from people, Samantha? You get everything from us. I've never felt so ashamed! What the hell is wrong with you? You stay the hell away from that flat, do you hear me?'

'I've heard you,' I said moodily, but inside I was thinking, *You don't know me at all! I'm not a thief! And I'm doing nothing wrong, nothing at all. What is wrong with having a laugh and spending time with a right good-looking guy who treats me like a princess?*

Chapter 9
'I'll wait until you're ready. I love you'

'Don't get involved with Ash. You're a good girl and he will ruin your life.'

'What?' I stuttered, wondering what the hell was going on. Bash was on the phone. He'd called Ash's mobile while we were in his car together and asked Ash to put me on. I looked at Ash and he started laughing. He'd heard every word but he obviously didn't care what his little brother said. I laughed too. How could Ash ruin my life? Bash was being over the top. I wondered if maybe Bash was jealous of his big brother, because of that time he kissed me when I didn't want him to?

Bash didn't give up easily, and he carried on with his warning even though Ash and I were both laughing.

'Sammy, I'm telling you; you need to stop seeing Ash. You're the one girl who could make it out of Rotherham and do something with your life. You need to listen to me. He's bad news.'

I didn't want to listen to any more of this, and so I muttered, 'All right, Bash,' and handed the phone back to Ash, who laughed loudly at his brother and hung up. Then Ash turned the music up and started singing loudly.

I was supposedly on 'total lockdown' now, as my dad had threatened, but I'd found a way to see Ash by skipping school. All pupils my age were allowed out of school at dinner time and so I wouldn't go back for afternoon lessons, or I'd sometimes walk out of the gates after registration, or even between classes. It was dead easy. I'd waltz off the premises, and Ash would be waiting outside the school gates in his car.

My heart skipped a beat every time I saw Ash. He drove quite a few different cars, and sometimes he turned up in a blue sports car with cream leather seats, gold-coloured alloy wheels and a personalised registration that spelled G8ASH, which he and Bash both shared. I felt like a million dollars whenever I climbed in the passenger seat.

'You look really pretty today,' he would tell me, even though I was in my school uniform and didn't think I looked great.

'Are you hungry? Can I get you something to eat? Where do you want to go?' I was flattered by Ash's attention and touched by how caring he was. He wasn't worried about us being seen together when I should have been in school. I took this as another compliment; Ash only cared about us being together, just like me.

Just before Bash called, Ash had leaned over, stroked my cheek and kissed me, then told me how beautiful I was. I couldn't believe how powerful my feelings were. I was exploding inside; I'd never experienced anything like it. He wasn't rushing me like other boys had, and he looked in my eyes and gave me the softest, most tender kisses ever. I was falling in love, in a big way.

I thought Bash must be jealous of us. How could Ash possibly be bad news for me? He made me feel like nobody had ever made me feel before. I felt like a princess, special and wanted, and he was my Prince Charming. Being with him was the best feeling in the world.

Holly, Tina and Alison skipped school with me a few times in those early weeks, and the three of us went to the cinema a couple of times with Ash and some other friends, including Richard. I didn't care what we watched, or that Richard was tagging along. There had never been anything serious going on between us, despite the fact we'd had sex, and Richard didn't seem to mind that I stopped seeing him as soon as Ash came along. In fact, it was the opposite. Richard had our backs, as he'd shown that night when he warned us the police were out looking for me. I didn't question this; Richard was a decent lad.

I sat next to Ash in the cinema and held his hand, and he bought me drinks and sweets. I was in heaven, and I always saved my cinema tickets as keepsakes, hiding them in my bedroom so Mum and Dad didn't see them.

One day Ash invited me, Holly, Tina and Alison to watch a film on TV with him. We went to a house I'd never been to before, which he explained was another one of the properties his family owned. It was near the flat, and must have also been waiting to be refurbished, I reckoned, because it was a bit old and scruffy, though none of us were bothered.

Ash put on a film called *Set It Off*. It was about four women who were struggling to make ends meet and started robbing banks. Ash said something about how we four girls could do armed robberies like that, how good it would be and how he could organise them for us.

We all thought he was joking and started mucking around.

'Can you imagine us lot?' we laughed. We all pretended we were holding out guns and joked 'Put your fucking hands up!'

It was no secret that Ash had been to prison and was therefore capable of getting involved in something illegal, but the idea of an armed robbery was ridiculous. I still didn't know exactly what he had been locked up for, but I continued to assume it was for some petty 'mischief'.

Me and Ash were starting to spend more time on our own, just the two of us. We went to the Meadowhall Shopping Centre in Sheffield quite a few times, wandering around window-shopping and hanging out together. We also used to drive for miles, and he started taking me to fancy restaurants.

I never had any money but Ash usually had a rolled-up wedge of cash in his pocket, often made up of loads of 20- or 50-pound notes. Once he had so much money he hid it under the seat of his car and asked me to keep an eye on it when he nipped out to pay for petrol. By the size of the rolls of cash there must have been thousands and thousands of pounds under there.

'Have you took owt?' Ash asked me when he came back.

I wasn't sure if he was joking or not, because he had this knack of saying serious things with a bit of a smile on his face.

'No,' I said defensively, thinking to myself that I wouldn't have dared touch it, let alone steal anything.

I was starting to realise that Ash made a lot of money from drugs, but we never talked about it. I'd known he was involved in drugs from the start, when he smacked Bobby, the heroin addict, but I closed my mind to it. I didn't want to know about anything that might put a barrier between us, because all I wanted to do was get closer to him, and keep him on the pedestal I had put him on.

'Let's go in here,' Ash said on one of our shopping trips.

It was a booth where you could get a big picture taken together, the size of four passport photos, and you could choose a border and a message to go on it. We squeezed in close and waited for the flash. I was wearing a silver coat and had my hair pinned up and Ash looked really good in a designer shirt and expensive jacket, with his thick gold chain around his neck. He chose a border with love hearts round the edge, and the words 'I Love You' were written in red above our smiling faces.

I was thrilled to bits with the photo and I hid it in my bedroom alongside the cinema tickets I'd kept as souvenirs. From that day on I looked at the photo every night before I went to sleep, dreaming of a day when Ash wouldn't be a secret any more, because I'd be properly grown up and could see him whenever I wanted to.

* * *

I still wasn't allowed out in the evenings. Mum and Dad were worried sick about me and ever since they'd called the police our relationship had been really strained. I was avoiding them as much as possible, because I was keeping secrets and didn't want to give anything away. It was easier to shut myself off from them and communicate as little as possible.

They knew things weren't right. For one thing, the school had been on to them about me playing truant. I lied through my teeth about what I'd been up to, making up any old story about missing a lesson because I hadn't done the homework, or skipping PE because I forgot my kit and went to the library instead, but forgot to tell the teacher.

Dad was keeping his ear very close to the ground, as was our Lisa, and they were hearing all kinds of stories. Inevitably, I'd been spotted with Ash around the town, and his name had been mentioned to my dad, though I didn't know this at the time.

My dad knew Ash of old, of course, from when he nicked Dad's car from outside the club. Dad knew that Ash had a bad reputation, linked to drugs and violent offences, and he was terrified that I was mixing with him and his mates and might get myself into trouble. But he had no clue about how my romantic relationship with Ash was developing.

One of the ways Dad tried to get through to me was by lecturing me about the importance of getting a good education.

'You need to knuckle down,' he would say. 'You're a clever girl, Sammy. Don't throw your education away.'

His words went straight over my head. Mum always told me I could make a living as a model if I wanted to, so even though I was clever and capable of getting A grades, why did I need to bother passing exams? That was one excuse I gave myself, but the truth was all my energies were focused on Ash. I could think of nothing but being with him and I was already starting to dream of marrying him and having a family with him one day. That had become my ambition in life. Even though I'd only known him for a matter of weeks, I wasn't interested in anything but Ash.

Some of my friends agreed to help me to sneak out at night, which I was desperate to do. Tina pretended to be her mother for me once, and invited me to their house, which my mum fell for.

'It'll be all right, she's with an adult,' Mum explained innocently to Dad. 'I've checked with Tina's mum. They're staying in and she'll be there all night.'

Dad wasn't happy but he let me go, and the arrangement was that Tina and her older brother would pick me up. In fact, Ash collected me at the top of our road and we went for a drive. He bought me a McDonald's, gave me some fags and we talked for ages. He knew I could dance and he said he was really impressed by this, and he told me I could be a big star one day, because I was so pretty and talented.

'I'm a good dancer too,' he joked. He put the music on full blast and started showing me his moves. I laughed and shook my head at him; he was so funny.

The next day I skipped the last lesson at school and met Ash again. He was in the silver Astra and he drove us up to the woodlands behind Clough Road, where we'd been on the first night and quite a few times since. This time, after he parked up, he reclined the passenger seat and lay back in it, pulling me on top of him, so I was straddling him. Ash then put his hand up my school skirt and started to reach into my knickers.

'I want to make love to you,' he said.

I felt right nervous and panicked.

'I can't,' I blurted out. 'I'm on my period.'

This was a lie but I didn't know what else to say to put him off. I wasn't ready, and I felt a little bit scared. The sex I'd had before was just kids messing around compared to this. This was a much bigger deal. This was making love, not just having sex, and I needed to get my head round it.

'Don't worry,' Ash said. 'I don't want to rush you. That's the last thing I want to do. I'll wait until you're ready. I love you.'

Chapter 10

'Keep your noses out of my business!'

I'd been with Ash for four weeks when I slept with him for the first time. I snuck out of school with Holly, who was now seeing Bono, and the four of us went to the house where we'd watched the film on TV. Ash said it belonged to his mother and told me his family lived mainly in another house on this road. I didn't question this. I knew he had a big family and I understood that lots of Pakistanis had a set-up like this, where close relatives lived near to each other in different houses. The arrangements would have been really strange in my family, but I accepted this was how he lived, especially as his father and several members of the family ran a property business.

'There's no one here,' Ash said as the four of us went inside. There were no carpets or furniture downstairs and he explained that the house was being renovated.

'We'll go upstairs,' he said. 'It's better up there.'

It was a four-bedroom house and Bono and Holly went into a room at the back while Ash led me to one of the bedrooms at the front, next to the bathroom. We hadn't talked about having sex, but as soon as I saw the room I realised that was what was going to happen. I imagined Ash thought I'd be more comfortable here than in the car, and he was right. The room was obviously lived in and the bed had nice covers on it. I felt happy that Ash had gone to the trouble of finding us somewhere like this.

We lay on the bed and he kissed me, but then I suddenly remembered I was wearing a horrible pink bra under my school shirt. The bra was on its last legs and had elastic sticking out of it. I didn't want Ash to think I was a scrubber, so I told him I didn't want to take all my clothes off. It was freezing cold in the house and he said he understood and it didn't matter. I was wearing a white Kappa jacket over my school shirt and my big blue bomber coat over that, and I had on my blue school skirt with buttons down the front. I took off my jacket and coat and my knickers.

Ash got on top of me, lifted my school shirt up and un-fastened my bra while kissing my lips and neck, then down to my breasts. I felt his hand go down in between my legs and he started rubbing me and asking, 'Do you like that?' He was taking his time, trying to please me and make me relaxed. When I'd had sex before it hadn't been like this at all. This gave me a feeling that was new to me, and felt nice.

Ash got inside me and he started off slowly, taking care not to do it too hard, even when he speeded up before he came inside me. The sex didn't last very long and once it was over I felt a little bit awkward. *What do I do now?* I thought. *What does he think of me?*

Ash jumped up off the bed and put his white vest on and started to get dressed, so I did the same.

'Did you enjoy it, Sammy?' he asked.

'Ye, of course I did.'

He looked very pleased with himself.

'I best get you home, love. We don't want anyone kicking off, do we?'

He softly put his hands on each side of my face, pulled me towards him and kissed me passionately. Then he smiled at me.

My and Ash's relationship had moved on to another level. We were closer now; that's how I felt, and that's what mattered to me. We were a couple now and we were going to stay together. I wanted to be with him forever, and I was glad we'd finally done it.

We had another trip to Meadowhall a few days later and afterwards Ash dropped me off at the bottom of our street. Dad was at home and he exploded with rage when I walked in.

'Have you been with Ash?' he demanded.

'Ash? No. What are you on about?'

I didn't care any longer what Dad knew or said to me. I had the same attitude towards school. I'd been getting into more and more trouble for missing lessons and the teachers were constantly on my case, but I'd reached a point where I really couldn't care less. Threats of detentions and suspensions meant nothing; they could call my parents all they liked as far as I was concerned. Expelling me would be a result not a punishment; I'd have had more chance of seeing Ash.

'You know full well what I'm on about!' Dad yelled. 'You've been seen in Ash's car, Sammy.'

Dad said he'd followed me, and he told me that Lisa knew I was seeing Ash too. He had phoned the police again, which was becoming a regular occurrence.

'You're talking crap,' I shouted back, 'and I don't give a shit what you think any more!'

I'd never spoken to Dad like that before and he hit the roof, threatening to lock me in the house and never let me out again.

Mum appeared and started crying and begging him to stop shouting. Even her tears didn't get through to me.

'Keep your noses out of my business!' I yelled.

'Stop it!' Mum sobbed. 'Just stop it! I can't take any more! Oh my God, what's happening to us? Sammy, love, can't you see we're worried out of our minds? Peck, what's happening to my babby?'

'She's out of control, that's what! The school has been on again. She's missing lessons and I know why. You're knocking around with that Ash. You can't deny it.'

'I'm not! Leave me alone, won't you?'

'Don't lie to me, Sammy! You think you know it all but you don't. He's a dickhead who goes around robbing people and selling drugs. He's using you and he's been in prison. I'm telling you, he's a dangerous man.'

Dad was clearly trying to shock some sense into me, but it didn't work because I knew Ash had been to prison, and the Ash I knew wasn't dangerous at all. My Ash was loving and kind, so what was Dad on about? His words went straight over my head. He couldn't tell me anything I didn't already know.

'And do you know what else?' Dad went on. 'He's married!'

Dad said this as if he was playing his trump card and I would have no comeback.

'That's a lie!' I spat, horrified that my dad could make up something so spiteful.

'It's not a lie. Everybody knows it. Ash is a married man, Sammy. He shouldn't be knocking about with a young girl like you. I don't know what his game is but he's not going to get away with it, not over my dead body!'

'You know what your problem is, Dad?' I screamed.

'Yes, you,' he said. 'You're the problem. You're tearing this family apart and making our lives hell. You're making a big mistake, Sammy, and you need to see sense.'

'No!' I screeched. 'You're the problem, Dad. You're jealous, that's what you are. You don't want me to enjoy myself and be happy. You want to control me because you're a sad, jealous old man. The police thought you were fucking stupid when you called them out. Fancy calling the police because I was an hour or two late home! I'm not a kid, I'm 14! You've lost the plot! Just fuck off and leave me alone!'

Dad growled and raised his fist, and I thought he was going to swing for me.

'For pity's sake!' Mum wailed, dissolving into tears. 'Stop it, Peck! Just stop it now, both of you!'

I ran off out of the house and rang Ash, who came straight over to collect me.

Scenes like this began happening all the time. Both my sisters tried to talk sense into me but I wouldn't listen to them and argued with them too. Some of the rows were terrible. We swore, traded insults and lashed out at each other, but they wouldn't get off my case.

Every night after I'd eaten my tea there was a new battle, with me shouting and screaming that I wanted to go out and telling my parents they had no right to stop me. Dad got more and more angry and agitated and Mum was falling apart, crying all the time and constantly pleading with me and Dad to stop fighting.

As my relationship with my family deteriorated, I became closer to my friends, because they were the only ones who understood me and knew how much Ash meant to me. Some other girls who were also dating Pakistanis in Ash's circle had been called 'Paki-shaggers' in the street, and I started to get this too. All this did was confirm what Ash said, that people were just jealous or racist or both.

Once I'd started sleeping with Ash he wanted to have sex with me every day. I wanted to please him so I hardly ever said no. I began to try every trick in the book to get out of the house and be with him. One night, when my dad was out at a Man United football match, I told my mum I was going to the chippy and would come straight back. She made me promise faithfully that I wouldn't go anywhere else, but Ash was waiting for me at the back of our house. He'd given me a mobile phone, so we could arrange to meet. It was a big brick Motorola one which I was careful to keep hidden from my parents. Whenever Ash's number flashed up I'd be buzzing and couldn't wait to see him.

When I explained the situation about my dad being out at the football Ash said he had an idea.

'Let's sneak back in your house,' he said. 'I wanna see what your bedroom looks like!'

I was nervous about it but agreed. We went off in his car to get some chips so I could prove to Mum I'd been to the chippy, and then I came in the back door.

'Mum, where are you? I'm back.'

'I'm in the kitchen, love,' she replied.

'OK. I've eaten my chips,' I called back. 'I'm off to bed.'

'OK, love, night!'

I then gave Ash the nod to sneak in behind me through the back door. He was all excited, like a child in a sweet shop. I was so nervous in case I got caught, but I was also buzzing. I knew what we were doing was really naughty, and it gave me an adrenaline rush. Ash crept in through the door and I sneaked him along the hallway, straight past the kitchen door, behind which my mum was sitting. We then stole up the stairs and into my bedroom, trying not to make a sound. It was thrilling, and we were both grinning like loonies.

Ash looked around my room. 'It's right nice, in't it, Sammy? You're right posh.'

I had two single beds that pushed together to make one big one, and there was a spare bed underneath that pulled out if I had a friend to stay. All my wardrobes and the dressing table were cream and matching and I had pale blue curtains, yellow walls and lovely bedding, which was all summery and bright and had tulip-shaped flowers printed on it.

I had a set of shelves by my bed where I kept my stereo and CDs. Mum and Dad had given me the stereo for my birthday and I loved it. I had a load of Craig David CDs stacked on the shelf plus some Spice Girls, Blue and Atomic Kitten CDs, and lots of dance music. Ash looked at my collection and seemed impressed. Also on display was a framed certificate I'd been given at primary school for cross-country running, and pictures of me and my family smiling on holiday. Ash looked at everything and grinned approvingly. Then he said: 'Come here, I wanna have sex in your bed, that would be right exciting!'

'We can't do that,' I said with a smile on my face, trying to keep my voice down. 'We'll make too much noise.'

Ash didn't take no for an answer, and so we lay on the bed in the darkness and started to have sex. I was feeling confident by now about my body, because Ash paid me compliments all the time. I was comfortable taking my clothes off, and when I was naked Ash said to me, 'Get on top and ride me, Sammy.'

'I don't know how to do that,' I said, hoping he wouldn't think I was silly.

'I'll show you,' he said, pulling me on top of him, putting his hands on my bum and moving me really fast.

It hurt and I was struggling to catch my breath. I wanted to yelp out because it was so uncomfortable, and I even put my hands over my mouth to stop myself making a noise.

Ash started to laugh, which made me feel a little bit paranoid. 'You fuck like a fucking rabbit, Sammy.'

I wasn't quite sure what that meant and didn't have time to ask, because at that moment I heard my dad's voice downstairs.

'Holy shit, my dad's home! You gotta get out, you gotta get out!'

Ash started to laugh and quickly got dressed and headed for my bedroom window. I threw on some pyjamas and got into bed with my heart beating so hard I thought it was going to come out of my chest. He escaped by dropping down on to the roof of the outbuilding my dad had built on the back of the house. It was butted up right under my window, so it was easy for Ash to jump down from there and then sneak out of the back gate undetected.

Another night I climbed out of my mum and dad's bedroom and on to the porch above the front door to escape after dark. It was a school night and Mum and Dad had sent me to bed while they stayed up watching telly in the lounge downstairs. They would have seen or heard me coming down the stairs and going out the front or back door, so I lowered myself quietly off the porch roof and then ran off to meet Ash round the corner.

I knew there would be an almighty row if they found out I was missing, but what was the worst that could happen? All Mum and Dad could do was ground me, and even then they couldn't lock me in the house 24 hours a day, could they? Shouting and arguing didn't bother me. I'd take any argument with my family if that were the price I had to pay for seeing Ash. Calling the police was no use to Mum and Dad either; that had been proved on countless occasions by now, when they were told the same thing every time: 'There's nothing we can do if Sammy herself is not putting in a complaint.'

My dad had to do some contract work in London around this time, which took him away for days at a time, and this made it easier for me to get out. I'd disappear before my mum got in from work and then face the rows and the pleading from her when I eventually got home. I didn't even watch the clock any more when I was out; I was oblivious to everything other than Ash's attention.

One night we went out for a family meal, while Dad was still in London. As soon as I'd finished eating I ran off, straight out of the restaurant and across the car park, and went to meet Ash. Mum called my dad in tears, telling him what had happened, and asking what she should do. Nanan was there, and she was in tears. I don't think Dad ever worked in London again after that.

If I had a drink when I was out with Ash I became even bolder. I still smoked weed from time to time too. Ash always encouraged me to have as much as I liked whenever he bought a bottle of vodka, alcopops or offered me a spliff. I'd typically only been used to drinking cider before I met Ash and the vodka made my head spin quite quickly. I didn't like it on its own and usually had to drink it with Coke or I couldn't stomach it. It was the same with weed. Before I met Ash I'd only ever had a quick drag on some-body else's joint, just to be cool in front of my friends. Now I could have as much weed as I wanted, because Ash always had loads of the stuff. I'd try not to go home drunk or stoned but I'd usually had a bit of something. That loosened my tongue and made me shout and argue even more when my parents confronted me.

Me and Ash usually had sex in one of the houses his family owned, or he'd ask me to give him a blowjob quickly in the car, at the back of some garages or in the woodlands. I didn't know what I was doing the first time, but he told me he would help me, and show me exactly how to do it.

'Put your mouth around it and suck it hard like it's your favou-rite lollypop,' he said. That became a very familiar phrase to me; Ash said it often.

I didn't mind if the sex was quick, or if I didn't really get any pleasure from it myself. If Ash was satisfied, I was happy. I thought I was being a really good girlfriend, and doing what all other good girlfriends did for their boyfriends.

One night I was lying in bed at home, waiting for Ash to ring me on the Motorola, when I accidentally fell asleep. Dad came in to check on me, found the phone and took it away. When Ash phoned, Dad saw his name flash up and answered the call. He went absolutely mental with Ash, telling him to leave me alone once and for all. He told Ash never to contact me again, but Ash simply listened silently and hung up. Dad called the police imme-diately, but they told him what they always did: that if I wasn't making a complaint against Ash there was nothing they could do.

The following night Dad watched me like a hawk. I guess he thought he'd scuppered my chances of linking up with Ash because

I had no way of contacting him without the phone – Dad never returned it to me – and I was stuck in the house. What he didn't know was that Ash had met me at dinner time from school, laughed about the telling-off he'd had from my dad, and given me a brand-new phone.

'You can't do this!' I shouted at Dad when he was hovering around me that night. 'You're treating me like a prisoner!'

Dad had started securing the windows in the house and being extra vigilant about bolting and locking the doors too, to stop me escaping without him noticing, but I was one step ahead, as I had a window key. He hadn't actually caught me climbing out of his bedroom window at the front, and the night I'd done that I managed to slip back in through the back door without him even realising I'd been gone, but Dad wasn't daft and he must have had his suspicions.

'I can't let you out, Sammy,' he said. 'I can't trust you and I can't trust him. Why can't you listen? He's dangerous. He's got a criminal record. He's a married man. Can't you see how wrong this is? You're 14 years old! You're putting yourself in danger!'

'I'm not! I don't know what you're talking about!'

That was my default position. I simply denied I was seeing Ash, to anyone in my family who asked me about him.

I went to my bedroom and slammed my door. When Ash phoned my new mobile and asked me when and where we could meet, I whispered to him, explaining the situation. Both Mum and Dad were in and they weren't going anywhere, and Dad was on red alert, so I wasn't sure what we were going to do.

'I'll come round to yours then,' he said. 'I need to see you.'

'What?'

'I'll sort it. Wait for me.'

'What? How?'

Ash hung up. A few hours later, when I had all but given up hope of seeing him and was tucked up in bed in my pyjamas, I heard a tap on my bedroom window. I opened the curtains and looked out to see Ash on top of the roof of the outhouse. I unlocked the window and quickly let him in.

'My dad's home, he'll kill me,' I hissed.

'He won't know,' Ash said. 'We'll have to be fast.'

'Fucking hell, Ash! Get in, quick.'

Ash took all his clothes off. He was never afraid to show off his body. He went to the gym all the time, had a six-pack and was really confident about his physique.

'Get naked, Sammy,' he said. 'Let me see that sexy body.'

I followed his instructions, lay in bed and opened my legs. We had sex while my mum and dad were in their bedroom just along the landing. It was exciting and gave me a real adrenaline rush but it was also quite scary. I was terrified of Dad hearing something and coming in and finding us. Thankfully he didn't. Ash slipped out the window and disappeared into the night, while I re-locked the window and hid my key.

Afterwards I lay in my bed feeling really lucky we didn't get caught. I was thrilled that Ash was prepared to go to all this trouble to be with me, and I started to think that it was only a matter of time before we'd be able to stop sneaking around. I would be 15 soon, and then as soon as I was 16, I'd be out of here, living with Ash in a house of our own.

After that night, we pulled off the same stunt several more times without getting caught. I thought we were really clever.

We'd lie in bed and have sex trying not to make any noise, and we'd laugh under the covers afterwards, feeling really naughty. I didn't care at all about breaking Dad's rules and disobeying him, but I did care about being caught red-handed, as that would have been too embarrassing to bear, and I didn't like to think what Dad would do to Ash.

One night we heard my dad getting up and I gasped in panic but remembered not to scream. Ash quickly jumped under my bed, naked, and I pulled the covers up over myself, because I had no clothes on either. Dad appeared in the doorway of my room then walked to the end of my bed.

'What are you doing?' I said nervously.

Dad's feet were inches away from Ash, who was holding his breath and trying not to make a sound.

'Like I said, I don't trust you.'

My heart was pounding and I felt really vulnerable. Being in bed with no clothes on like this was bad enough, but having Ash hiding under my bed made it terrifying. I wanted Dad to leave my room as quickly as possible. He sniffed the air and then walked out, thank God, and when the house eventually fell silent again Ash got dressed and slipped out of the window.

I was really scared that we'd nearly been caught but Ash laughed his head off about it afterwards. He thought it was right exciting and daring, and again I was flattered he took the risk for me. He wasn't scared of anyone, even my dad, but he *was* bothered about us having our fun spoilt. Not being able to see me, and not being able to have sex with me, was the very last thing Ash wanted.

If I'd skipped school at dinner time we often drove some-where secluded to have sex. Afterwards he bought me my favourite foods like burger, chicken nuggets and chips from McDonald's, or cheese salad sandwiches and crisps. I felt like no expense was spared and I jokingly began to call him my 'walking bank machine'.

'You're worth it,' he'd say. 'I like to look after you, I like to feed you. I care about you.'

I really did feel very well looked after. Ash was the perfect boyfriend and didn't put a foot wrong in my eyes.

This changed one day when I went to an out-of-town shopping centre with Holly and Tina. We were sitting on a bench and a girl called Melanie, who looked to be a year or so older than me, came up to me and asked if my name was Samantha Woodhouse.

'Yes,' I said. 'Why?'

'Have you been seeing Ash?' she asked aggressively.

'Yes,' I said, frowning. 'What's this about?'

'I'm with him,' she said. 'And my friend is going out with Bono.'

My throat tightened and I could feel myself getting right upset and angry, but I tried to brazen it out and told her she was lying, and to go away and leave me alone.

'I'm not lying,' she laughed. 'I see him all the time. We have a right good laugh, we do.'

I stood up and went to walk away, but then Melanie started bragging about how she usually saw Ash in the flat on Clough Road, and how Ash and Bono had made her sit in the bath one time, and poured cola all over her while she still had her clothes on.

'It was right funny!' she laughed. 'We always have the best laugh together, me and Ash.'

What she said sounded too real for me to ignore and I felt sick to my stomach. *How can he cheat on me when he's told me he loves me?* I felt like shouting at Melanie that if Ash was a two-timing cheat like that then she was welcome to him, but I was too gutted to spit the words out. I'd been seeing him for months now and really didn't want this to be the end, but what choice did I have?

'Come on, Sammy,' Holly said. 'Just ignore her, she's jealous.'

We headed to the bus stop. Ash was meant to be picking us up to give us a lift home but I told Holly and Tina that I didn't want to see him.

'I can't be with him any more, can I?' I said, feeling dazed and angry. 'I thought he really loved me, but he's made a right idiot of me!'

My friends could see how upset I was and told me again to ignore Melanie. 'She's lying,' Holly said. 'You see Ash every day. How can he be seeing her as well? She's trying to wind you up.'

Holly wasn't very happy about the stuff said about Bono either, as she had an on–off relationship with him, but she wasn't floored like I was. Me and Ash were the couple who were serious. I believed we were faithful to one another; this had ruined everything.

My mind went into overdrive. If this Melanie was older than me she could easily have left school, and Ash could have been seeing her when I was in lessons. I was skipping school a lot, but there were plenty of other hours in the day when Melanie could have been seeing Ash too, because I usually only ever managed to see him for an hour or so each day.

I saw Ash's car in the car park and decided to walk down the tunnel into the bus station to avoid him.

'Sammy!' he called out angrily when he saw me walk away. 'Where are you going? Come back!'

He ran up to me asking what was going on, so I told him exactly what Melanie had said, and that it was over and I was getting the bus home.

'No! She's my ex, Sammy. She won't leave me alone! Don't listen to her crap!'

'I don't believe you.'

'You have to believe me! Honest, she's a jealous slag who doesn't want me to be with anyone else. That's the truth. Don't let her split us up. She's talking shit!'

Ash was shouting at me. He was absolutely livid, which scared me a bit. However, the fact he'd called Melanie a slag made me think his story could be genuine. I'd never heard him be so rude and disrespectful about a girl like that before; he was normally the opposite, and in my experience he was always a complete charmer.

I didn't want to make a mistake I might regret and so I turned around and got in his car. I really wasn't sure I'd done the right thing. Ash had never raised his voice at me in that way before and I suddenly felt a pang of fear as I sat in the passenger seat. I froze and felt as stiff as a board, thinking about how his shouting scared me.

Ash grinned and my friends were pleased I'd got in the car. They climbed in the back seat. Nobody wanted us to split up, and I didn't want to lose Ash.

Back in Rotherham, Ash dropped my friends off and then pulled into the Aldi car park not far from the centre of town. We were still talking about what Melanie had told me because I couldn't get it out of my head, and that's why he'd pulled over, so we could talk through what had happened without any distractions.

I told Ash I loved him and I didn't want to stop seeing him, but that I had to be sure he wasn't cheating on me. What my dad had said, about him being married, was in my head too. I'd always felt sure that was just my dad's desperate attempt to split us up, but after this Melanie episode I wanted to be certain there was no truth in it. I repeated what he had said, and Ash got angry.

'Look, Melanie's a dirty horrible little slag and your dad hates me cos he's racist. Why the fuck are you believing them over me?'

Ash was shouting again and I was getting scared, but I still wanted reassurance.

'So, you're definitely not seeing Melanie?'

'No, Sammy. Why would I want anyone else? You're taking the piss now.'

Ash's phone rang.

'More trouble,' he muttered, frowning and looking at the number.

'What is it?'

'I need to go and sort a guy out who's giving me trouble. You better wait here.' He said this angrily, and issued a threat: 'I mean it, Sammy. Stay here. I'm leaving my car keys and if I come back and you've gone, I won't be happy.'

Ash put a Craig David CD on for me, gave me a couple of cigs and said he'd be back as quickly as he could.

'OK. I'll wait for you.'

As I listened to the music I thought about how Ash's image had subtly changed since I met him. He modelled himself on Craig David, and he looked really good. He'd eat chicken and eggs for breakfast before going to the gym, and I'm sure he'd got even more muscles than he had when I first met him. He'd even grown a thin beard around the edge of his chin. He said he had done it for me, because he knew how much I liked Craig David.

Ash was gone for about half an hour, and when he came back he told me he'd dealt with the problem.

'How?'

'I had to kick someone's door in and give him a smack,' he said, looking right proud of himself.

I gave a nervous little laugh.

He thought for a moment and then said, 'I'm surprised you're still here.'

I wondered what I was doing there, but I'd stayed bolted to my seat, despite having been scared by his shouting.

'I'm glad you're safe,' I said. 'I was worried about you, Ash.'

'You're beautiful,' he replied, in a soft voice. 'You're my princess. I love you. You're the most beautiful girl in Rotherham.'

His words made my heart melt. He kissed me tenderly, stroked my face gently and told me again that he loved me. My heart filled with love for him, even though I also felt really anxious.

As I'd sat alone in his car I'd realised how deep my feelings were for Ash. I didn't just fancy him; I cared about him, a lot. I really did love him. It didn't matter that I was still only 14. I'd made up my mind that I wanted to be with him, forever.

'Shall we go and get some food, princess? You must be hungry.'

'OK,' I said quietly, still trying to take in everything that had just happened.

When he drove off my head was telling me I wasn't sure about this, but my heart was pounding with feelings for him. I was staying with him. That's what I wanted to do. Leaving him was unthinkable.

Chapter 11

'No one will find out, trust me'

'I want to teach you how to drive,' Ash said.

'Really? You'd do that for me?'

'Of course I would. I like teaching you things, Sammy.'

Ash had a cheeky, knowing smile on his face. He'd taught me a lot about sex by this stage. We'd been having sex every day for a few months and he'd shown me different positions and told me he wanted me to enjoy myself, like he was.

The first time I experienced an orgasm I started freaking out, because I didn't know what was happening. I don't think I'd ever even heard the word before. Ash was really sweet and patient. He explained everything and told me it was normal, and that it was what happened when two people who loved each other made love. He was quite responsible too, bringing condoms and teaching me how to put them on, although there were many times when we didn't use any protection.

'Here, this is for you,' he said one day, presenting me with a ring. It was Asian gold and decorated with green and purple stones. When we were intimate, he'd tell me he wanted to marry me and that he wanted me to have his children.

'I'll look after you, Sammy,' he always said. 'You'd never have to worry about anything. I'll take care of everything. You'll never have to work. You're too beautiful to work.'

Often we'd be curled up together on the old mattress in Clough Road when we had these conversations, and I'd look around the room and dream of the day when we wouldn't have to sneak around. We'd have our own lovely home, and everything would be clean and neat and perfect.

The ring took my breath away. 'What's all this?' I asked.

'It's for you. Try it on. We're going to get married!'

I put it on my ring finger but it was way too big, which was disappointing. I could tell he hadn't bought it from a jewellery shop as it wasn't in a box or anything, but I was still right chuffed he'd gone to this trouble. I gave it back to him, and he said he would get me another one that fitted properly.

I couldn't wait to learn to drive. Ash took me to Morrison's car park in his Astra and explained all the basics about the gears and the clutch and the brake, and then I got behind the wheel. It felt brilliant, even though I was barely five foot tall and had to have the seat raised up as much as it would go, to give me a good view over the steering wheel.

'You're right good,' Ash said, encouraging me every step of the way. 'Take your time. You're doing brilliant.'

He said this even when I was crunching his gears and narrowly missing other cars and obstacles in the car park. It was thrilling but also a bit terrifying. Eventually, Ash began to take me to other car parks and empty spaces around the town so I could practise. When I started to get the hang of driving I could feel a buzz rushing through me, and I felt proper grown up. Ash was right pleased with me. He said I was really clever and encouraged me no end when I finally got on to the roads.

It was nerve-racking, but Ash's reckless attitude was rubbing off on me by now. Instead of thinking, *what if I had an accident?* I was thinking, *whatever happens, Ash will fix it. Ash has other cars. Ash is a hero. He can sort anything out.*

In fact, my confidence was soon so high that when we eventually got spotted by the police one day I brazenly pulled over and swapped seats with Ash, right under the officer's nose.

'I saw you driving that car,' the officer said to me accusingly when he approached Ash's car.

My heart was thumping in my chest.

'Fucking prove it!' I said, giving him a defiant look and shocking myself in the process, because I hadn't planned to be so shameless, brash and rude.

The police officer was shocked too. He looked absolutely gobsmacked, muttered something under his breath and shuffled away. Ash burst out laughing and was clearly impressed that I'd behaved like a horrible little madam. I was pleased with myself too, because having Ash's approval was everything, and he'd always taught me not to like cops.

I began to carry this reckless attitude into school with me, so if I wasn't truanting, I was causing no end of trouble in the classroom. One day me and my friends drew rude pictures of a teacher's wife and pinned them up around the school. Another time we graffitied five-foot-high penises on the school walls, not giving a damn who saw us.

I was regularly hauled in front of the teachers, given detentions and threatened with letters and phone calls home, suspension and expulsion. 'I don't care,' I said. 'Throw me out. You'll be doing me a favour.' I could see the teachers getting right frustrated, because when they tried to discipline me it was like talking to a brick wall.

* * *

'We're gonna do a burglary,' Ash said to me one day, completely out of the blue.

'What are you on about, "we"?' I said, laughing.

Ash explained that the job was 'tit for tat'.

'I'm owned money so I'm taking back what's rightfully mine,' he said.

Ash told me that a man called Jim owed him a lot of cash, and he wanted me to climb in a window at the back of Jim's house and get the cash back. As it happened, I knew who this man was, as Jim used to go to the same school as our Kate.

'What if he finds out it's me and tells me mum and dad?'

At 14 years old, all I was worried about was being told off or grounded by my parents; being caught by the police for breaking and entering or burglary didn't enter my head.

'No one will find out, trust me,' Ash said.

Jim was a local drug dealer and lived in a terraced house in the town. Ash said I would be able to sneak in, grab the money from where he knew Jim stashed it, and do a runner. I could see why Ash wanted me to do it. I was a very slim and a petite size 6, with no hips and a very child-like body. Ash assured me that Jim would be out, as he went out at the same time every night, like clockwork.

'There'll be no comeback, Sammy. It's not his money anyway. He can't even report it.'

It sounded simple enough but I was still fretting about getting in trouble with my mum and dad.

'You love me, Sammy, don't you?'

'You know I do.'

'Then do it for me.'

'OK, I will.'

Ash drove to the back of the house in a black car, another of the many cars he and his brothers owned.

There was a tiny window at the back of Jim's house and me and Ash crept up to it. Then Ash lifted me up and started pushing me through the window, whispering at me to grab the money fast as soon as I was inside. He described where I should look, downstairs in the living room of the house.

My heart was beating fast. Suddenly, just as I was about to drop through the window, I saw a light go on in the hallway, and then I heard footsteps. It sounded like they were coming down the stairs and I froze.

'Shit!' I hissed. 'Someone's in! Someone's coming!'

Ash pulled me back out of the window and we ran to the car. I thought Ash would drive but he got in the passenger seat and told me to get behind the wheel.

'Shit!' I said again as I struggled to start the car. Ash was getting frustrated with me as I was taking so long to get going, while I was panicking and shaking and thinking Jim was going to come out and see me.

Ash was so agitated, and he suddenly lost patience. He threw open the passenger door, jumped out and ran off, telling me to meet him at the bridge.

Oh my God, I'm on my own and Jim's gonna come out and beat me up.

Just at the moment when I expected Jim to come charging out of the house, the engine finally fired up and I managed to drive off. The bridge was only down the road and I knew how to get there, but I was still scared stiff. I'd never driven a car on my own before, and it was dark. I was furious with Ash for leaving me by myself. I didn't even know how to switch on the headlights.

I headed down the road, and when I was approaching the pub at the bottom I saw someone waving their arms in the air, shouting that I had no lights on. To my relief I realised it was Holly, so I stopped the car and she jumped in.

'Sammy, what the fuck are you doing? You can't drive and you haven't even got your lights on!'

'I had no choice. Ash fucking left me. I can't believe it, I'll kill him!'

Holly helped me work out how to switch the lights on and then I drove us to the bridge, where Ash was waiting. He was laughing his head off when we both got out of the car.

'You left me!' I shouted, punching him on the top of the chest. 'I can't believe you left me!'

I wasn't usually as brave as this towards Ash, but fear and adrenaline were pumping through my body.

'Listen, everything's fine. He didn't see you. I knew you'd be fine on your own. I trust you, Sammy.' Ash carried on laughing. 'Come on, it were right funny! Don't be a mardy cow.'

I didn't want Ash to think I was a mardy cow, so after I calmed down I laughed it off, and so did Holly. Ash was my bad boy, so what did I expect?

We'd been together for nearly four months by now and I knew Ash was very heavily involved in crime and drug dealing.

The property business he'd told me about when we first met did exist, and his family did own other legitimate businesses too, but I never saw Ash do any regular work. He was becoming more open with me about his drug dealing, and he'd started teaching me a bit about the drugs world too.

I knew he had lots of people working for him, selling the drugs, and Ash said they were called 'runners'. Richard, my old boyfriend, was one of his runners. That explained how he knew Ash in the first place, and why he watched Ash's back. I learned that drug dealers had 'patches', certain areas where only they sold drugs. If anyone else muscled in, there would be massive consequences.

I took all this on board, still naïvely failing to see what a dangerous, evil trade Ash was involved in. Ash was clean and healthy, and he was a businessman. I thought all he was doing wrong was dealing in something that it wasn't legal to sell, and my childish understanding stopped there. I didn't question the wider consequences, or the morality of what he was doing.

One day Ash told me that a man and a woman had started dealing drugs on his patch, near my dad's old club.

'I'm going round to the flat, come on,' he said.

Ash left me in the car and I watched as he and another man he worked with went up to the white front door of a flat. It was near Nanan's place and I was worried someone might see me. My heart was beating fast as I watched Ash kick the door straight off its hinges. Then he and his mate went inside.

'Sammy, come here,' Ash said a few minutes later, sticking his head out of the door.

I did as I was told and darted in the house. Ash and his mate were trashing the place, looking for money and drugs, and Ash showed me loads of shopping bags stuffed with women's clothes, all still with designer labels on.

'Take what you want,' he said. 'They owe me. Take the lot if you like.'

It was like Christmas. The only designer clothes I'd ever worn were the odd items I pinched from my sister when she wasn't looking. I grabbed loads of stuff and ran back to the car, buzzing. Ash was pleased to see me like that.

'I don't know who these dirty bastards think they are,' he said. 'This is my fucking town. You'll look miles better wearing them clothes than his girlfriend.'

The clothes were amazing and I thought how lucky I was that they were brand new, and hadn't even been taken out of the bags. It never occurred to me that they didn't belong to the drug dealers either, and were probably stolen goods. I believed Ash's story every time. He was just taking what was rightfully his, what he was owed. It was tit for tat, which wasn't a big deal, was it?

Chapter 12
'The police have got to listen now!'

'I'm pregnant,' I said, my heart missing a beat.

Sophie was in the school toilets with me, and we both looked at the blue line on the pregnancy test. I'd bought it in the chemist after missing a period, and I was hoping it would come up positive.

'Oh my God!' Sophie exclaimed. 'What are you going to do?'

'Keep it, of course. There's no way I'm getting rid of it. We're in love. We're going to get married, as soon as I'm old enough. I can't wait to tell him. He's gonna be so excited!'

Sophie was still my best friend, but she'd told me she felt as if she'd lost me to Ash, as I was now spending all my time with him. She knew Ash and his brothers and also hung around with them, but she looked a bit doubtful and worried about my reaction to the pregnancy. I'm not sure she approved of me wanting to keep the baby, but she didn't argue with me. We'd been very close friends for ten years, and she said she'd do whatever she could to help me.

When I thought about having a baby I imagined it would be like having a doll, but one that breathed. I pictured how its skin would be a gorgeous colour, and I really hoped our baby would have Ash's big brown eyes. I didn't care if it was a girl or a boy. I wanted Ash's baby, and for us to be together forever, bringing our little girl or little boy up, and then having another baby, and another.

I was so thrilled to be pregnant that before I even talked to Ash, I blabbed to a girl at school called Jennifer. I'm not sure why I did that, because I couldn't stand her and she was a horrible bully. Perhaps I thought I was proving to her how grown up I was. To me, being pregnant was proof I had a boyfriend who loved me enough to want to have babies with me, which made me better than Jennifer, didn't it?

'Don't you dare get rid of that baby or I'll kick the shit out of you,' Jennifer said. I was used to girls talking aggressively like that. There were arguments, slanging matches and scraps all the time around school and on the housing estates.

Thanks to Jennifer, my news spread like wildfire all over the school, and one of my teachers got wind of what was being said and phoned my mum, who confronted me the second I got home from school.

'Are you pregnant, Sammy?' Mum looked worried sick. 'I've had a phone call from the school.'

'No,' I said, bold as brass. 'I can't believe what you're saying to me!'

I knew Mum would go mental if she knew the truth, and probably want me to have an abortion.

'Then why did the teacher phone me? Why are the girls at school talking about you being pregnant? Apparently, you've admitted it to one of them—'

'It's just one of the bullies at school spreading lies, Mum.'

'Are you sure, Sammy?'

'Course I'm sure! What do you take me for? That Jennifer's a right lying cow. Honestly, Mum, it's all a load of crap.'

Then Dad turned up, and he began ranting and raving and threatening to press charges against Ash.

'I knew he was bad news! I knew this would end in tears. The police have got to listen now!'

'Peck! You can't jump to conclusions,' Mum cried, leaping to my defence. 'I believe our Sammy's word. My babby would never lie to me, would you, Sammy love?'

Mum looked me in the eye, searching for what she wanted to see, and Dad was staring at me intently. It was like he was holding his breath. If I admitted I was pregnant he'd explode, but if I denied it, he'd be able to breathe normally again.

'No,' I said brazenly. 'I'll do a pregnancy test if you like, to prove it.'

Dad slumped on to the settee. He said it was a good idea to do a test, as he didn't know whether he could believe me. Despite it being my suggestion I kicked off again, saying what a waste of time it was, as I wasn't even sleeping with Ash or anybody else for that matter. Dad's mention of the police scared me, because I didn't want Ash to get into trouble with the cops. I had never been concerned about the law until this point. I knew it was illegal to have sex at my age, but I hadn't dwelled on the possible consequences for Ash.

I asked if Sophie could be there when I did the test, and then I asked her a big favour.

'Can you do it for me?'

'What?'

'The test. Can you do it instead of me? You only have to wee on it.'

'Oh God, I don't know, Sammy …'

'Please, Sophie! If you don't they'll know I'm pregnant and they'll make me get rid of the baby, and Ash might go to jail! There's no way I'm getting rid of my baby. Please can you help me out?'

I'd put my friend on the spot, which wasn't fair, but the seriousness of the situation was sinking in and I was desperate. Sophie reluctantly agreed and then did the test for me in the bathroom. I waved the negative pregnancy stick under my parents' noses triumphantly.

'See, I'm not pregnant!' I crowed. 'Now will you believe me?'

'I believed you anyway. Thank God, Sammy.' Mum smiled with relief even though she looked so stressed and exhausted. 'I knew my babby would never lie to me.'

Dad looked relieved too, but he wasn't smiling. He began shouting about the police again, threatening to have Ash arrested for being involved with me.

'What would they arrest him for?' I taunted. 'I'm not sleeping with him! You've got no proof. It's all in your sick mind, Dad.'

I felt I'd won. I'd not only hidden the pregnancy, but Dad couldn't get the police involved. As far as anyone knew, nothing had changed since the last time he'd called them. I wasn't complaining about my relationship with Ash, far from it. There was no proof he was having sex with me, and it wasn't against the law for a 14-year-old to have a 24-year-old boyfriend, was it? Mum and Dad wouldn't find out I was pregnant until it was too late, and when the baby arrived everyone would just have to accept it and move on.

I met Ash after school the next day and told him the news. We'd parked up behind a pub, in an alleyway where the woods were. I announced the pregnancy in a breathless, excited way, like a wife would to a husband, because in my mind that's what we were like, only we hadn't got married yet, because of my age.

Ash smiled and looked right pleased.

'I'll do all I can to support you, you know that,' he said, which made my heart swell. That was exactly what I thought he'd say.

'Come here.'

He pulled me over to him and kissed me, and then we had sex. I'd never felt so happy and so loved.

Chapter 13
'I don't know what I'd do without you'

My head was all over the place once I started to really think about the fact I was pregnant, and my next memories are quite blurred.

From my Social Services file, I know I had a doctor's appointment in February 2000, and that Ash came with me. We saw a GP, who confirmed my pregnancy and subsequently informed Social Services that I was 14 and the father of my child was a 24-year-old called 'Mad Ash' who was 'apparently on a probation order'. In my Social Services file it is noted that 'Sammy is not making any complaint regarding "Ash" and being pregnant, in fact she is happy with the relationship'. It goes on to say 'there does not appear to be a role for SS at this time'.

After this appointment, I do remember that Ash started to fret and worry. I would only be 15 when the baby was born, and he began to talk about DNA tests and the law.

'What are you saying?' I asked, feeling hurt and upset. 'Don't you want me to have our baby?'

'Of course I do, Woodypoo,' he said.

I liked it when Ash called me that. He also stroked my face the way he had done when we first met. 'All I'm saying is it could get me into trouble. I don't care about getting myself into trouble, I can handle that. But what about you?'

'What d'you mean?'

'I could be locked up, and then I wouldn't be able to support you and the baby. And then there's my family. If I got locked up because of you, they'd kill you.'

My eyes widened. I hadn't thought of any of this. I didn't think for one minute that Ash meant his family would literally kill me, but I knew how tight-knit they were, and I knew there would be big trouble if he went to prison because of me.

'What shall we do?' I asked, my eyes searching his for answers.

'Like I say, I'll support you. I'll do all I can to help if you want to keep the baby, but it's risky.'

That night I lay in bed with my hands on my stomach. I wasn't showing at all yet as it was very early days, but I felt different and I couldn't sleep. I wasn't afraid of what was going to happen to my body – strangely, this didn't bother me at all – but I was right scared of what was going to happen when the baby arrived. I was terrified of losing Ash to prison. I had no idea what to do, and I couldn't talk to Mum and Dad because I was still denying to them that I was pregnant at all.

Not long after we'd been to the GP, Ash came to pick me up from the shops near school. It was dinner time and so there were lots of other school kids around, and as he pulled up in his car he saw me walking along, talking to a boy the same age as me. I'd known this lad for years and there was nothing going on, but Ash didn't like to see me talking to him. I didn't realise he was angry and jealous until I got in his car.

'What the fuck are you doing?' he screamed, his knuckles turning white as he gripped the steering wheel hard.

'What d'you mean?' I asked, shocked and confused.

Ash suddenly picked up a lighter, threw it in my face and hit my head on the dashboard, demanding to know why I was talking to a boy, and calling me a 'fucking whore'.

'Oh my God!' I screamed. My nose started bleeding and it really hurt, but Ash didn't let up. He sped off, driving way too fast and through red traffic lights, and all the time he was ranting about what a fucking whore I was, what a white slag I was, and accusing me of sleeping with other people.

'Stop it!' I shouted. 'You're gonna harm the baby!'

'Good!' he yelled. 'You're not good enough to have my kid!'

'I'll have it on my own then! I don't want to be with you any more!'

'I'd like to see you try,' he said, sneeringly. 'You know what's gonna happen to you, don't you? You'll end up a scrubber in a council house with loads of kids, and no one will know your fucking name.'

I looked at him, horrified.

'I'll kill your whole fucking family,' he ranted. 'And your dad will be the first to get it.'

He then started grabbing at my hair, pulling it so hard I was being flung around like a rag doll. I kicked him and managed to climb in the back of the car, where I cowered on the back seat and started to cry. Ash didn't let up and tried to grab me with one hand while he continued to speed along. I kept kicking to get him away from me, and eventually he calmed down and pulled over.

'I'm sorry, Woodypoo,' he said. 'I'm really sorry. I don't know what came over me.'

'That was horrible. What the hell is wrong with you?'

'It's your fault. You made me like this.'

He told me he cared for me so much that he couldn't stand seeing another boy even talking to me.

'I love you,' he said. 'I only reacted like that because I love you so much. Look what you made me do! Do you still love me as much as I love you?'

I nodded and wiped away my tears.

'You're not going to leave me, are you, Woodypoo? I can't live without you. I'd never hurt your family. I was just mad, you know that, don't you?'

Again, I nodded my head. I was extremely quiet and withdrawn and Ash was really fussing over me. It seemed like he was afraid I was going to leave him.

We went to get some food and Ash made sure my nose was all right.

'It's fine,' I said. 'Let's forget it.'

* * *

Both my sisters soon discovered the truth about my pregnancy from friends of friends, and they confronted me at home. Kate went absolutely mental, telling me that I had to face up to the mess I was in.

'It's not true!' I lied again.

'Admit it, Sammy! You need to start telling the truth.'

'You're mad!' I shouted. 'Just leave me alone.'

Lisa started shouting and screaming and saying, 'I can't believe you're doing this. What the hell is happening to our family?'

It was around the time of her 16th birthday and she'd been given a TV for her bedroom as a present. I screamed back at her, telling her to keep her nose out of my business.

'How the hell can we do that?' she yelled. 'We *know* you're pregnant. You can't keep lying. You need to admit it and we need to sort it out.'

Lisa then said she would raise the baby while I was at school. I told her to fuck off and leave me alone, adding, 'This is my baby, not yours!'

I'd admitted it now and Lisa gasped as she took this in, but I immediately told another lie, saying Ash wasn't the father like everyone was saying. Kate screamed in my face that I was lying. She also yelled that I had no choice but to have an abortion.

Something in me snapped. I picked up Lisa's brand-new TV and threw it straight at Kate's head. Mum appeared at the top of the stairs, screaming and crying and begging us to stop fighting.

The next few days are a blur to me. I started thinking that maybe it was a bad idea to have got pregnant in the first place as it was causing so much trouble for everyone.

Mum and Dad said they were going to get a DNA test on the baby, whether I kept it or had an abortion. They also told me that if they had DNA, they could press charges without me making a complaint myself, so Ash was done for and would be locked up either way. Ash really started panicking when I told him this, and he began to suggest ways to bring on a miscarriage, so I didn't have to have an abortion. One of his ideas was for him to beat me really badly in the stomach, and another was to throw me down the stairs.

'You can get fucked,' I told him. He then suggested I ran a red-hot bath and drank a bottle of castor oil. He said that would end the pregnancy, the baby would suffer no pain and it would be peaceful for everyone.

'Will you do it, Sammy? I think that's the right thing to do.'

I reluctantly said yes, because I agreed to nearly everything Ash wanted me to do, and I didn't want him to go to prison. I was in emotional turmoil, and I could see no other way out.

He gave me a bottle of castor oil. 'Here you go, Sammy. Make sure you drink it all. Just remember it's the best thing. I love you.'

I nodded robotically, took the oil and went home and ran a hot bath. Then I sat in it, holding my stomach and crying. All I could think about was that I was about to kill my baby, the baby I had already grown to love and planned to bring into the world. I had to do it though, because if I had the baby Ash would be locked up, and even if I went to hospital for an abortion, he could still go to prison.

I picked up the bottle and started to pour it down my throat, and the next minute I was vomiting everywhere in the bath. Mum and Dad heard all the commotion and came rushing upstairs. I'm not sure why but my vomit was a dark red colour. 'What's going on?' both Mum and Dad called in a concerned way.

'Nowt. I'm OK, I've just been sick.'

They didn't believe me, and when they saw the bathwater, once I'd got myself out of the bath, they thought I'd put tomato sauce or some other red liquid in the bath, to fake a miscarriage, so I could secretly go on to have the baby.

'You think we're stupid,' they said. 'He's told you to do this.'

'It's not true, I've just been sick.'

I was shouting at them but they weren't believing a word of it. I'm not surprised; I'd spent the last six months telling them lie after lie.

My miscarriage attempt didn't work. Mum and Dad were worried to death and wanted me to have an abortion but I dug my heels in and refused to admit or agree to anything.

Not long after this, I was moved in with Kate for a while. Mum and Dad were prepared to try anything that might help the situation. They were struggling to cope, and I'd had another massive row with Dad.

I was running a bath again and Dad started shouting and screaming at me, telling me what a mess I was making of my life, and how I was ripping the family apart. I grabbed the nearest object and swung it at him. It was a tall iron candlestick with a tulip-shaped top, and I very nearly clobbered him with it. He grabbed hold of my neck and put my head under the water, and Mum had to drag him off.

Dad was absolutely mortified afterwards that he had done this to me. I'd completely pushed him and Mum to breaking point, but of course I used this against him.

'You're mental,' I taunted. 'You're round the twist. I'm not listening to you! You're out of control. I hate you! I hate all of you!'

Mum broke down in tears, and I got dressed and ran off out the house. Ash and his friend came and met me at the top of the street. I felt so grateful and relieved.

'I don't know what I'd do without you,' I gasped.

'Your family are bastards, Sammy, but don't worry, I'm going to look after you. You don't need them, you've got me.'

Ash was right: the only person I needed was him. He kissed me and told me everything would be all right now. He was going to look after me and make sure I came to no harm.

Ash drove us to a small terraced house not far from the town centre, where he introduced me to a woman called Sarah. She was friendly enough and made me feel quite welcome, even though the house itself was cold and a bit untidy and scruffy. Ash suggested it was somewhere I could stay if need be, to get away from all the shouting and arguing at home. I didn't ask questions.

When I was moved in with Kate she took my mobile phone off me in an attempt to stop me having any contact with Ash. At the first opportunity, when Kate had to go out and locked the door behind her, I tore the place apart, searching for my phone. I found it hidden among a pile of towels in Kate's bathroom and immediately called Ash. I told him my family wanted me to have an abortion, and that Kate had locked me in the house while she went out.

'I'm on my way,' he said.

I waited anxiously, but not for long. I heard the engine on 'Scooby', which was the nickname he had for his blue Subaru. I looked out of my sister's bedroom window and spotted Ash driving down the street. He signalled me to come out.

I got out somehow – I must have climbed out of a window – and I ran to meet him.

My family didn't understand how I felt. They were trying to split me and Ash up, and how dare they do that? Didn't they realise this wasn't some stupid teenage romance? I was in love with Ash and he was in love with me.

So Ash took me to Sarah's house and stayed with me all night. I was tired but he said he wanted to make love to me, and so I agreed.

'We'll get a place of our own one day,' Ash said, as he lay beside me on the floor of a room downstairs. We used a thin mattress that was old and a bit tatty, like everything in the room, but I wasn't bothered. At least I wasn't alone, lying in my bed at home, worrying about the future all by myself.

The next day Ash went out for a bit, and when he came back, he said he wanted to make love to me. I didn't feel like it but I didn't like saying no after everything he had done for me. We had sex for quite a long time, but Ash wasn't satisfied.

'I want to make love to you all day,' he said.

I was flattered and I didn't want to upset him, so I agreed to carry on. We had sex for hours and I wondered how Ash carried on. I was getting sore and badly swollen, and asked him to stop loads of times.

'Ash, please stop! It's hurting loads, it's really burning.'

He squeezed loads of moisture cream from a pot in between my legs, and then carried on.

'Ash, it still hurts, please stop!'

But he kept going, telling me not to be 'mardy' and saying, 'Just keep putting moisturiser on it, you'll be fine.'

In the end we had sex all day and all night. The only time we had a break was to go to the toilet. I found it almost impossible as I was in so much pain and so badly swollen. Afterwards I lay on the floor holding myself, complaining about the pain and wanting it to go away.

* * *

Mum had called the police and reported me missing. She explained that I'd run off after arguments about me being pregnant, and she said that she believed I was pregnant by a 24-year-old Asian called Ash. This was noted in my Social Services file, written up by a member of the 'Family Crisis Response Team', on 1st March 2000.

I'd been missing for a couple of days when Ash's phone suddenly lit up. It seemed everyone was ringing, telling him to get me home. His brothers, Bash and Bono, both called, as did another relative called Jahangir Akhtar. I'd never heard of Akhtar before, but Ash told me that he was well connected. Someone in the police had contacted Akhtar and warned there would be 'too much police involvement' if Ash didn't get me home 'sharpish'.

Ash took all of these calls on his mobile, and then he parked up and went to a phone box, where he rang a police officer he knew called PC Sadat. I'd met this officer a few times when I was with Ash. He was quite young and cool and had a goatee beard, and he was always right nice to us whenever we saw him.

'Look, Sammy, I really do have to get you home,' Ash told me after he had spoken to PC Sadat.

'No, I don't want to go home,' I replied. I couldn't face the rows again, I just wanted to hide away with Ash.

'You have to. You can run away again, but I've got to get you back today, or I'll be in trouble.'

I didn't want Ash to get into trouble, and so I told him I'd agree to go home, at least until the dust had settled and I could run away again. I thought he would drop me off at the top of my road, or near our Kate's, but Ash explained that he had been told to drop me off at a local petrol station. If he did that, Ash said he'd been assured that he wouldn't be questioned over his involvement in my running away from Kate's house. The last thing I wanted was for Ash to be in trouble with the cops on my account, so I agreed to go to the petrol station with him.

We drove to the garage where Ash had arranged to hand me over, and as we pulled up I saw there were quite a few men in police uniform waiting for us, as well as Ash's relative, Jahangir

Akhtar. I didn't know why he was there. I think he was a taxi driver then, though later on he went on to become a councillor, and then the deputy leader of Rotherham Council.

I was taken out of Ash's car and put into the back of another car with two men in the front. It was a long, dark-coloured, unmarked police car. Then I was driven to Main Street Police Station in Rotherham, from where police called my mum and told her they'd found me. After the call was made, one police officer told me I should be ashamed of myself. I started crying and arguing, telling the police I didn't want to go home. I brought up the fight I'd had with my dad, telling the police that Dad had tried to strangle me, and that I was scared he might hurt me again.

The police told me that if I didn't go home I'd have to be put in a children's home or placed with an emergency foster carer that day. I thought that if I were in care it would be much harder to see Ash, because a children's home or foster carer would have even stricter rules than my mum and dad. Because of this I very reluctantly agreed to go home, consoling myself with the thought I'd run away again, as soon as I could.

While I was at the station, a police officer asked me for Ash's surname. I told him I didn't know it, which was true. All I knew was that his nickname was Mad Ash and I knew his real first name was Arshid, but I didn't know his last name and had never bothered to ask. Ash knew everything about me, yet I realised I knew next to nothing about him.

I was also questioned about my pregnancy. I admitted it but lied and said I'd got pregnant on a one-night stand with a teenage boy, because I was so desperate to protect Ash from getting into trouble with the law.

I don't think the police believed me about the one-night stand. I was made the subject of a Police Protection Order, and another note went in my Social Services file. Written by a police officer, it said: 'Samantha Woodhouse has been missing from home since 28/02/00. She is suspected of being two months' pregnant. Due to her age she is considered to be morally and physically in danger. The people she has been associating with during her period missing are known to the police and social services. Due to her association she is considered to be in further danger'.

A social worker subsequently phoned the probation service to ask if they knew of a 'Mad Ash', describing him as an Asian male in his twenties who had recently ended a prison sentence. The probation officer refused to give out information to the social worker without knowing Ash's full name and date of birth, so that trail went cold.

Nevertheless, Social Services did have information on Ash, because over the next few days several other notes were written in my file. One said that further details had emerged on him that had a 'bearing on my situation', and that it should be stressed to my mum how 'at risk' Social Services felt I was 'without divulging' what these further details were. Someone from Social Services told my mum they had serious concerns for my safety and that she must not let me out. They also said they would contact my school and work out a strategy for my education. If I went missing, Mum was to call the police, and if I had any trouble from the 'Asian community', she was advised to call 999.

The next day a social worker phoned my school to set up a meeting about me. 'I explained we had serious child protection concerns regarding Sammy,' the social worker wrote in my file.

This meeting never took place in the end, because a water pipe burst and the school had to cancel the appointment.

I knew none of this and, as advised in my file, my parents were kept in the dark about the further details that were known to Social Services about Ash but not shared. To this day, I do not know exactly what the social workers knew at this point in time, because when I got hold of my file many years later a large section from this particular entry, dated 2nd March 2000, was marked with an asterisk, completely blacked out and had these words written in the margin: 'CONFIDENTIAL DO NOT DIVULGE OUTSIDE OF TEAM'.

Chapter 14
'I'm only like this because I love you so much'

'OK, I'll have the abortion,' I said flatly.

My family were so relieved, but I wasn't doing it for them. I was doing it for Ash and only Ash, because I didn't want him getting into bother with the police or locked up. I felt deflated, miserable, very angry and was too tired to argue any more. My brush with the law had brought me to this conclusion. It seemed the only way out.

Members of my family took me to Rotherham Hospital. I have no recollection of how I got there, and very little memory of the events of the day itself. I have an image in my head of being in a white, chemical-smelling room at the hospital, after it had happened. People were talking about my situation and everyone seemed to know the truth by now, that Ash was the father, but I really didn't care what my family or anybody else thought. The previous few weeks had been a nightmare, with social workers talking to my mum a lot, poking their noses into my business and going on about how they were going to get me back to school when this was all over. I couldn't give a shit about school or anything else and I was very uncooperative. All I wanted was to get out of the hospital, get back on my feet and see Ash again.

My dad had begun to slowly withdraw into himself. Instead of ranting and raving he became very quiet and sad, almost like he was depressed. One day he went to watch a Man United game with his brother and started crying. My uncle disowned me after that, as did a lot of other members of our extended family.

Mum was suffering from stress and anxiety. She'd start crying very easily, and then would have a few drinks to calm her nerves, which usually made her even more tearful. She and my dad argued when I was out of the room. I'd had enough of both of them, and I thought we'd all be better off when I'd finally left home and lived with Ash.

It was decided that I'd have a few weeks at home to recover from the termination and return to school after the Easter holidays, closely supported by my family and teachers. I think my mum thought the shock and upset of the pregnancy, and the fact the police and Social Services had got involved, would finally make me see sense and stop seeing Ash, but the way I saw it, we were more closely tied than ever. I'd lied for Ash and made the biggest sacrifice possible to keep him out of trouble with the police, and he said he was prepared to stand by me despite the risks, and wait until the time was right for us to try again to have a baby together.

Mum and Dad both had to work for some of the time once I was at home; it wasn't feasible for them to guard me 24/7, even though they wished they could. Whenever I had the chance I'd sneak out of the house and see Ash. He usually picked me up at the top of the road in his car and we talked, listened to our favourite music, went for a drive and had some food. He fetched fags and spliffs sometimes, which I'd kept off when I was pregnant, and then we'd park somewhere private and chill out.

Our relationship now felt edgy all the time. The good times were brilliant, but when we had a row it could get really explosive.

One day Ash asked me what I wanted from the shop. 'A cheese salad sandwich, a bottle of Lucozade and a packet of beef and onion crisps, please,' I said.

'You can't eat them,' he snapped.

'Why not?'

'Because I'm Muslim and I don't eat beef, it's against my religion. If you eat them you won't be able to kiss me.'

'But Ash, I eat them all the time. You've never said anything before! That's stupid!'

'Don't call me fucking stupid, motherfucker!'

Suddenly, his eyes were blazing and he looked right nasty and was snarling at me. I recoiled in my seat, trying to shift myself as far away from him as possible. I was scared he might hit me, because by now he'd hit me lots of times.

I can't remember the exact way it escalated, but violence had crept into our relationship and become the norm. Sometimes it was a slap or a punch, other times he grabbed my hair. I thought that was what boyfriends did to their girlfriends when they had a row, because Ash told me that's what people did when they had strong and passionate feelings for each other, like we did. I always hit him back, but I didn't stand much of a chance as I was so tiny. A lot of the fights got extremely aggressive, and Ash said those ones were always my fault for making him angry.

This time, over the beef crisps, I thought he might attack me very badly.

'You want to be with me, you do as I fucking say!' he shouted.

'OK,' I whispered, shocked by the level of his anger.

We drove on in silence, and a few minutes later, Ash apologised.

'I'm so sorry, Sam,' he said. 'I'm only like this because I love you so much. You know that, don't you?'

I nodded. I hated it when he got angry, but I knew he didn't upset me on purpose. He was very protective of me, that's all, and I took that as a compliment.

* * *

We both agreed we had to be careful about our relationship for the time being, because we didn't want the police getting involved again. We had to keep things secret, and I also had to be careful not to get pregnant again. We used contraception and me and Ash carried on having a lot of sex. Sometimes we went to a hotel in Rotherham; other times he parked up at the garages or in the woods, where he asked me to give him oral sex in the car. I always did it if that's what he wanted; at least I wouldn't fall pregnant that way.

If I couldn't get out of the house during the day, Ash sometimes climbed in my bedroom window in the middle of the night, and we had sex as quickly as we could while my parents slept next door. Ash sometimes put his hand over my mouth, to stop me making any noise. He didn't seem nervous at all, but I always was.

I thought we'd got away with this, but it turned out we hadn't. One of our neighbours told my dad that they'd seen a man matching Ash's description on the roof of the outhouse under my bedroom window, and when Dad investigated, he found footprints and told the police.

I didn't know this at the time. Nor did I know that Dad was falling apart as much as Mum; he just didn't show it in the emotional way she did. After he went quiet and stopped shouting and fighting with me, Dad gradually stopped speaking to me completely. It had got to the stage where he would walk straight out of a room when I walked in. *Arsehole*, I'd think. *I can't wait to get out of here.*

* * *

I hadn't been back at school for long when Ash phoned me on another mobile phone he'd given me, in a right state. He said he'd had a fight with my dad and we should run off together. I ran straight out of school in a blind panic and our Lisa was there, screaming and going mental. She'd been coming up to school to find me, and she was shouting that Dad had gone round to Ash's house and Ash had battered him. Lisa was so angry that the teachers had to put her in a room to calm down. Meanwhile, I ran off to meet Ash, who was parked up outside school. As soon as I got in his car I saw that he had scratches on his face.

I asked Ash if Dad was all right and he told me my dad had turned up at the house where Ash's mum, dad and family lived. Dad tried to warn Ash off seeing me, and he accused him of having a wife and kids in the house, which had really pissed Ash off.

'I didn't want to hurt him,' Ash said, 'but he went for me, and I had no choice but to fight back. I feel right bad. I broke his chain.'

Ash handed me the expensive gold chain that my dad always wore around his neck. I was gutted to see it in pieces. I didn't want my dad to be hurt, but I was also blazing that he'd fought with Ash and scratched his face. It confirmed what I'd suspected from the start: Dad wanted to interfere in my life and spoil my happiness. Why couldn't he leave us alone? This was my life, not his, and I was absolutely livid and embarrassed.

'I'm sorry,' I said to Ash. 'I feel right ashamed of my dad, doing that.'

Ash shrugged it off, and then his phone rang. It was my dad, and he knew from the school that I'd gone missing.

'Tell Sammy to come home; she's not in trouble. You can drop her off outside the house.'

Ash couldn't believe this, but Dad said very calmly that he would rather know where I was, and he just wanted me home.

In the past, my dad would have gone mental if Ash had come anywhere near the house. This was the first time he had moved an inch in my direction, but Lisa told me afterwards that the reason he did this was because he was scared I wouldn't come back at all. Apparently, he had heard rumours that Ash was planning to take me away somewhere, and he feared he would never see me again.

I let myself into the house and went up to my bedroom, holding Dad's broken chain. I thought there was nobody in because it was so quiet, but then Dad appeared at my bedroom door. I gasped in shock; I scarcely recognised him. He'd clearly been given a right good hiding. His lips were swollen and split, and one side of his mouth looked like it had been turned inside out and was stuck up on the side of his face.

'Here's your chain,' I said softly, feeling right bad for him. 'I'm sorry it's broken. I'm sorry you got hurt.'

I found out later that Ash had charged at Dad when his back was turned, as Dad was shouting to members of Ash's family, telling them what Ash was up to.

Dad looked like a defeated man, but I didn't feel like I'd won. It was really sad to see my dad in that state. I was used to him being my hero, the kind of bloke who defended his family and always came out on top. Dad stayed very calm and quiet as he began to talk. He said that even though he had asked Ash to drop me at the house on this occasion, I was not allowed to go near him again. That wasn't going to happen, but it wasn't the time for an argument. I thought I'd just have to get better at sneaking around.

Our Lisa now says it felt like our house went through three phases during our childhood. In the beginning, it was like a youth club, full of laughter and fun and kids, with Mum as the Pied Piper, always the life and soul of the party. Then the shouting and screaming came. Mum got hysterical and emotional; Dad came out fighting and flexing his muscles. After that there was this terrible sadness and silence. Dad looked cowed and kept very quiet, for what seemed like a very long time. Mum started drinking more, and became a crumbling, emotional wreck.

We'd reached a crisis point. I loved my parents and I hated to see them like this, but I wasn't prepared to do the one thing that would make them happy: I wasn't going to give up Ash. Even that day, when there was fresh blood on my dad's face, I was preoccupied with getting out of the house again to see my boyfriend.

Ash had a new plan. He got various women he knew to phone up our house and pretend they were the mothers of friends of mine. I thought this worked like a dream as it got me over the doorstep and we didn't get caught out, but in fact my parents were suspicious every time I left the house, and terrified I was continuing to see Ash. Unbeknown to me they were on the phone to the police all the time, reporting that I was missing or out with Ash, but getting the same feedback every time: there's nothing we can do if Sammy is not prepared to put in a complaint herself.

There were loads of occasions when I was seen by police officers in Ash's car but nobody stopped us, or the officers would chat to Ash and leave us alone. I understood very well by now that he had friends in the police, and that some of them must have been looking out for us.

My mum and dad were living on their nerves, filled with fear all the time. In desperation, they decided to take me and our Lisa on holiday to Spain for a week, hoping the time away would make me see sense, and sever the ties with Ash once and for all. I didn't want to go, not because I thought my parents' plan would work, but because I knew how much I would miss Ash.

Also, I'd heard all kinds of rumours that he was seeing other girls. This had happened on and off for ages, ever since the incident with that girl Melanie at the shopping centre. Now I was hearing tales more often, and from lots of different people. I didn't want to believe them, but why were so many people making up so many lies?

'They're just trying to make trouble,' Ash said, every single time I reported another story back to him. 'Don't believe them, Sammy. There's nowt to worry about. They're just jealous, I swear.'

Going away for a whole week made me anxious, because what if one of these girls sharked in while I was away?

Lisa helped convince me to go on holiday, saying what a good time we'd have, swimming and sunbathing and having a laugh like we did in Kos the year before. That holiday had only been about seven months earlier, just before I met Ash. It was unbelievable how much had happened in such a short space of time.

Before I knew it, the flights were booked, the suitcases were packed and we were going through the familiar routine of flying out of Manchester Airport. Thankfully, Dad wasn't completely ignoring me as he had been doing for a while, which was a relief. Two of Lisa's friends came with us, and having them there helped ease the tension within the family. Nobody wanted to mention

Ash and risk having trouble in front of Lisa's friends, and that suited me fine. I didn't want anyone to know I was still in love and had no intention of breaking up with him.

Once we arrived at our resort I found myself feeling less stressed than I had in ages. It was like I was in a bit of a bubble, away from Rotherham and all the bad stuff that had gone on.

As usual, me and our Lisa spent loads of time in the pool, swimming and fooling around. Meanwhile, Dad went off cycling and Mum took root on a sunbed, catching her tan. We had some good meals out and saw a few shows, and all in all, it was a right good holiday. The only thing that spoilt it for me was that I missed Ash, really badly. Every night I slipped out to the phone box near our hotel and secretly called him for as long as I could before my money ran out.

Mum and Dad had given us spends and I must have put all of mine in that phone box. Sometimes we had a snatched call on Ash's mobile, which ate the money, and sometimes I called him on a landline phone at whichever house he was staying at, as it was a bit cheaper. Either way the calls were never long enough, and I couldn't wait to get home and see him.

'Will you meet me as soon as I get back, Ash?'

'Of course I will, love. I can't wait.'

'I miss you.'

'I miss you too, Sammy. I bet you'll look right pretty with your tan.'

I lived for those nightly calls. Thank God Mum and Dad had absolutely no idea I was calling Ash; they'd had gone mental.

I'd lie in the sun and dream of the future. I was very nearly 15 now, and then I'd be 16, and of age. I couldn't wait for the day when I could do as I pleased. I wanted to be Ash's wife and have his babies. We'd had our ups and downs, but I loved him so much. He was my destiny, no question at all.

Chapter 15

'He's dangerous. He's going to ruin your life'

'Oh my God, look at your tan, it proper suits you,' Ash said. 'You look like a right sexy bitch, Sammy.'

The moment we landed back at home there was only one thing on my mind. I dumped my suitcase and ran straight out of the door, not caring what Mum and Dad thought, running as fast as my little legs could carry me.

Ash was waiting for me in the car, down what we called the snicket, the narrow alleyway running along the back of the row of houses I lived on. I jumped straight in the front seat, and he was clearly buzzing to see me.

'Do you really think so?' I grinned. 'I've missed you loads, Ash. I've been dying to see you.'

'I've missed you loads, Woodypoo. I've been lost without you. I didn't know what to do with myself.'

We drove off in the Scooby with the windows down and music blasting. Ash was bouncing on his seat with one hand on the wheel, singing away to me and waving his other arm around to the music. We both had massive smiles on our faces and I was giggling at him. People walking past were looking at us, as the music was so loud and the engine on the Scooby made such a noise. Ash always loved the attention, and he slowed the car right down and then paused the music and started shouting out of the window to passers-by.

'Na then, ya motherfuckers! I've got my baby back. Woo-hooooo!'

'Oh my God, Ash, stop! It's embarrassing.' I was laughing my head off and I put my hand over my eyes and sunk a little in my seat. It was a beautiful sunny day, which added to Ash's good mood. He loved it when the sun came out. Summer was his favourite time of year.

We drove to one of the hotels we'd used before, planning to spend some time on our own, making love and catching up.

Afterwards Ash held me in his arms and we cuddled for hours, talking about our week away from each other and watching TV. Ash loved soaps such as *Emmerdale*, *Coronation Street* and *EastEnders*. I lay in his arms as we watched TV and nothing else mattered in the world. Everything faded to the back of my mind. Getting home was the very last thing I was thinking about.

When Ash finally dropped me back it must have been about 6 a.m. and our house was in darkness. I didn't have a key and so I banged on the door. Despite the lovely family holiday we'd just had, I didn't care about the consequences. Spending the night with Ash was worth the hassle I was inevitably going to face.

A light went on and my dad appeared, looking drained and exhausted. He opened the door and then walked off, not saying a word to me. Mum appeared and was all tearful, and wringing her hands. 'I wish you'd stay in, stay away from him.'

I denied I'd been with Ash, and then Mum repeated all the crap I'd heard before. Ash was dangerous, she said. Ash was too old for me. Ash was married.

'I'm not listening,' I said.

I'd spent the night with Ash. As if he was married! How could he be?

'Your dad's heard he has two kids, Sammy. Did you know that? I don't know what this man's game is, but I know you're making a big mistake going back to him. He's dangerous. He's going to ruin your life.'

'I'm not even seeing him!' I lied.

'Then who were you with last night?'

I didn't answer, and instead stormed off to my bedroom and slammed the door.

My education was another ongoing worry for my parents. I'd been an A-grade student in several of my GCSE subjects before I got involved with Ash but I'd missed so much work that now the teachers were talking about strategies to help me achieve Cs and Ds in a reduced number of subjects. I didn't care about my education in any way at all.

The only good thing about school was that I could play truant. I was being monitored, because I was on Social Services' radar, but the teachers couldn't lock me in or watch me every minute of the day.

I'd do a bunk at every opportunity. It was so easy. I'd get myself registered and then I'd ask to go to the toilet and slip out, or I'd not return after dinner. When this got reported back to my parents, the rows started up again at home, and I was hauled before the teachers time and time again. I'd take the rap, but nothing anybody said got through to me. I'd be standing there thinking about where I was meeting Ash next, or daydreaming about the day I'd be married to him, and all this shit would be in the past.

Ash was taking me to hotels and B&Bs around town a lot now. Sometimes I'd stay in the car while he went in and booked the room, but most of the time I went to the reception with him. There was only one occasion when we were turned away as the woman said he was an adult and shouldn't be with me. She followed us out of the hotel, and as I got in the car she started arguing with Ash. Of course, he didn't listen to a word she said, and nor did I.

Ash would sometimes go out and buy alcohol and we'd always have sex all night. I was getting bolder now, and I was staying out regularly, no matter how much grief it caused my family.

I was always asking Ash about his life, and what he did when we weren't together. I didn't want to know any more than I really had to about his drug-dealing or criminal activities, although Ash talked openly about what he got up to. I was more interested in his life in general; what he thought and felt about things, what he liked doing and his plans for the future. I still didn't know as much about his life as he knew about mine, but I didn't believe for one minute he was married and had kids. Ash would talk about the gym or his music, but more often than not he turned the conversation round to me, saying he wanted to know all about my life, because I was so interesting and intelligent.

My dad was still on the phone all the time to the police. He'd gathered so much evidence about Ash by now that he handed them an 11-page statement, detailing registration plates, names of hotels he suspected I'd been in with Ash, and specific dates when I'd failed to come home. He also gave the police my diary, which he found in my bedroom and contained loads of detail about my sexual relationship with Ash. Dad had torn the room apart looking for it when I was out.

In the beginning, I used to keep the diary under my pillow, but I'd started pulling up a corner of the carpet by my wardrobe and hiding my diary under there, thinking nobody would find it. I wrote down absolutely everything, in typical teenage girl style. Alongside details of what top or jeans I had on, who'd been on *Top of the Pops* or what I'd eaten for my tea I'd detailed everything about Ash, in graphic detail. My poor dad; no father should have to see that. I described how Ash kissed me, how he touched me, where and when we had sex, what we did afterwards, how we plotted to get together, how I lied to my parents and how I couldn't wait to leave home and live with Ash.

* * *

I was on my own in a hotel room above a pub in town when the police caught up with me one day. An officer turned up, knocked on the bedroom door and ordered me to open up.

'Piss off!' I shouted. 'Leave me alone.'

'Open up or I'll have to force entry. I know you're in there, Sammy.'

All I had was a fluffy black bag with me, and I hastily stuffed the few belongings I had with me into it, opened the door and then gave the officer who picked me up a load of abuse all the way to Rotherham Police Station. I wasn't scared of the police. In fact, I'd started to hate them. They were always mean to me and called me names, so I did the same to them. I didn't care what they said. All I was bothered about was getting away from them as quickly as possible, so I could run off with Ash again.

When I was eventually taken home, Mum and Dad were in the front room, talking to a police officer. Thankfully, it was PC Sadat, the officer who was friendly with Ash and had been involved in the handover at the petrol station. I tried to listen in to what was being said, and to my surprise I heard PC Sadat comment that I looked 'sweet' on one of the photographs of me that was on display in the front room.

Dad started kicking off, saying the police should be doing more to keep Ash away from me, and Mum was having another meltdown, crying and begging for help. She felt guilty for having to go out to work, but she didn't have any choice, as the family needed the money. It was the same for Dad. They couldn't afford to give up their jobs to guard me full-time.

Foster care was mentioned and my parents agreed that it might be worth considering, if it was a way of keeping me safe. 'We'll do anything to keep her away from him,' Mum cried.

The mention of care made my ears prick up. The prospect of leaving home didn't bother me at all – I wanted to leave, I wanted to get away from the control of my parents – but I didn't want to be monitored even more by people in authority, so I didn't want to go into care.

While Mum and Dad chatted to PC Sadat I crept into their bedroom and climbed out of their window on to the porch over the front door. Then I lowered myself down and ran off along the snicket. Ash called me on one of the spare phones he always made sure I had. He came to meet me, and we talked about running away together, to get away from all this hassle and live happily ever after.

Ash said he had a place where I could hide for the time being. I wasn't sure what I was letting myself in for, but I wasn't worried. I trusted Ash and if this was the only way we could be together, I'd do it.

Chapter 16
'It's me and you against the world'

Ash drove me to a small, terraced house on the corner of a narrow street. It was similar to the one where Sarah lived, although it was a bit tidier and cleaner. The woman who lived there was called Lorna and was in her thirties. I smiled shyly and said hello and the three of us went into the kitchen. Ash said he had to go out for a bit as he had stuff to do, but he'd be back later.

Lorna was kindly allowing us to use her bedroom while she slept on the settee. The idea was that Ash would go about his daily business while popping in and out through the day, then stay with me at night. This was only a temporary set-up, he said, until he got something better and more permanent organised.

I wasn't particularly happy to be in a strange house with a person I didn't know, but I was prepared to do it for the time I got to spend with Ash. If I went home I knew I'd only go back to an argument, or I'd get nagged by my mum or ignored by my dad. Lisa had a serious boyfriend and was spending most of her time out of the house, and I didn't blame her. The atmosphere was terrible, and why would anyone want to be there? I certainly didn't, not when I could sleep with my boyfriend, do what I pleased, and not bother with the charade of going to school.

Lorna didn't seem to mind having me in her house, or having to sleep on the settee. She and Ash seemed to get on well, but I didn't feel threatened by her. I could tell she wasn't involved with Ash in any sexual way, and that was all I cared about.

Lorna smoked weed, and Ash had loads of that. I think when I stayed he gave her more, or gave her weed for free, as a thank you. I don't know this for sure, but that was the impression I got. I'd occasionally smoke a bit of weed or have a drink at night with Ash, but I never had much and this wasn't a big part of my life.

I lived for Ash's visits. The days seemed to be getting even longer and more drawn out. I wasn't allowed to go out in case I was picked up by the police, and I had nothing to do all day but sit for hours drinking coffee and smoking fags in Lorna's kitchen. I felt like I was losing touch with reality.

I always imagined running away with Ash would be exciting. We'd drive off into the sunset, having the time of our lives. It wasn't like that at all, not yet in any case. At least we had each other, and things were going to get better when Ash worked out the next part of the plan.

I gradually got to know Lorna quite well. She was in a relationship with a Pakistani man, who she told me was married. I was horrified, and asked her how she could put up with that, going out with a married man, and playing second fiddle to his wife.

'They have these wives from arranged marriages,' Lorna explained in a matter-of-fact way. I didn't know about arranged marriages and was very shocked by this. 'It's their family duty. It's not like our marriages, it doesn't bother me.'

'People keep telling me Ash is married,' I said.

'I've heard that. I've heard his wife is really pretty,' Lorna said, looking unfazed.

I felt a stab to my heart. Even though I'd been like a broken record telling everybody this was a complete lie, I had my doubts about Ash being married, because I'd heard it from lots of different people by now.

'Do you think it could be true?' I asked nervously.

'What does Ash say?'

'He says it's rubbish and that people are telling lies to split us up.'

'Well, like I say, Asian marriages aren't like ours, and he obviously wants you. Does it matter?'

It really did matter to me, because I wanted to be much more than Ash's girlfriend. I wanted to marry him and raise a family with him.

I confronted Ash one night and he laughed. 'Look, I have been married,' he said. 'But my wife had an affair and I got divorced. So now you know the truth, OK?'

'Right, so why didn't you tell me? You've lied to me!' I said crossly.

'I didn't want to upset you or ruin what we have, Sammy. I got married when I was really young. It was arranged and I was a kid myself. It's what happens, we don't have a choice. We're not together now so it doesn't matter. It's not like we had kids or owt. It's me and you, Woodypoo, against the world.'

I was upset Ash hadn't been completely honest with me, but I also felt a bit sorry for him for having to marry someone he didn't even know or love, when he was so young.

I was also on Ash's case about how bored I was, stuck in the house all the time. I nagged him so much he started to take me on the odd drive so I could get some fresh air. I'd have to wait until the coast was clear before I left the house, and Ash would use different cars all the time so we didn't get spotted by the police. I'd duck down and hide as we drove along, so nobody saw me.

We were in a car park one time when the marriage issue came up again. This time Ash said I could speak to his lawyer – Wazir – about his marriage, if it would reassure me it was all over.

I'd heard Ash mention Wazir loads of times before. He had told me that if ever I got into trouble with the police then this man could handle things for me, because he was a very good lawyer and had acted for Ash in the past. Ash explained that Wazir had handled his divorce when the marriage broke down. He said he'd phone Wazir and before I knew it, Ash had dialled a number. I listened as he explained why he was calling and then he handed the phone straight to me.

'Speak to him, he'll tell you he did my divorce,' Ash said.

Sure enough, the man on the phone confirmed that he had handled Ash's divorce papers. He asked if there was anything else I wanted to know, and I said that was all, thank you.

'Do you feel better now?' Ash asked in what seemed like a genuinely concerned way.

'Yes, but from now on you're always to be totally honest with me, Ash. There's something else. Why have people said you have kids? Is it true?'

Ash sighed and reluctantly admitted he had two children with his wife before their marriage broke down. Then he stroked my face and said he didn't tell me because he didn't want to upset me, and that he wanted to have kids with me now.

It was a lot to take in, but I was glad he was being honest with me at last. For the time being, Ash wasn't hitting me like he had before. I was pleased we were getting on so well and having these heart-to-hearts. He then went on to tell me that his children still lived with him and his immediate family, and that he wanted me to meet the kids so I could get to know them.

'They're beautiful, Sammy. They're going to love you and your gonna be a great stepmum. I'll take you to meet them, right now.'

We drove round to the main family home and parked outside. Ash's nephew came out, and Ash told him to bring out the kids. I felt really nervous about meeting them but also really excited. I loved kids and had babysat lots of times for friends and neighbours for some extra pocket money.

When the children came out of the house Ash picked one of them up and sat her on his knee as he introduced us. She was the cutest little girl I'd ever seen. Ash had a big smile across his face as he joked with her and tickled her.

'I love kids, Sammy, and kids always love me,' he said.

'You're a great dad, I can tell,' I said.

Once I'd met both of Ash's kids it confirmed to me that I wanted a family with him. I thought that just because I wasn't their mother it didn't mean I wouldn't care for Ash's kids any less than for my own. As we left I kissed Ash's daughter on the cheek and we arranged a day out to spend some family time together, and to get to know each other properly.

* * *

According to my records I'd been missing from 15–24 May. A social worker wrote on my record sheet: 'Police won't do anything because they say she won't make a statement'. Again, my mum was tearing her hair out, shouting, 'She is a child! She is being exploited! Why is it up to our Sammy to make a complaint or a statement? She is the victim here! Why can't anybody see that?'

On 6th June, a Strategy Case Conference was held to discuss me and 'other young people associating with Ash, Bash etc. and other undesirable Asians with criminal records'. Minutes were recorded, more notes were made in my growing Social Services file, but nothing changed, because I still wasn't complaining about Ash, and I certainly wasn't going to make a statement to police or press any charges.

Far from it. He was my boyfriend and we were in love.

Chapter 17

'I'm gonna teach you everything I know'

'I've got a surprise for your 15th birthday,' Ash said as he walked into the bedroom.

My heart leapt. My birthdays at home were always really special. I'd have a big party with all my family and friends and there would be a bouncy castle, loads of cake and sweets and pop, and stacks of presents, all organised by Mum. I'd been at Lorna's for what felt like weeks, and in the circumstances couldn't expect my parents to throw me a party. But now Ash was the one who was going to make a fuss of me and make it a birthday to remember, and I felt right excited. I wondered if he was going to get me flowers, because I love flowers.

'What's the surprise?' I asked excitedly.

Ash leaned down at the side of the bed and looked straight at me with a smile from ear to ear. 'I'm going to take you on your first armed robbery. Are you excited, Sammy?'

I laughed. 'You're crazy! Who does an armed robbery for their 15th birthday?'

I laid my head back on the pillow, giggling at Ash and his crazy ways. He was making it all seem like a laugh, and like something exciting. I didn't think for one second about how wrong it might be, or the consequences. I'd seen how he got away with loads of stuff now. He must have got pulled over by the police about three times a week and nothing ever seemed to happen to him, so what could go wrong?

One time, we were in the blue Scooby Subaru with the G8ASH registration plate and Ash was speeding along a road. The windows were down and he had the music blaring, and I was asking him to put the windows up because my hair was getting blown all over the place and I didn't want to look a mess.

'Stop moaning, woman!' Ash said. 'You look sexy, you always look sexy.'

PC Sadat and another officer saw us, pulled us over and started looking around the car.

'What's happening?' Ash said.

'How's you, Ash?' PC Sadat replied, shaking Ash's hand.

'I'm good. Just chillin'.'

PC Sadat came round to my side of the car and asked me to get out while he had a search inside.

'Ey up, Sam, how's you?' he said.

'I'm good, thanks. How are you?'

We had a friendly chat and then PC Sadat told Ash he could go, but that he should get the car taxed.

It was like Ash had some sort of immunity to Rotherham – like he was invisible to certain police officers. This is why doing an armed robbery with him didn't frighten me. I knew Ash would never let anything bad happen to me, and I was flattered that he trusted me and wanted me involved in his business.

'I'm gonna teach you everything I know,' he said. 'I know you're a fast learner, Sammy. You're clever. Just don't tell anyone else and do exactly what I say, and everything will be good.'

Once I'd agreed to get involved Ash didn't hang around. He and his mate Paddy stole a car to use in the robbery, and then Ash said he wanted me to sit in another car and listen to the police scanner while the two of them carried out the raid, so they would know if the cops were on to them.

'It's the post office we're robbing,' Ash explained.

'Nanan gets her pension in there,' I fretted, eyes widening.

'Don't worry, it'll be fine,' Ash laughed. 'There's no CCTV. I've robbed it loads of times before. There won't be any problems.'

I didn't like that it was so close to home, but Ash seemed to know exactly what he was doing, and he made out it was no big deal at all. He even got hold of two all-in-one white suits and masks for him and Paddy, the kind I'd seen forensic investigators wearing in TV dramas.

On the day, my nerves were jangling. Ash placed me in the back seat of the second car that was parked next to some garages. He and Paddy put the suits on then quickly drove the stolen car to the post office, which was about a hundred yards up the hill from where he'd left me, listening to the police radio.

'Stay here, Sammy,' Ash instructed. 'Listen on the scanner, and if you hear anything, ring my mobile.'

It seemed to be pretty amateurish but I did as I was told and sat there listening to the crackle of broken conversations between police officers, not really deciphering anything that made any sense. Ash and Paddy set off in the stolen car looking like something out of *CSI*. Ash was holding a black-handled pistol-type gun in his hand.

I was starting to get used to seeing weapons. Six weeks before this Ash had given me a baton, which he told me to keep in my bag 'for protection'. I did as he asked without question.

My heart was racing faster and faster the longer Ash and Paddy were gone. Thankfully, after only a few minutes, the two of them pulled up next to me, got out of the stolen car and started taking off their white suits.

'What happened?' I asked.

It turned out an old man who was shopping in the post office had tried to tackle them, and in the heat of the moment Ash and his friend decided to scarper empty-handed. I was relieved. I didn't want anybody getting hurt, and I felt right bad for the old man. Nanan might have known him, and what if she had been in there getting her pension? It was possible, and the thought made me shudder.

* * *

Some time later Lorna's house got raided by the police, so I was sneaked out and moved across the road to her friend Sandra's place.

Sandra's house was a very similar set-up to Lorna's. It was a small, terraced council house and she also seemed to have an understanding with Ash. No questions were asked. She knew I was hiding from the police and, again, we were allowed to use a bedroom, and Sandra smoked weed, which I think Ash supplied.

One day, when I was staying at Sandra's, Ash took me out for a drive with Paddy. I got on with Paddy and liked him a lot. He was always telling jokes and had a crazy side, like Ash.

We were in a white car. Paddy was in the front and I was in the back seat behind Ash, and he went to fill up with petrol. The next minute Ash jumped back in the driving seat without paying and sped away.

I knew Ash did what he called a 'petrol run' all the time. He'd usually put bits of black tape over some of the letters and numbers on the car's registration plate, and he always got away with it. He could afford to pay for the petrol but he loved the rush it gave him to do something he shouldn't.

This time he'd done the petrol run on the spur of the moment and hadn't put any tape on the number plate, and the next thing we knew, the police were on to us, giving Ash a chase with the blue lights flashing.

'Let's have a police chase, Sammy, fuck the dirty piggy bastards!' he whooped.

Ash kept driving fast but was eventually forced to pull over. The officers searched all three of us and the car.

'Have you got anything sharp or dangerous in your bag, madam?' one police officer asked me.

'No, I don't think so,' I said, but the officer began searching my black fluffy bag and pulled out a shaver I used on my legs.

'WHAT THE HELL IS THIS?' he demanded.

'Oh, that's just my shaver,' I said.

'You've lied to me,' the officer replied.

'It's only a shaver, chill out!'

'I want your name and date of birth.'

Of course, I wasn't going to tell him, and so I gave my sister's name and details.

By this time another police car had arrived. Ash and Paddy were arrested and driven away by the first police car and I was placed in the back of the second one.

'Where would you like to be dropped off, madam?' the officer behind the wheel asked me. I thought it was funny that he was calling me madam when I was just a kid.

This police officer was really nice and so I said I'd like to go back to Sandra's. We chatted all the way there and he dropped me off at the door. As I got out of the car quickly I was thinking to myself, *How the hell did I pull that off? Aren't I clever?*

Ash was teaching me well, moulding me to be a criminal like he was.

Chapter 18
'Thank God Ash has friends in the police'

As soon as Ash was released he came to find me at Sandra's and we went upstairs together, laughing about our little adventure. Ash wasn't bothered that he'd been caught nicking petrol; it was nothing at all to him, and he made light of the fact he'd been picked up by the police, so I did too.

Ash wanted to have sex, and we got into bed together, in the bedroom we'd been using upstairs. Both of us were naked when we suddenly heard a really loud bang. A male voice shouted, 'This is the police!'

Ash panicked, jumped out of the bed and pulled on his blue tracksuit bottoms, while I grabbed my knickers, put them on as fast as I could, and dived under the bed to hide. Two police officers burst into the room moments later. I held my breath, but it was a waste of time.

'You might as well come out from under the bed, Sammy,' one said. 'I can see your feet sticking out.'

I crawled out and put my clothes on as quickly and discreetly as I could. I was embarrassed, and when I stole a glance at Ash he was pulling on his T-shirt and looked right scared. It alarmed me to see him like that. Nothing scared Ash, ever. He was normally the big man, unflappable and completely untouchable.

One of the officers searched my handbag that was on the bedroom floor, and he pulled out the baton Ash had given me for protection.

'Samantha Woodhouse, we're arresting you for possession of an offensive weapon,' the officer said.

'You what?' I gasped, gobsmacked.

I lied and said I'd found it in a field, but the officer read me my rights and said he was taking me down to the station.

Ash had a very relieved look on his face. If this was the only charge they were throwing at the two of us after he had been caught red-handed, having sex with me, a 15-year-old girl who had run away from home and was reported missing, it was a great result for him.

The police went downstairs and arrested Sandra for possessing cannabis. I was taken to the station and cautioned for possession of an offensive weapon.

I was held in a cell while calls were made to my parents, and Dad came straight to the police station. At one point a policeman I'd seen before appeared and said, 'You're Ash's girl, aren't you? I'll look after you.' I couldn't place him at first, but then I remembered where I'd seen him. It was when I'd been sitting on the grass by the big shopping centre, not that long after I first met Ash. A police car had pulled up with two officers in, and Ash gave a little silver package to one of them. It was this man. Ash told me the package contained steroids, and I can remember him laughing and saying, 'They're right dodgy bastards' as the police car drove off. Ash called this officer 'Jonesy'. *Thank God Ash has friends in the police*, I thought.

A handwritten police report noted 'Child has been MFH (missing from home) since 01/06/2000 in the company of a

A cheeky grin for the family album. Mum always took so many pictures. This one was taken in 1989 when I was about four and couldn't wait to start school.

Here I am at around two years old with my blonde curls, smiling for a family portrait. I was always happy to get dressed up and Mum bought me loads of pretty clothes.

I was thrilled to bits at winning the Little Miss Hawaiian competition in Cleethorpes. I loved going on holiday to the caravan park every summer and I managed to come home with a beauty contest prize every time!

I was well chuffed to be crowned Junior Princess and given a shiny tiara and sash. This little white dress with the red piping on the collar, and the pink hairpiece, were favourites of mine for ages.

Here I am taking to the stage once again with a big grin on my face as I came first in the Little Miss Princess competition in 1991, when I had just turned six. 'That's my babby!' Mum shouted. 'Well done, our Sammy! I'm right proud of you!'

This was a picture taken in my last year at primary school. I was a good pupil and the teachers said I was very bright, but I'd much rather have been dancing than stuck in a classroom.

My first day of secondary school, aged eleven. I felt like such a big girl. Mum even let me walk to school on my own with friends. I was so excited and felt very grown up in my brand-new uniform.

A quick pose as mum took a picture of me wearing my favourite striped trousers. I'd been dancing round the bedroom showing her my new dance moves. On the bedroom walls I had posters of pop stars and footballers.

This was taken at my secondary school when I was aged around thirteen. It was the fashion to pluck your eyebrows like this and I always tried to make them into perfect arches!

I attended a family wedding just a few months before I gave birth to my son, James. I was 15 years old in this picture. There's a haunted look to me – I'm like a ghost.

Holding onto James so tightly on our first holiday abroad together.

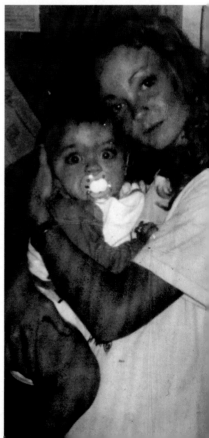

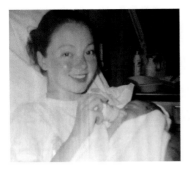

Here I've just given birth to James in the hospital and I'm giving him his first bottle. I immediately felt very protective of him and wanted to be the best mummy ever.

Another picture that was taken just after arriving home with my little angel. I'm shocked now at how young I look. I thought I was so grown up.

Here I am on the settee at home, cradling James.
I'd just come back from the hospital after having him.
I was 16 and had no idea how to care for a baby.

NEWSPAPER OF THE YEAR

THE TIMES

Friday August 23 2013 | thetimes.co.uk | No 70971 · Max 29C Min 6 · Only £1

Goals! Goals! Goals!
You can't afford to miss any

Join the football revolution
See pullout inside

Grooming scandal of child sex town

Under-age girl in care allowed to go out with known criminal, 25

Continued from page 1

as a couple and was said in a hospital report to be "friendly" with Hussain, told *The Times* that the child was the dominant partner in the relationship: 'He didn't control her; she controlled

girl repeatedly went missing from home, spending days and sometimes weeks with Hussain and his associates at houses and hotels in the town.

Last September, when *The Times* revealed confidential documents detailing a ten-year history of police ...ces failing to act on spe-

...estigations
...w Norfolk
...roid tablet editions

...ilfully blind
... culpability
page 34

Girl in care allowed to meet known c

Andrew Norfolk
Chief Investigative Reporter

A child in the care of social services was allowed extensive daily contact with a violent adult offender who was suspected of grooming more than a dozen young teenagers to use and sell for sex, it is revealed today.

Police and social services held detailed intelligence about the activities of Arshid Hussain, who twice made the girl pregnant, yet he has never been prosecuted for a child-sex offence.

Among those who became aware of the relationship was a local politician,

He stroked my face
and said: 'You're not
really 16, are you?'
News, pages 6-8

related to the offender, who is now the deputy leader of a Labour-run council and vice-chairman of a police scrutiny body. Jahangir Akhtar said last week that he was unaware Hussain was ... child

affray, and was soc
for violent disorder
Before their re
social services
warned that Hus
was among a sma
were suspected o
sexual exploitati
young teenagers
Yorkshire, inclu
dozen who "exp
Ash was their bc
The child's d
unable to keep t
that she would
was given an e
ment after poli
with Hussain,
under a bed.
Police and
the incident i
after the girl's
she was "kno
relationship"
thought to be
Once she
was allowed
The married ...
permitted to attend medical appointments with her. A social worker told the girl's mother that the local authority ... "no power" to end the relation-

News Grooming scandal

He bought me chicken and chips from a place just up from the petrol station. He stroked my face and said: 'You're not really 16, are you?'

DAILY Mirror

What have I Don?

HORRIFIC BETRAYAL OF 1,400 CHILDREN

Asian gangs' appalling sexual abuse of young girls lasted 16 YEARS because people in authority were scared of being labelled racist if they tackled it...

Arshid Hussain – aka Ash - photographed by a newspaper when my story came out. The net was finally closing in and his past was catching up with him.

I'm proud to be a part of the community-led iMatter campaign that is raising awareness of CSE in schools in Walsall. It is funded by the Palfrey Big Local partnership and supported by the police.

I'm involved with *Loose Women*'s Never Too Late To Tell campaign, alongside Maggie Oliver (right) and Saira Khan. It's been a huge success, raising awareness of grooming and abuse on a national scale.

I spoke about my experiences at a conference in Bedfordshire, addressing a range of different professionals to help give them a better understanding of grooming. I'm pictured here with David Moss, a member of Luton's care leavers information panel, and Lisa Robinson, CSE Coordinator for Bedfordshire.

A picture that always makes me smile. Me and Andrew Norfolk, the chief investigative reporter for *The Times,* and the hero who helped me expose the Rotherham scandal.

25-year-old male with criminal convictions with whom she is known to be having a sexual relationship. When found at his house drugs were also found. Child found in possession of an extendable baton (offensive weapon) for which she was arrested and warned. Danger of significant harm if released without supervision'.

My parents got a call from Social Services, and at this point they reluctantly agreed it was best I went into care; they felt they had no choice. I'd put them through hell for months, and the fears they had been passing on to Social Services for so long had proved to be alarmingly accurate. They couldn't keep me in the house, they couldn't keep me out of trouble and, most importantly, they couldn't keep me safe. When I was missing, they had been terrified that I was going to be found dead. They were searching for me every day, quizzing all my friends and hoping to catch one little glimpse of me or hear one word that would put their minds at rest. Instead, they were met with a wall of silence every way they turned, because all the friends who would have been able to help were involved with Ash and his brothers and associates too in some way, and they kept quiet.

Putting me in care was a desperate measure and a decision Mum and Dad didn't take lightly at all, but they were not too proud to admit they needed expert help. Their own relationship was breaking under the strain of trying to deal with me. As a family, we'd hit our lowest point yet.

Emergency foster care accommodation was found for me while I was still being detained at the police station. When I was told I was going into foster care and didn't have to return home I wasn't bothered; in fact, when the news properly registered, I was jubilant. I couldn't go back to Sandra's, and it was a result that I wouldn't have to go home and deal with my dad's moods and silent treatment, or my mum's weeping and wailing. I'd had a bellyful of my parents. Even before my latest escapades, the atmosphere in the house was so toxic and loaded with stress and anger that I don't think anybody wanted to be there.

I was officially under 'child protection' now because, according to my police file, 'if this was not done Sammy would suffer significant physical, moral and mental harm'. I was also automatically referred to the Youth Offending Team, because of the offensive weapon caution. Basically, I was marked out as a kid in danger, a kid to keep an eye on. South Yorkshire Police knew about me, Social Services knew about me and Rotherham Borough Council knew about me.

I was put in the back of a blacked-out riot van and told I was being taken to the home of an emergency foster carer, out of town. This was an attempt to shake Ash off, but it didn't work. He followed in his car to the foster carer's house and watched as I was moved in.

'This is your room,' the foster carer, Maggie, said.

It was a nice room and Maggie was friendly and made a big effort, but I didn't take much notice, because all I was thinking about was how I could get out of the house to meet Ash.

'We are quite strict here,' Maggie said. 'We don't have a television and I always get up at six o'clock to feed the horses. Would you like to come and meet them?'

'No, you're all right.'

'Right, then. If there's anything you need, just ask.'

'Thanks.'

I can't remember what time it was, but I think it was quite late, and I was really tired. I still had a mobile phone on me. It was a new flip-up one Ash had given me. He always made sure I had two phones, in case my parents took one off me, or the police, though they could only do that if I was put in a cell. I'd managed to keep hold of this one and I called Ash on it and told him I'd try to get out of the house the next day, as early as possible.

* * *

Alone in my bedroom, the reality of the situation hit me. I felt lonely in this strange house with its weird rules, away from my family and away from Ash. I got into bed and cried myself to sleep, trying to tell myself that everything would be fine tomorrow, because Ash would come and rescue me.

I went to see the horses when I got up and after breakfast, when I was alone in my bedroom again, Ash phoned.

'Come outside, I'm here,' he said.

I went downstairs and asked Maggie if I could go and have a look around the local area, to get to know the place and see where things were.

'Of course, love,' she said, smiling and waving me off. 'Have a good time!'

I had a couple of bags of belongings with me – I think the social worker must have fetched them for me from home – and Maggie didn't seem to notice that they were now sitting in the hallway, packed and ready to go. I took them with me when I walked off down her drive. My head was all over the place. I was feeling emotional and worn out and wanted everything to be OK, but I knew that wasn't going to happen, at least not until Ash came up with another plan.

Ash was parked up a few houses down the road and Lorna was in the car with him. I was pleased to see both of them; I trusted them to look after me.

As we drove off Ash smiled and winked at me through his rear-view mirror, as I was sitting in the back seat.

'I told you no one could have you but me,' he said.

According to my Social Services file, me and Ash were now subject to an 'inter-agency strategy/investigation'. Dad had reported that he had heard locally that Ash had got several other teenage girls pregnant, and this was noted by a member of the Youth Offending Team who visited Dad at home. My parents were now so worried about me that they had talked to some relatives in Ireland and were seriously considering moving me there, to get me away from Ash.

I had no intention of even being found, let alone taken abroad. Ash was on my side; we were stuck together like glue and he had a great new plan for us.

Chapter 19
'I can't stay here forever, can I?'

'You'll be safe here,' Ash said. 'I'll bring you everything you need so you don't have to go out.'

'Thanks,' I smiled.

He had a friend called Fraser, who had agreed that I could stay in his council flat. Ash took me there straight from the foster home. It was a small, modern, first-floor flat in a terraced row, with a neat little patch of garden in the back. Fraser was in his late twenties, he worked and he spent a lot of time either at his girlfriend's place or his mother's house, so I would have the flat to myself most of the time. Fraser came and said hello and seemed quite nice. The flat was bright and fairly clean and tidy, much nicer than the scruffy old houses I'd stayed in with Sarah, Lorna and Sandra.

'Make yourself at home,' Ash said, showing me where the kettle was. He gave me cigarettes and told me he'd fetch me a takeaway later.

'You're not going to run off?' he asked.

'No,' I said, thinking that was a bit of a strange thing to say, considering I was always running off with him.

Before Ash left we had sex on the floor of one of the flat's two bedrooms. The sex ended up going on for hours, and I remember complaining really loudly, as I was sore and we'd been having sex for so long. Fraser was in his bedroom next door and must have heard everything that was going on, which I found embarrassing. Ash didn't care.

'You know you need to lie really low for a while,' he said afterwards. 'Are you all right with this?'

I said I was. I'd hated it in that foster home. 'It were right lonely without you,' I told him. 'What will we do next, though? I can't stay here forever, can I?'

'Don't worry, I've got a few ideas. I'm looking for a house for us to move into together. I'll take care of everything.'

By the time Ash left, Fraser had gone out too, so Ash locked me in the flat. I didn't mind, because I knew it was only in case anyone came to take me away from Ash, and that he didn't want that. This was the first time he had talked properly about us living together, so I was trying to be positive and focus on that.

As I sat alone in Fraser's living room, drinking coffee and smoking fags, I fantasised about my life with Ash. I'd buy nice matching containers for the teabags and coffee and sugar. I'd cook Ash's tea every night. I'd decorate the bedrooms, and we'd be able to finally start our family, with nobody interfering this time. There would be no more running away and hiding all the time. We could live a normal life.

We didn't always use condoms when we had sex. Ash said they didn't make the sex feel as good as it did without them, and I didn't mind. As far as I was concerned, the sooner I fell pregnant again, the better.

I lived for Ash's visits to the flat, because just like at Lorna's and at Sandra's, there was nothing else going on. I was cut off from everybody. I hadn't really noticed this happening, but I'd not been in contact with my friends for ages. I wasn't in touch with anybody in my family at all, including my sisters, because I didn't trust anyone not to tell Mum and Dad where I was.

Fraser only came in and out of the flat occasionally. All I did was hang around all day and night, waiting for Ash. I'm surprised I didn't go crazy, and I started to tell Ash how homesick I was feeling. I didn't want to live with my parents again, but I was missing the small, normal things in life that I had always taken for granted. I thought about my clean, neat and tidy bedroom, mucking about with my friends, and listening to my CDs of the Backstreet Boys, Atomic Kitten and the Spice Girls. Most of all I missed a home-cooked meal. Mum always put a healthy meal on the table the minute my dad walked in from work. Her topside of beef with Yorkshire puddings, veg and roast potatoes was one of my favourite meals, followed by apple pie.

At first it was great living on the takeaways Ash bought all the time – it was a teenager's dream – but after a while I was really longing for a proper meal. Ash's mum cooked a lovely curry and on occasions, when he knew I was craving some home comforts, he'd put some in a container and fetch it for me.

'My mum's a wicked cook, isn't she, Sammy?'

I'd nod and gobble it down as quickly as I could, happy to have something homemade, but I would have much preferred my own mum's cooking.

Fraser didn't appear to be bothered that I was staying in his flat, though he didn't say much. Bash came round one time and did something illegal to the gas meter and electricity box, which meant Fraser was getting supplies for free. I assume this was his payment in kind, as I don't think Fraser was involved in drugs. He seemed decent like that.

Eventually, two police officers turned up at the door, looking for me. I was used to Fraser coming in and out and when I opened the door I thought it was going to be him.

'We'll have to take you to the station,' one officer said.

'Fine,' I said, rolling my eyes.

I don't think I was in my right mind because I didn't fight or argue at all. I remember something the officer said to me before we left, because it struck me as odd.

'Why don't you write Ash a note, so he knows where you are, and that you're safe?'

I did exactly that, thinking to myself that this was a strange thing for a police officer to suggest. Surely they knew or at least suspected Ash was the reason I'd absconded from care? Why would they want him to know where I was? I was so confused, but I was also pleased they let me write the note. I wanted Ash to know exactly what was happening, so we could work out our next move, and most of all I didn't want him to think I'd run away, as that would have caused trouble between us.

I was interviewed at the police station, and asked loads of stuff about Ash. I told the police I met him through my friend Richard, who was a friend of Ash's brother Bash, rather than telling the truth, that I'd met him through Holly.

I did admit Ash had arranged for me to stay at Fraser's flat, but I denied that I was in a sexual relationship with him, as I knew he'd go mad if I told the police that. My phone had started beeping and I knew Ash was trying to call me and message me. I was worried he hadn't seen my note so I dialled his number and hid it under the table so he could hear what was going on.

The police thought I'd been taking drugs, and noted that when I was interviewed my pupils were 'enormous' and I was 'very laid-back'. I have no recollection of taking any drugs. I hadn't smoked weed for ages and I was scared of all drugs besides cannabis; I'd seen what heroin did to people and it terrified me. I would never willingly have taken any hard drugs, so I've no idea why I had enormous pupils and looked drugged up. The vodka Ash gave me used to mess my head up at times. It was strong and it tasted weird, so I thought maybe that was what affected me, even though I couldn't remember the last time I'd drunk any.

A note from the Family Care Unit was added to my file, saying, 'she is mixing with a bad crowd involved in prostitution etc., needs urgent placement tonight'. I didn't know about this at the time, and if I had, I'd have laughed at the suggestion I might be involved in prostitution. I only ever slept with Ash.

From the police station I was taken to another foster home to stay with foster carer Sue Smith and her husband Brian. A social worker took me there, and on the way she explained that Sue was a very experienced carer. The placement would be temporary to begin with, while Social Services worked on a long-term plan for me.

I didn't take much notice, because I had no intention of being stuck in care. I couldn't live without Ash, and I imagined there was no way an experienced foster carer was going to let me see him. It would be worse than being at home, so I'd have to do a runner as soon as possible.

I can remember feeling right nervous when I walked in the house. The social worker explained to the foster carer that the windows in my bedroom had to be locked to stop me escaping, and Sue looked alarmed. I wondered what she had been told about me, and I was scared of how I was going to be treated.

When the social worker left, Sue made us a cup of tea and sat me down for a chat in the kitchen. The house was cosy and welcoming, and I started to relax a little. Sue seemed like a kind person. I felt calmer than I had in ages, and surprisingly at ease in her company.

Sue told me a little bit about her life. She had an older daughter who had left home, and Brian worked locally. He liked to go to the pub for a pint before his tea, and on Sundays she liked to cook a roast. It sounded nice, and normal.

I'd told Sue I was only in foster care because my mum and dad didn't like my boyfriend, and she nodded and gave me an understanding smile.

'I got told you were on heroin and you were a prostitute,' she replied, 'but you aren't like that, are you?'

'Of course not,' I laughed.

I explained to Sue the truth about Ash, telling her we were in love and had been seeing each other for about nine months. She listened without judging me, and I really started to like her. Nobody had treated me like this when it came to Ash. Perhaps this placement could work out after all.

Chapter 20

'If you want to see her, you do it by my rules'

'It's lovely to meet you,' Ash said, smiling politely.

He was shaking Sue's hand at the local fair after I suggested they should meet, so she could see for herself how nice Ash was. It was only a day or so after I'd moved in, and Sue had allowed me to phone Ash and arrange a time to meet.

He turned up on the dot in the blue Scooby, looking well turned out and being very charming. The way he was reminded me of the day I first met him. Sue seemed impressed and accepted Ash was my boyfriend.

'If you want to see her,' Sue said, 'you do it by my rules, and she has to be home by 10 p.m.'

Ash grinned and thanked Sue. 'If there's anything she needs, let me know.'

I don't think either of us could believe our luck. There was me thinking it would be loads harder to see Ash once I was in foster care, but thanks to Sue it was going to be much easier than it was at home. Sue had done what my parents never had. She'd met Ash with an open mind, shaken him by the hand and given him her blessing to see me. I could finally be normal again and me and Ash could be happy together. This proved that my family had been unreasonable and overprotective.

It was summer time, and for a week or so Ash picked me up from the top of Sue's road every night. We went for a drive, had chips, maybe had a drink, and we always had sex, usually in hotels that Ash paid for, or in one of the houses his family owned or the flat on Clough Road. For some reason – I think it possibly had something to do with Sue's other fostering commitments – I had to move out for a few weeks, to another foster home in a different area. The idea was that I'd then move back in with Sue, which I was very pleased about. I was having nothing to do with my family at this time, and going home, even for a few weeks, wasn't an option.

I was allocated a social worker called Margaret Brown, who worked on long-term cases. She was a friendly, middle-aged lady, and I can remember that when she dunked a biscuit in her tea it fell in. *Are you a bit ditsy?* I thought to myself the first time I met her, but Margaret seemed kind-hearted, and she genuinely appeared to want to help me.

I told Margaret I was seeing Ash regularly, because the way Sue had behaved made me think that Social Services had agreed to this. I assumed Margaret would be fine with it too, and sure enough she didn't seem to object. In her notes she wrote that I was 'doing it willingly and would not make any form of complaint'.

According to my file, Sue says that *I* told *her* Social Services had agreed to let me see Ash, but I can't remember saying that.

Anyhow, Margaret visited my mum and explained that Social Services had no power to prevent contact between me and Ash. Mum had no idea Sue was allowing us to see each other every night, but she knew we were still in contact. Evidently, Margaret suggested that my parents had more chance of breaking the relationship if I stayed at home, but Mum didn't agree. Having me at home hadn't stopped me seeing Ash so far, and she stuck to her belief that a foster carer, supported by Social Services, would have a much better chance of keeping me safe, which was her priority.

My memory of staying at the temporary foster home is very sketchy, which is odd, as according to my files I stayed there for four weeks. I remember there was a little girl there who had an eating disorder and took two hours to eat a slice of toast, and I know the foster carers allowed me to see Ash. I have memories of him being in the house and one night, when the foster carers went out, he stole some money from a purse. The carers reported this to Social Services, and the next day I was moved back in with Sue and Brian Smith.

It was brilliant. Just like before, Ash picked me up at the top of Sue's street at 6 p.m. every night and we laughed as we sped off to spend the whole evening together. We had four whole hours together; Ash never failed to drive me back by 10 p.m. prompt, to keep Sue happy. Sometimes we'd go for a spin up to a park to see who was out and about, and we'd nearly always go and get some food.

On a few occasions he took me to the house where his mum and dad and several other members of the family lived. His father never acknowledged me, but one time his mum smiled at me and said something I didn't understand. Ash told me that his mum had said I was really pretty but looked very young. I thanked her and smiled back. I met two of his sisters too, who were quite friendly towards me.

Ash and I had stopped being careful about contraception. I never asked him to use condoms and he rarely did. 'I want your babies,' I told him often.

'I want you to have them,' he always replied, 'loads of them.'

It was a bit of a honeymoon period. Ash was being kind and loving and was treating me really well. He would often talk about when I'd been pregnant before. He always said that if I'd had the baby it would have been a little girl, and he would talk about how beautiful she would have been, 'just like her mummy'. He said how upset he was that I had an abortion, and that he thought about that baby all the time.

* * *

I was still living at Sue's house in September, when it was time to return to school. I had barely shown my face there in eight months. There had been various meetings about my return, and it was decided I would go back on a reduced timetable, to help me settle in. The teachers wanted me to pass at least a couple of GCSEs but I wasn't bothered about exams, as I believed that in the future Ash was always going to look after me. I only wanted to go back to see my friends, because I'd missed them.

I felt very settled in Sue's house and she had agreed to be my long-term carer, at least until I was 16 the following summer. When I went back to school she made another rule: I could only carry on seeing Ash if I didn't skip school. That was fine by me.

Back at school I really enjoyed spending time with my friends again. I'd hardly seen them in months but we picked up where we left off, having a laugh and getting into trouble. My mind wasn't on my GCSEs at all, and if one of my friends suggested we went and had a crafty fag instead of going to a lesson, I readily agreed. I didn't mind how much cheek I gave the teachers when I got caught.

At the time, I reckon there were about 20 girls from my school year who were involved with older Pakistani men, many in Ash's circle of friends and associates. There would be gossip going around all the time about who was sleeping with who, and all kinds of 'girl wars' started kicking off.

One girl in particular, Cheryl, became the bane of my life. She was seeing Ash's brother Bash, but Holly still had a thing for Bash, which led to all kinds of fights and arguments. Then lots of rumours began flying around that Ash was sleeping with other girls behind my back, and Cheryl's name was mentioned more than once in connection with him.

More insecurities were creeping in about my relationship with Ash every day, and I began fighting and arguing with other girls all the time. I was turning into a right nasty bitch, and at the same time I wanted to please Ash more than ever, because I was scared of losing him.

I was quizzing Ash all the time now about whether he was sleeping with other girls. I'd check his phone and messages whenever I could, but he laughed and always said the other girls were telling lies because they were jealous. I wanted to believe him, but I was brooding on the girls' comments all the time and they were starting to really get to me.

Ash would come down to the parade of shops near school at dinner time to meet me, or he'd pick me up at the gate. Sometimes I'd be going absolutely mental, saying I was going to kill whoever had told me lies. If Cheryl's name had been mentioned, I'd be like an absolute madwoman because I detested her so much. After I had the abortion, she had gone round telling people that I'd had a funeral and a grave for my baby, which wasn't true and so cruel. I hated her so much for saying that.

Ash's reaction to these girl wars was always to laugh. He seemed pleased that I cared that much, and encouraged me to have a go at whichever girl was giving me trouble.

I did have lots of fights with girls, and dinner time by the shops had turned into a complete war zone. I was prepared to take any girl on, and we'd kick and punch each other, pull hair, swear and call each other all kinds of names.

I told myself all the time that Ash couldn't be unfaithful, because he didn't have time. I was having sex with him at least once a day, when he picked me up from Sue's in the evenings. We were always together from 6 p.m. to 10 p.m. and therefore how could he be with other girls?

We were also talking a lot about our plans for the future, discussing how we'd be able to live together the following summer when I turned 16, in June 2001. One night, Ash said he'd found a house for us. I was absolutely buzzing. A woman called Karen MacGregor and a Pakistani man whose name I didn't know were involved with this house. Ash explained he had to keep Karen 'sweet' over it but he never explained why.

He drove me to the house to have a look from the outside. It was a little terraced house that was quite decent from the front, but when I looked round the back I noticed it had bars across the windows, which I didn't like the look of. Ash reassured me there was still work to be done before we moved in, but he was getting it sorted and it would be perfect for us when it was finished.

Seeing the house helped put my mind at ease about the stories I was hearing about other girls and Ash, but even so I was still ready to blow my stack if anyone dared suggest he was cheating on me. The sooner we moved in together the better. Then the rumours would have to stop, and me and Ash could focus on being happy and starting our family.

Chapter 21

'Who else have you brought here?'

My phone rang one day when I was in the kitchen at Sue's, eating my tea. It was another of Ash's brothers, Siggi. He was the youngest of the brothers, and was a year or so younger than me. He told me he had some bad news.

'What?' I asked nervously.

'It's Holly. She's sleeping with Ash.'

'Fuck off,' I said. 'You're just making trouble.'

Sue told me off for swearing and I hung up, stormed out of the kitchen and phoned Ash.

'Siggi told me you're sleeping with Holly.'

He laughed.

'It's not fucking funny, Ash. Is it true?'

He laughed again and told me that of course it wasn't, but I wasn't sure I believed him.

When I saw Holly at school the next day I confronted her in the toilets. She denied it and tried to walk out, and I saw red and grabbed the back of her hair.

'It's true, isn't it? You fucking little bitch!'

She didn't admit it but even so I totally flipped and laid into Holly, punching her. There was blood up the toilet walls when I'd finished, and the teachers had to clean Holly up and send her home. I was put in isolation for the rest of the day and the teachers had a meeting about how to deal with me. At home time, Ash came to pick me up. My friend Alison spotted his car before I did and ran over to him, saying, 'Oh my God, Sammy hit Holly!'

Ash had a grin that stretched from ear to ear.

'Have you, Sammy?' Ash laughed as I got in the car. 'You little motherfucker!'

'Is it true about you and Holly?' I shrieked, searching into his eyes. 'You have to tell the truth. It is true, isn't it?'

'Fuck 'em, Woody. It's me and you against the world!'

I knew Ash loved girls fighting over him, but this was different. This was Holly, one of my best friends. I was hurting and this could split us up. Couldn't he see that?

I asked him why Siggi had got involved, grassing him and Holly up. Did the Hussain brothers want us girls fighting over them? Was it all some fucking big ego trip?

'Oh my God, Sammy! Just chill. I love you. I can't help it if other girls are jealous of that and make up lies.'

He was in his blue Scooby car with the G8ASH number plate and gold alloy wheels, and he put his foot to the floor and sped off down the road.

'Let's listen to some music,' Ash said, and he put on some dance music and started jumping up and down in his seat like he always did when he was pumped up. He had the windows down and started singing loudly, clearly enjoying the fact that yet again I'd had a fight over him, and that I was getting myself deeper into trouble.

'You're crazy,' I said.

'Let's go somewhere quiet, just the two of us,' he said.

I sighed. I loved it when he said that; it made my heart melt, and I couldn't say no.

* * *

The care order I was under was known as a 'Section 20', which meant that my parents retained full parental rights over me but had voluntarily agreed to place me in care. This meant I was free to see them when I wanted to. I'd started talking to Mum on the phone and I'd made one or two brief visits home, but things were still very strained. I spoke to Lisa more than anyone. She asked me to come and stay for a weekend, and I said I'd think about it, maybe when Dad wasn't there.

Not long after the fight with Holly, Mum phoned me, sounding very upset and angry. She told me that Holly and another girl had been making nuisance calls to her, mucking about and hanging up, saying things about me and Ash.

'I can do without it, love, I really can,' Mum wept.

'I'll kill her!'

'Now don't go getting yourself into more trouble,' she cried. 'You've known Holly a long time. Surely you can talk to her, talk some sense into her?'

I told Ash what had gone on and he came to meet me in his car at the top of Sue's road.

'Take this,' he said, handing me a small canister that looked like a can of Lynx deodorant.

'What is it?'

'CS gas.'

'What's it for?'

Ash sniggered. 'Let's go and find the little bitch,' he said, putting his foot to the floor.

We spotted Holly by the shops.

'Spray it in her face,' Ash said. 'That'll shut the silly bitch up.'

I did exactly as Ash said, jumping straight out of the car and spraying the gas in Holly's face.

She let out a piercing scream and started staggering around, clutching her eyes and screeching obscenities at me. I had no idea what horrible stuff CS gas was, and I was shocked at how Holly had reacted. My own eyes were streaming and burning as I got back in Ash's car and we drove away.

I heard later that Holly had to go to hospital to get checked over. Then the police got involved. I was taken to the station and questioned, and I lied and said it was only a can of hairspray, not CS gas.

I was cautioned and released, though the incident was still listed as a 'firearms offence' and now I had a growing criminal record. Holly had told the police it was like being in a horror film when the spray hit her eyes and she couldn't see. I didn't care how bad it was for her. I don't remember feeling any remorse or sympathy towards her at all. It was like some of my emotions were switched off, and sympathy was definitely one of them. In my mind Holly deserved to be punished because of the nuisance calls she made to my mum.

* * *

Things were still going well at Sue's, and she continued to let me out every night to see Ash. I couldn't keep away from him, despite the fact we were fighting and arguing a lot, and this seemed to be getting worse. It was as if he was a drug and I was addicted to him, so even when I was hurting inside I was drawn to him and couldn't say no to him.

We carried on having sex every day, even when we'd had a falling-out or we'd been fighting like cat and dog. I didn't enjoy having sex with him after a row or a fight, so I'd lie there, like a dead body.

One night we went to a hotel on the outskirts of town, where we'd been three or four times before. Ash did the check-in, as he always did, and was given a card along with the room key, which listed all his previous visits. I saw that these amounted to a lot more than three or four.

'What's that?' I said, looking at the massive list.

He laughed.

'It's not funny. Who else have you brought here?'

'For fuck's sake, not this again! Look, Bash and Bono use this hotel too. We're all on the same account, that's all.'

We argued in the lift and then I brooded for a while in the room. Part of me hated him and part of me loved him; it was so confusing. Ash told me I needed to chill out.

'Why are you getting mardy?'

'I'm getting mardy because I'm starting to believe what everyone is saying to me. I'm starting to believe you've slept with Holly and loads of others while you've been with me.'

'Look, you're the one I want to spend the rest of my life with. Remember how special it was when we first met? I've never felt that with anyone else. I still don't. You're the one, Sammy. Nobody else matters.'

* * *

The rumours about Holly and Ash persisted, and so did the girl wars. One day I was in town with my sister Lisa, my old friend Sophie and another girl when I got a random call on my mobile from a girl I didn't like, asking where I was.

I sensed there was trouble brewing. The four of us walked out of a shop at the top of town together and there were about 15 girls I knew all standing on the pavement, outside the door. Holly was among them. The girls started circling around me. One of them spat out something about Holly sleeping with Ash, clearly trying to get me going. I told her to shut her mouth.

'Make me,' she said nastily.

The other girls moved in tighter around me, looking like they were all spoiling for a fight. I didn't want any trouble, not least because Lisa was expecting a baby with her long-term boyfriend, and was heavily pregnant. I was worried she would get involved, as she'd never let anyone hit me. I told Lisa to leave, but she didn't.

'Holly's not the only one Ash has been shagging,' another girl taunted.

'That's enough!' Lisa shouted, trying desperately to stop things kicking off. 'Stop it, all of you.'

Then Holly's mum appeared. She saw the commotion, assumed it was my fault, and said something along the lines of, 'At least I know what my daughter is up to, at least she isn't in care.'

This really pissed me off. It was Holly who'd introduced me to Ash in the first place, and she was as involved as I was with him and his circle. It was a right cheek of her mother to say what she had, and I was furious. I couldn't contain my anger any longer and I totally flipped.

'I'll fight you all, one-to-one,' I yelled.

The girls had started backing off when Holly's mum turned up and were walking away down the hill, but I screeched after them.

'I'll put you all in a box!' I yelled. 'Come on, come and fight me! I'll put every single one of you in a box!'

'Oh my God, we need to get out of here!' I heard one of them say. 'She's crazy, let's leave it.'

I called Ash and he pulled up in his car almost immediately. He always seemed to know my whereabouts and so I didn't question how he managed to appear so quickly.

'Don't worry, you can get them one-by-one,' he told me.

I felt safe when I climbed in Ash's car. All I wanted was for all this shit with other girls to end, and for me and Ash to live happily ever after.

Chapter 22
'I thought you'd like it, or I wouldn't have done it'

One night Ash suggested we could go to a hotel in Attercliffe in Sheffield.

As soon as we got in the room, Ash said he wanted to have sex. Halfway through he turned me around and started having sex with me from behind. Everything was fine at first but all of a sudden I felt his hands grab tight hold of my hips. Then I felt a piercing, burning pain shoot up my backside. My body flew into the headboard and I started screaming my head off in panic and pain, not knowing what had happened.

'What the fuck was that?' I shrieked, gasping and reeling. I ran quickly to the bathroom, holding myself and slamming the door shut behind me. I was in extreme pain and floods of tears.

Ash stayed on his knees on the bed, laughing like it was the funniest thing in the world.

'It's not fucking funny,' I screamed, still sobbing.

'I thought you'd like it,' he said, still laughing. 'I'm sorry.'

'You fucking bastard! It hurts!'

I got myself on the toilet, though it was agony. I was torn and bleeding and crying hysterically, asking Ash again and again what had just happened. When he told me I was horrified; I'd never even heard of anal sex, let alone done it. I was shocked and confused; I had no idea that was even physically possible.

'I don't get why anyone would do that,' I said. 'Why the fuck did you do it?'

'I'm sorry,' he said again. 'I thought you'd like it, or I wouldn't have done it.'

'You thought I'd like it? Well, I fucking didn't.'

'Do you still love me?'

'No.'

'I don't believe you.'

I didn't know what I felt. I could tell Ash wasn't really sorry, and I found the whole experience so disturbing.

It took me a while to calm down. I got dressed and then Ash took me back to Sue's for 10 p.m. I started to wonder if other people did that, and whether I was just being a boring girlfriend.

The next day, Ash acted like nothing had happened. He was all sweetness and light, and he asked me if I fancied going to a nightclub at the weekend. Before I met him I had only ever been to the teen 'pop 'n crisps' disco at a nightclub in town, which was for young teenagers. Ash had first taken me to nightclubs when I started to run away from home. We stuck to certain ones where he knew the bouncers, because they let me in, even though I only looked about 12 or 13. It was always exciting to go to a proper grown-up club with Ash, and when he made this suggestion I pulled out all the stops to make sure we could go. I arranged to stay back at my family home for the night to avoid my 10 p.m. curfew with Sue. For some reason, only our Lisa was at home that night, although I didn't tell Sue this. Then I lied to Lisa, telling her I was going on a special night out with my mates.

I got myself all done up in heels and a skirt that Ash liked and he drove us into town. It was a great night. Ash bought me lots of drinks and I danced for hours, having loads of fun and really enjoying myself. At the end of the evening he dropped me back home and disappeared.

As soon as I walked in the house I started freaking out. Lisa was up and she started shouting at me, asking me what was wrong.

'Can't you see?' I asked. 'Oh my God, the spiders!'

'What, Sammy, there are no spiders!'

'Are you joking? There's massive tarantulas everywhere.'

Lisa was really alarmed. She could tell I must be hallucinating.

'Sammy, have you taken something?'

'No! It's not me. Can't you see the spiders? They're absolutely massive ...'

I was screaming and going hysterical. Eventually Lisa calmed me down and put me to bed.

When Ash picked me up at the top of the road the next day I told him what had happened, and said I thought someone must have spiked my drink.

'It were me,' he said, laughing. 'I put an ecstasy tablet in your drink!'

'You did what? You could have fucking killed me!'

I was fuming, but Ash told me I was overreacting and being a mardy bitch. He had a friend with him in the car and they both started laughing. I felt stupid, so I let it go, not feeling sure if I really was a mardy cow or not.

Chapter 23

'You're too young. You're just a babby'

'I'm pregnant,' I announced proudly.

It was early December 2000 and I was in a hotel room on the outskirts of town with Ash.

For weeks before this we'd been having a lot of fights. There were still rumours going around about Ash seeing other girls, and I hadn't got over what he did to me in that hotel room in Sheffield, and how he spiked my drink with ecstasy.

One fight was particularly bad. Ash hit me after an argument and I ended up curled in a ball, crying, on the living-room floor of the flat in Clough Road. I'd seen him kick off in that room before, breaking furniture and kicking the fireplace in when he was mad about something. Now I was the target for his anger, and I was terrified. Ash was as mad as hell, and he had a vein bulging in his neck, which always happened when his blood was up.

'I want me mum,' I said.

Ash looked really offended by this. He didn't like the fact I wanted somebody else and not him.

'No, you don't. You want me.'

'No, I want me mum,' I sobbed again.

Ash hugged me after that, and then he said he was very sorry, and that he didn't know what had come over him. He'd only hit me because he had such strong feelings for me. He loved me, and he wouldn't have hit me if he didn't love me so deeply, and care so much.

'You need *me*, don't you, Sam?'

I cried in his arms. I wasn't sure what I needed. It was like he'd cast a spell on me, because even after being beaten by Ash I stayed with him.

I would always think that it was my fault he hit me and it must be something I was doing wrong that made him do it. I thought I shouldn't ask questions; I shouldn't get him mad, I shouldn't provoke him. It was my fault, and I was the one who needed to change, then he would.

Now I'd missed a period and done a test, and I was sure this pregnancy would change everything for the better. We could put the past behind us once and for all.

Ash's face lit up as soon as I told him the news. He kissed me and hugged me, and he seemed right happy and excited. I was so relieved to see him like that. I really believed the fact I was pregnant would make us so happy. Ash wouldn't hit me again, and he'd go back to how he was when we first met, which is what he always promised, whenever he lost his temper.

We had sex and afterwards I was laid on the bed in the hotel. Ash started rubbing and kissing my belly, saying the baby would be spoilt, because he was going to buy it everything and it would want for nothing.

I felt flooded with happiness. Having the abortion had been the lowest point ever. I couldn't turn back the clock, but at least I was lucky enough to have another chance to have Ash's baby. This time there was no way in the world I was going to give in to any pressure from anybody. I was keeping our baby and nothing and nobody would make me change my mind.

We talked about how this was so different to last time, when I was living at home and everyone was against our relationship. Now that Sue was letting us see each other, the fear that Ash might be prosecuted seemed to disappear. I didn't even think about this risk, even though I would be just two months past my 16th birthday when the baby was born the following summer.

I'd done the pregnancy test in Sue's bathroom, just before I told Ash, and I told Sue straight away that it was positive. I'll never forget her reaction. She was walking down the stairs, one step ahead of me, and when she got to the bottom step she turned around and looked me in the eye.

'I'm not even going to ask if you're going to keep it,' she said calmly, raising her eyebrows. 'I already know the answer.'

Sue had accepted Ash was my boyfriend in a way my parents never did, and now she was accepting the pregnancy, almost like it was inevitable.

* * *

There are two notes in my Social Services file in the months leading up to my pregnancy that show how Sue's view of Ash as my boyfriend was shared by people in authority at Rotherham Borough Council. The first note, in a 'Looked After Child' review of arrangements, summarises that 'Sammy's relationship with her parents became difficult as Sammy had pursued a relationship with a male older Asian, Ash, who the parents felt was not appropriate. The relationship difficulties appear to be her continuing relationship with her boyfriend'. Another note refers to her 'boyfriend who is 25 years of age, of Asian origin and married with two children'.

By this time I had met Ash's children more than once. We'd taken them to a fair together and a few other places. It seemed normal. I accepted this was what a father did when he had got divorced and had a new partner in his life, and we always had a nice time.

Sue offered to do up her spare room for the baby and was very supportive, chatting to me about what colour walls I'd like, and what I needed to buy.

My social worker, Margaret, arranged a meeting at my family home, and I can remember sitting around the table with Mum. She started crying and had her head in her hands.

'My babby can't have a babby,' she sobbed. 'You're too young, you're just a babby.'

I was glad I was living with Sue. I couldn't stand scenes like this. Mum and Dad's marriage had reached breaking point. Mum was drinking way too much. Our Lisa told me she had caught Mum drinking vodka first thing in the morning, trying to pretend it was tea or juice. One day she was spilling bleach all over the carpets as she tried to clean the house straight after breakfast. Dad was falling apart too. I knew people in the family were blaming me for pushing my parents to the edge like this, but it was like I was a robot when it came to anyone other than Ash. He got 100 per cent of my emotions and there was nothing left for anyone else – no empathy, no compassion, nothing at all.

* * *

'Sam, I've been arrested,' Ash said.

He was calling me from the police station and he asked me to go down and see him.

My heart leaped. I was sorry he'd been arrested but pleased he'd called me, and wanted me there.

'What for? What's happened?'

Ash told me he'd had a fight with Richard over money, and that he'd stabbed him. He blamed me, saying he did it because he needed to get money he was owed, to provide for me and the baby.

'How the fuck is it my fault?' I asked. 'I didn't tell you to do anything to Richard, and you've got loads of money.'

Ash was released on bail and was eventually charged with kidnapping and stabbing Richard with a screwdriver 12 times. He had some other charges to face too, for other offences. It would be a while before he'd have to go to court, which I was relieved about. At least Ash would be with me through the pregnancy, I thought, even if he had to spend some time inside once the baby arrived.

Chapter 24
'If I can't have you, nobody can'

I was sitting at the table in Sue's eating chips, beans, two burgers and some fish fingers for my tea. In the early stages of my pregnancy, I craved food like this all the time, and I was really enjoying my meal.

Siggi rang my mobile. 'I think you ought to know that Ash is shagging Emily. Has been for a while. He's gone to meet her now.'

My gut dropped and I pushed the plate of food away.

Emily was a very good friend of mine, someone I would have trusted with my life. Though we didn't see each other very often we had a close bond and I thought we'd always be there for each other.

I felt physically sick.

Members of my family, and some of my friends, had been telling me they'd seen Ash and Emily together, but I'd not wanted to listen. She didn't hang around with the same people as I did and I didn't want to believe she could be with Ash – how could she? The people who were telling me wouldn't lie though, and now I couldn't deny it any longer. I called Ash straight away.

'Ash, come and meet me at the end of the street. I need to talk.'

He didn't argue or ask why, and when I saw him I started screaming and shouting and telling him I wanted to finish with him.

'That's it, it's over,' I yelled. 'I know it's true this time. I know it. We're done. I've had enough.'

I had one of his jackets on and I took it off and threw it at him.

'Sammy! You can't do this, you motherfucker. Get in the car, you crazy bitch, and let's talk.'

'No.'

'I said, get in the fucking car.'

Ash's eyes were blazing and the vein in his neck was pulsing. He wasn't used to having anyone standing up to him, because most people were scared of him. He grabbed me by my hair and manhandled me into the car as I kicked and fought.

'Get off me! You're mad! What are you doing, you fucking bastard?'

Ash started speeding away like an absolute maniac while I was kicking and punching him, trying to get him to stop the car.

'If I can't have you, nobody can.'

'What? Are you mad or what?'

'I'll kill you, and I'll kill myself.'

Ash had threatened to kill my family when we'd had rows before. I was petrified. He seemed deadly serious. I grabbed for my seat belt and buckled myself in, as I was scared he was going to crash the car.

Ash began driving down a residential street with cars parked on both sides. There was a gap between two cars in front of a church wall, and he suddenly swerved off the road, steered into the gap and smashed through the parked cars and head-on into the wall.

I screamed and felt the seat belt tightening across me. Ash ran off, but I stayed put. My stomach hurt and I was afraid I was having a miscarriage. He then ran back and started telling me to get out of the car. There was a woman driving up behind us and he was afraid she was calling the police.

'I'm not moving,' I said, and Ash called me a stubborn bitch.

I think the woman must have called 999, because both me and Ash were taken to hospital in an ambulance, although I have no memory of this.

I woke up in a bed next to him, but then he was moved to another ward. I was told members of his family had come in to see him. I was checked over – my baby was fine – and then Ash came to see me, and he was unscathed too. He apologised.

'I forgive you,' I said robotically.

I started to have a constant hurting feeling inside because of Ash. It was like a ball of pain and worry in my chest, yet I could never imagine leaving him. I'd become so used to how dysfunctional our relationship was that I accepted that this was how things were, even when frightening and outrageous things like this were happening.

I was pregnant and despite Ash's behaviour and my feelings of hurt and pain, I believed we truly loved each other. Besides, who would I turn to if I left him? I was totally immersed in his world, and how could I live without him?

Me and Ash were both discharged from hospital that same day and he told the police the accident happened when a dog ran out in front of his car. I backed up his story.

My social worker, Margaret, came out to visit me at Sue's a week or so later and I also saw my mum. I went round to the house and we had a civilised talk. I wanted Mum to know I was definitely keeping the baby, and there was no way I was changing my mind. Mum didn't argue or cry this time, but I could tell she was very sad and bitter.

Mum told me she had put money away for when I was 16. She said she would give it to me now, and we could go shopping together for baby clothes and toiletries, nearer the time. I thanked her and left.

Providing for the baby was one of the things Margaret had come round to Sue's house to discuss. We had a cup of tea and chatted, and I told Margaret that Ash had offered to buy everything I needed. I'd already been window-shopping in Meadowhall and seen a turquoise-coloured pram I wanted, plus the best cot ever, which was a bit like a wicker Cinderella carriage. Ash had promised to buy both. Sue explained that she was doing up her spare room. We'd decided to paper it yellow, which would work for either a boy or a girl. Margaret seemed to approve and I was relieved that I had her and Sue's support.

With plans taking shape for the baby, I began to feel more settled and calm, but it wasn't long before there was more trouble with Ash. He told me that because he was on bail, the police were keeping an eye on him and he couldn't go about his normal business, which I assumed meant drug-dealing. With no money coming in, he could no longer afford to buy everything he had promised for the baby.

My heart sank, but then Ash said he had a plan.

'There's a post office,' he said. 'I can't rob it because the police are watching me, but I thought you could do it. I'll help you, because it's for the baby. You'll do it, won't you, Sammy?'

I nodded mechanically. 'I'll do it,' I said.

Ash took me down there to check out where the security cameras were and said he'd give me his gun. I'd seen his gun several times and on one occasion he'd held it to my head. It was such a terrifying experience I'd tried to push it out of my mind. It had happened in his car, outside the Clough Road flat. I can remember the feeling of absolute terror and I can see a flashback of the gun in Ash's hand as he held it to my head. The rest of the details are blurred, the memory too traumatising to hold on to. Despite this, now I readily agreed to take his gun. I felt no fear; it was like I was numb to normal emotions.

Fortunately, I never did the robbery. Bash got wind of what his brother was planning and went mental. He told Ash he wasn't to make me do it, and if he did then he would grass us up to the police. Ash was spitting tacks, but he dropped the idea.

'What about our house?' I asked. 'Will we still be able to live together if you haven't got any money?'

'Don't worry about money, Sam. I've got plenty of other irons in the fire. The house is nearly all sorted anyway. We could start staying the night there sometimes if you like.'

'Really? I'd love that. I'll ask Sue what she thinks. She might let me.'

A little while after this, me and Ash collected the keys from the Pakistani man who was also helping sort this house deal out. I still didn't know who he was, or what Karen MacGregor's involvement was, but I was thrilled Ash and me finally had the keys.

It was March now, and a note was written in my Social Services file stating, 'Sam saying Ash now has a house, asking permission to stay overnight. Explained parents' consent needed. However, if they agree Social Services would oppose this. Explained the department's concerns. When Sam was 16 would be able to make her own choices, however, there would be issues re the baby given Ash's previous history'.

I knew nothing about what Social Services were saying. I took Sue to show her the house, but she took one look at it and said there was no way I was staying there. 'You need to get somewhere better,' she said. 'This is a bloody shit hole.'

Sue was right. It was scruffy and dirty inside. Nevertheless, I started to go over there a lot in the evenings. I'd cook chips and beans and burgers for Ash. I bought the burgers from the halal meat section at the local Kwiksave, after Ash gave me some money to go shopping.

'Look at you, you're like a little wife.' I loved it when Ash said that, I felt right grown up.

Ash soon got involved in another money-making plan, involving stolen car parts, which he stored at the house. Unfortunately, the police were on to him, and he found out they were carrying out a raid.

'Sammy, will you go in, see what's what? They won't arrest you, but if I go in, I'll get arrested.'

'Yes,' I said, without questioning him. I took the house key with me.

'If anything happens, say nowt until I get Wazir.'

I walked towards the house and I saw Bono being arrested and handcuffed. The officers then told me they were arresting me.

'Fuck off, you can't arrest me!' I said. 'This isn't my house. I don't live here! How can a 15-year-old girl own a property?'

'Then why have you got the key to the house?'

'It's not mine!'

I was taken down to the custody desk at the police station. Bono was already there and was shocked I'd been arrested too. I was taken for questioning and Wazir turned up. Then something happened that completely threw me. An officer came in and said Ash had called. He put down a piece of paper with a phone number on it and asked Wazir if he could call Ash on that number. Wazir said he'd call later.

I looked at the phone number and my blood ran cold. I recognised it immediately as Emily's.

I was released, and Sue picked me up from the police station. I felt sick to the stomach about Emily being with Ash but I didn't show my emotions to Sue. I stayed really quiet and calm, but inside I was in absolute turmoil. Ash being with Emily was the worst thing in the world that could happen, the worst betrayal.

I asked Sue if she could take me to a phone box, as I wanted to call Emily's number. She agreed. My mind was whirling.

If Ash answers the phone, that's the end. I'll know it's true about Ash and Emily sleeping together and I'll have to leave him, but then what?

I called the number and Ash answered. I hung up. In that moment I felt like my insides were being ripped out. It felt like my entire life had turned to dust, because I had no other world outside of Ash.

I would have to appear at Rotherham Youth Court because of my supposed involvement in the stolen car parts. I didn't give a shit; all I could think about was Ash, and whether he was cheating on me.

A few of my friends decided to beat Emily up by the shops, because they were so appalled that she could be messing around with Ash behind my back. I felt right uncomfortable with this, despite the pain she'd caused me, and I managed to stop the fight halfway through.

What's happening here? It was like my life was getting more and more out of control. I was nearly four months pregnant and I wasn't happy at all, but I didn't have a clue what to do to make things better.

Chapter 25
'You need to start to trust me'

Ash had insisted he could explain everything, but I'd had enough. On the night I was released from the police station I told him to get lost and that I never wanted to see him again.

Ash insisted we had to talk and I reluctantly agreed, but only because of the baby. I didn't think it was fair to cut him off from his child, and so I said I'd meet him at the top of Sue's road.

'Sammy, you need to chill.'

'Chill? And you're sleeping with Emily behind my back?'

'Who said that? I was with her, that's all.'

'Well, what were you doing?'

'Sam, I'm with you now, what more d'you want?'

I wasn't falling for his charm so easily this time. After he dropped me back at Sue's I switched my mobile off so he couldn't contact me. A few days went by, and I was really miserable and uptight. I'd never felt so lonely and unhappy in my life; it was sheer hell.

Then Ash called Sue's home phone.

'I don't want to talk to him,' I told her.

Sue smiled, rolled her eyes and tut-tutted. 'You might as well, love, because you know you'll get back with him eventually anyway.'

I took the call and agreed to see Ash that night, on the understanding he was to keep well away from Emily and any of the other girls I'd heard rumours about in the past.

'Just chill,' he said.

I felt trapped. I knew I shouldn't go back to him, but what choice did I have? I'd glimpsed how I felt when he wasn't in my life, and I didn't want to live like that.

In the midst of all this uncertainty about my future with Ash, I had a terrible fight with Cheryl one dinner time at school. Cheryl was always being a clever bitch and there was so much bad blood between us. I saw red and started really laying into her, going completely overboard.

I was so fired up I didn't even let my pregnancy hold me back. I was blazing and punching her for all I was worth.

After the fight, someone took Cheryl into the butcher's to get cleaned up. Her dad was called, and when he arrived I argued with him too. He began making all kinds of threats to me and two other girls she'd also been fighting with. They went quiet and didn't say a word but I didn't care, and I argued back.

'What's happened?' I heard a person standing nearby ask.

'I'm not exactly sure but that girl's face made me feel physically sick.'

I hadn't realised how brutal I'd been, but I'd made a complete mess of Cheryl's face, cutting her mouth and damaging her teeth. She had to go to hospital to be treated, and I know she needed some kind of reconstructive treatment, as she tried to sue me for it afterwards.

I have no memory of going to the Youth Court over the stolen car parts but my records show I was let off with a warning and after that there was a 'personal education plan' meeting at school about me. Now I was back in court again, this time charged with a Section 47 assault. It was noted in my file that the assault would appear to be 'related in some way to Ash and disputes with other girls over him'.

I was told I would have to attend a 'victim awareness programme' as well as take part in discussions on things like anger management, peer pressure, Asian culture and adultery, pregnancy and birth. Ash was invited to attend the parenting and birth classes with me.

'No problem,' he said. 'It might be a bit of a laugh.' He seemed proud of me for having the fight and he treated my punishment like a trip to the shops. He also said he'd come with me to the victim awareness programme.

Ash was true to his word and he fetched me to and from all my sessions, even the ones he wasn't invited to attend. I can't recall learning much; most of the time it was just me and Ash, sat there watching birth videos.

'I think they're trying to scare me,' I said. 'Maybe they don't want me to have any more kids after this one.'

'Well, that won't work,' Ash replied, squeezing my hand.

I was back under his spell, wanting to cling on to him, even though I knew there were so many reasons I should leave him.

Mentally I was all over the place. One day I'd feel so much pain, hurt and anger, then the next I'd experience a burst of happiness and feel on top of the world.

In the 'observations' section of the report that was filled in by the youth offending services officer after I completed the victim awareness programme there is a note that sums up my dilemma.

'She recognises all the reasons why the relationship is not healthy but at this time feels unable to disassociate herself because of her emotional attachment to him.'

A strategy meeting about me and 'allegations regarding Ash' had been held within Rotherham Council by this time, though I knew nothing about it. The minutes of the meeting show that sexual exploitation was discussed, but the police said they had 'no formal evidence or allegations regarding Ash'. However, one youth worker stated a concern, saying she felt my life was at risk.

Nobody told me this, and presumably nobody told Sue this, as she organised a holiday to Skegness and agreed that Ash could come too. Me, Sue and her husband Brian all stayed in a caravan, while Ash drove himself down separately and was booked into a B&B on the same site.

'When are we going to make love?' Ash asked at the first opportunity.

'I'll have to try and slip away,' I said.

It was easy. I didn't even lie or sneak about. I simply told Sue I was going over to the B&B to see Ash, and we had sex. I was heavily pregnant now and having sex was starting to become difficult with my bump, though Ash still wanted to do it every day. I wondered if it would hurt the baby, but he said, 'No, of course not, love.' I told him to do it gently, just in case.

Ash was meant to stay in Skegness for the whole trip, but on the second day he said he had to leave. It turned out he'd robbed the B&B.

Then I took a phone call from a friend. 'Sam, do you know where Ash is?'

'No.'

'I'm sorry to tell you this, but he's with Emily.'

I sat on the caravan steps and cried. Emily was meant to be my friend. How could she do this behind my back?

I began constantly ringing and messaging Ash to put my mind at rest. Of course, he told me it was all lies, but when I got back from Skegness some other suspicious things happened. One day I got in his car and the windows steamed up, revealing the name 'Emily' had been written on the glass. I lost the plot, shouting and screaming at him.

'So I gave her a lift,' he laughed. 'You're paranoid!'

'I don't believe you.'

'Well, fuck off then, Sam. Get out of my life if you don't like it!'

I stormed off out of the car. Holly was with me – we'd managed to patch things up after our fighting and falling-out – and so were my friends, Tina and Jennifer.

Ash came after me, screaming at me to get back in the car. Then he spat in my face and head-butted me. He'd spat in my face before and knew I hated this, but the head-butting was something new. Holly, Tina and Jennifer saw it all and were terrified.

I started screaming and crying. Ash's friend Paddy was with us too. He stepped in and told Ash to leave it. Suddenly Ash was full of remorse, telling me he was so sorry, and that he loved me so much. I continued screaming at him.

'Let's all get back in the car and calm down,' Paddy said. 'I swear, Sammy, he's not cheating on you. Trust me, I'm his best friend. I'd know and I'd tell you. He gave Emily a lift, that's all. Nothing happened.'

I wanted to believe him.

'Oh, right then. Well, I didn't know that, did I?' I said.

'You need to start to trust me, Sammy,' Ash told me, 'Or this is not going to work. Think of the baby.'

Ash was right. I was paranoid and I needed to chill. It must be all my hormones; I'd been warned they would be all over the place while I was pregnant. I had marks on my face after the head-butting, but I accepted it was all my fault he'd hurt and humiliated me in front of my friends.

After that Ash told me he'd got the money together for all the stuff for the baby after all, and we could go shopping the next day. I agreed.

He'd already bought me the pram I wanted, and he took me to Sheffield to get the wicker cot I'd picked out too. I was thrilled to bits, but also so scared. I needed him and wanted him, but deep down, I'd also started to realise that the last thing I needed, or truly wanted, was Ash.

A text then arrived on Ash's phone, from Emily. We were driving at the time and Holly and a couple of other girls were in the car with us. I saw the text clearly: the message was flirty and it was obvious Emily and Ash were arranging to meet.

I exploded and started screaming and shouting at Ash, asking him what the hell was going on.

'Don't get him mad,' Holly said, but I didn't care what she and the others thought and started accusing Ash of cheating on me yet again.

'You stupid bitch, you need to shut up!' Ash shouted.

I twisted round in my seat and kicked him in the head.

'Bitch!' he screeched, skidding over to the side of the road. As soon as the car stopped I got out and began stomping away. Ash jumped out too and grabbed my arm. I hit and kicked him again, and as I did so a police car started driving down the road.

'Stop it, you stupid bitch! You'll have the police on us.'

'I'm not fucking bothered!' I screamed, kicking and punching him even harder.

The police car slowed down as it passed us, but then it carried on. I think, subconsciously, I'd wanted it to stop, and for the police to come and help me. I was so angry I'd have told them everything, but it didn't happen. I thought that nobody could help me. Somehow Ash calmed me down, and eventually I got back in the car. I didn't know what else I could do.

I felt like I was going round the twist. When I wasn't with Ash I did normal stuff like listening to my music and sticking pictures of Craig David in my scrapbook. I didn't feel angry and aggressive all the time, but I didn't truly relax, or feel any strong emotions at all. It was like I was disconnected from reality.

The spare bedroom at Sue's was nearly decorated now, and I'd been to Mothercare with my mum to buy some clothes and bath stuff for the baby, which were the only things Ash hadn't bought. He came to nearly all my antenatal appointments, driving me there and back and sitting with me. I was glad all the preparations were going well, but I didn't ever feel happy. It was like this was the calm in between the storms with Ash, that was all. I was going through the motions when I wasn't with him.

At school I sat two GCSEs in English and Maths, and the teachers were pleased with me for turning up and doing them when I was so heavily pregnant, and after all the work I'd missed. I didn't expect to do well and wasn't bothered what the outcome was.

All I cared about was what my future held with Ash, *if* we had one.

Chapter 26
'You're scaring me'

One night me and Ash were driving past the shops near my school when we saw a girl we both knew called Stephanie. It was late and she was on her own so Ash pulled over and offered her a lift. I wasn't happy about this because she was mates with Emily, but I didn't say anything.

I also knew Ash had his gun in the car that night and suddenly, out of nowhere, I found myself grabbing for it. Stephanie was sitting in the back of the car and I turned around and pointed it at her head.

She screamed and asked me what the hell I was doing, but Ash stayed quiet and waited to see what I'd do next.

'You'd better fucking tell me if Emily is shagging him,' I threatened.

'No, Sammy, no,' Stephanie said. 'She isn't. Honest, she isn't.'

Stephanie looked absolutely terrified, and when I saw how scared she was I put the gun down.

I stayed sitting next to Ash in the car. He told me I was a fucking stupid bitch. 'You can't leave it alone, can you?'

'I wouldn't have really used it,' I said. 'It's your fault anyway. You made me like this. All I want is to know the fucking truth. It's driving me crazy. Just tell me!'

Ash laughed. He had a proud look on his face, like he was glad I was the way I was.

Once again I told him it was all over and that I was definitely finishing with him, which seemed to be happening every other day.

'I mean it this time,' I said, wishing I did, but not believing it myself.

The next day we were back out together, in his blue Subaru. He'd told me he needed to see me, and that he wanted me and nobody but me. That was what I wanted to hear, so I agreed to meet him at the top of the road. It was still typically my routine to be with Ash for a few hours every night. Even when we were arguing we always had sex, sometimes in a hotel or in the house, and I continued to stick to Sue's rule of being home by10 p.m. If I hadn't been seeing Ash on a nightly basis I don't know what I would have done; I didn't know anything else.

I started quizzing Ash about what he did after 10 p.m., because this had been playing on my mind. For somebody who broke all the rules, he was always more than happy to drop me back at 10 p.m. prompt, as Sue instructed. I knew some of the other girls, including Emily, were allowed to stay out later than me, and I wanted to know who he saw and what he did after he took me home.

'Do you ever stop?' he snapped.

'Do *you*, Ash?'

'Stupid bitch. Can't you keep your mouth shut for once?'

'That's it. I want out of this relationship. I'm fucking sick of you treating me this way.'

Ash began to accelerate. We were on the main road by the hospital now and he was driving faster and faster, frightening the living daylights out of me.

'Stop Ash! You're gonna kill us!'

'That's right,' he snarled. 'I've warned you before and now I'm gonna do it. I'm gonna kill both of us.'

He veered off the main road and up a steep side road that led to one of the highest vantage points in Rotherham, looking out over Boston Park and Moorgate Cemetery. There's a car park at the top, leading to a cliff-top edge with a sheer drop. Ash had taken me there when he was teaching me to drive, and we'd had sex there once too, as it was deserted at night.

'Please, Ash!' I screamed. 'Slow down. You're scaring me.'

'You want to finish with me, do you? Well, d'you know what? If I can't have you, nobody can.'

We'd reached the top of the steep side road and Ash sped through the big metal gates that opened on to the car park. Then he kept driving, towards the cliff edge. It's only a small area, and he was speeding really, really fast.

I screamed and screamed because I honestly thought he was going to drive the car right over the edge. There was no space or time to stop, and I could see the whole of Rotherham below, and the road running out.

'Ash! Stop! Pleeeeeaaaase!'

I screwed up my eyes and put my arms across my bump, to protect the baby. A moment later Ash slammed his foot on the brakes really hard and the car stopped with the front tyres just inches from the edge of the cliff. I got out of the car and threw up all over the wheel on the passenger side, and then I collapsed to the ground. Ash got out really calmly, picked me up and stood me on the edge of the cliff. I'm afraid of heights at the best of times, and I was so frightened, I wet myself.

Ash burst out laughing.

'Come here,' he said. He picked me up again, threw me in the car and had sex with me as calm as anything, as if nothing had happened. I was too terrified to stop him. The passenger door was open and I was flat on the back seat with him on top of me. I lay there like I was a corpse on a slab in the mortuary. My head was turned away from him and I was staring into space while tears ran down my cheeks. I was hoping it would soon be over, and he was moaning in my ear and doing it really hard.

Afterwards he took me back to Sue's, on time. I was very quiet and she could tell something was up and was kind and sympathetic.

'Been arguing again? I'm sure it's something and nothing,' she soothed. 'You'll work things out like you always do.'

I looked at her and thought, *You wouldn't believe what just happened to me.*

I went upstairs and put my soiled clothes in the laundry basket, got in the shower and sobbed while I was curled in a ball.

The next day I felt ill with stress and worry and I decided I was never, ever going to see Ash again. I told Sue that if he phoned the landline she was to tell him I didn't want to speak to him, and she nodded and agreed.

I tried to concentrate on the baby and on anything other than Ash but I couldn't stop thinking about him. He had been my life for nearly two years and I was reminded of him everywhere, every day. Wherever I went in town I'd think about having been there with Ash, and when I did something mundane, like buying a cheese salad sandwich for my lunch, it would make me think about how he used to always buy my favourite foods. Friends talked about Ash, I saw people he knew all the time; it was impossible to escape reminders of him. I was carrying his baby, and I was thinking about him every minute of the day.

Then my friend Alison told me she'd seen Ash and Emily going into a hotel. Alison was a very good friend who didn't tell me stories to wind me up like other girls. She knew I was trying to break ties with Ash, and she probably thought this would help me realise I was doing the right thing.

'Right,' I said robotically.

Inside I had the same feeling I'd experienced when I saw Emily's phone number at the police station, and when Ash answered her phone. It was like I was being ripped apart from the inside out. I'd never experienced deep pain like it. I had to know if it was true. I wanted Ash to tell me it was lies, and that he loved me and we could mend things.

I sat on a wall near Sue's, crying and texting and ringing Ash. He didn't answer for hours, and when he did, his message devastated me. 'Go and top yourself,' he said.

I staggered out on to the main road. My life was over anyway, so I might as well kill myself. Through my tears I saw a bus coming down the road. I stepped out into the middle of the road and stood there, sobbing. As I did so I put my hand on my stomach. 'Sorry,' I said, and then I waited for the bus to hit me.

I got out of the way with seconds to spare. There was a man at the bus stop who saw everything and came up to me.

'I don't want to be here any more,' I cried.

He was shaking his head.

'Sorry,' I stammered, but I wasn't really apologising to him. The only thing I was sorry about was that I was still alive.

I walked back to Sue's and cried myself to sleep.

Ash phoned me the next day, and said he was sorry for what he'd said.

'Too late,' I said. 'I can't take this any more.'

Now it was his turn to have his texts and phone calls ignored. Sue was asking me what was going on, because Ash was phoning the landline all the time. I simply told her we'd fallen out again, and that I didn't want to talk to him. 'Oh dear,' she said. 'I'm sure you'll patch things up, love.'

Ash's trial for stabbing Richard was coming up soon, and I was worrying about that too. I didn't want to see him, but I didn't want him to be locked up and not be there for the baby either. My head was all over the place. I had no clue what I really wanted, and I felt lost and confused and extremely low.

'You'd better come in here and have a look at this lot,' Sue said one day. I'd been to town, and when I walked into the house I couldn't believe my eyes. The whole kitchen was filled with flowers of every type and colour. There were dozens and dozens of them, including potted plants and big shrubs.

'Ash brought them round for you,' she smiled.

I smiled too, for the first time in ages. I thought this was so sweet, and I phoned Ash, giggling.

'Have you done all this for me?'

'Course I have, you motherfucker!' he laughed. 'I've told you, I'll do anything for you.'

Ash confided in me later that he and a mate had been out all night long, robbing flowers from petrol stations, gardens and shops. I didn't care where they came from; this was the loveliest thing anyone had ever done for me.

'One of the reasons I love you is because I could put flowers in front of you and a Ferrari and you would always pick the flowers,' Ash had said to me once. This was true. I never cared about money.

It was love and romance I wanted, and I felt smitten as I stood in Sue's kitchen, breathing in the smell of the fresh flowers.

This feeling didn't last long. I got back with Ash, only for us to fall out again, badly. We could barely go a day without a big blow-up. It was one of those arguments that escalated quickly, and ended with Ash kicking me, me punching him, and both of us screaming and swearing at each other.

I felt exhausted and I wanted it all to stop. The more pregnant I was, the more I hated the rows and the fighting. I thought Ash should show me more respect, but he seemed to have the attitude that now I was having his baby he didn't need to try any more. I was having his kid and so I was stuck with him, that's what it felt like. Ash thought he could get away with treating me badly and that I'd have no choice but to keep coming back.

When our latest fight and argument ended, Ash said he was very sorry, and that he only got so wound up because of the strength of his feelings for me. Then he wanted sex, as always. We were in a hotel, and I remember very clearly that I looked up at him as we were having sex, and suddenly I felt repulsed. It wasn't like the times I'd lay there feeling resigned to the fact I was going to let him satisfy himself. This was a strong feeling of pure and utter revulsion: I'd had enough.

'Get off me,' I said.

Ash was shocked and called me a mardy bitch.

'I mean it. Fucking get off me.'

He started kicking off and calling me a slag and a bitch, but he did get off me, and he took me back to Sue's.

The next day, when I woke up, the first thing I thought, very clearly, was: *I need to leave him.*

This time I knew I truly had to, but I didn't know how. I felt numb and hurt. It was a right uneasy feeling that I'd had for a long time, like I was dying inside.

I wanted my family to help and I wanted to talk to Mum and Dad and Lisa and tell them how desperate I was feeling, but I was so worried that they'd say 'I told you so'. The only person I really had was Ash, and he was making me feel this way, so really I had nobody at all.

Ash picked me up the next evening as normal. He had no idea what I was thinking and we didn't mention what had happened the night before. I hadn't made my mind up about how to handle this. I was quieter than normal, but if Ash noticed he didn't say anything. We didn't have sex, and if he'd suggested it I would have said no. I never wanted to have sex with him again, but I still couldn't bring myself to actually leave him. Ash was like an addiction. I knew he was bad for me, but I couldn't give him up, even when he made me feel like shit.

* * *

Ash had to appear in court on some separate charges to those he faced over stabbing Richard. He told me I didn't have to go to court to support him, and I didn't. I was worried sick about what would happen though, and I was on pins waiting for news.

Ash was remanded in custody at Doncaster Prison. He was looking at several months inside, and while he was locked up he would face the charges relating to Richard.

I had very mixed feelings. The chances were Ash wouldn't get out of prison for at least four or five months. It would be nearly Christmas and the baby would be a few months old by then. My head told me this was the end, but my heart told me we had unfinished business. I wasn't ready to let Ash go, because then what? I had nothing else, and I had his baby.

I missed Ash when he was in prison. He phoned me a lot, and I enjoyed talking to him. I got myself a little part-time job in a discount shop called Honest Freddie's in the centre of town. Ash called me one day on my mobile as I was walking up through the bus station to work. He asked me why I was working, because it was his job to look after me, and he repeated what he always said, about me being too beautiful to work.

'I'm saving up to get you some trainers,' I told him. 'I'll send them to you in prison.'

I was earning £2.10 an hour, so it was taking me a long time, but I wanted to get them for him because I felt sorry for him being locked up with no new things. He told me I shouldn't, but I said I wanted to, and anyway it gave me something to do. I was only doing part-time hours at school and was about to leave for good, and I was bored and lonely.

I didn't admit it to myself, but I was clinging on, wanting things to go back to how they were when we were happy and Ash wasn't hitting me and cheating on me. He couldn't do those things when he was locked up, and so it was easy to push them out of my mind. I liked it when he said I was beautiful and that he'd look after me. That was the good side of Ash, and that was what I focused on.

When Ash was due in court again I'd reached the point where I was missing him really badly. I was feeling quite excited when I walked in and sat in the public gallery. I couldn't wait to see him, and I was looking forward to seeing how he would react to seeing me, especially as I was now very visibly pregnant and had a large bump under the purple flared trousers I was wearing.

Things didn't go to plan. When Ash was fetched into court he looked at me with a right nervous expression on his face, like a naughty puppy might have when he'd been caught out. He wouldn't take his eyes off me and he mouthed 'I love you' across the courtroom. I didn't know what was going on, but something wasn't right. Then a girl who looked to be about 18 or 19 was fetched out by a guard and placed next to Ash in the dock.

Who the fuck is she?

I sat and listened to the proceedings with a sickening feeling seeping through me, hearing how Ash was accused of falsely imprisoning and blackmailing Richard, and stabbing him with a screwdriver. The girl was called Janet, and she was accused of being Ash's accomplice, acting as his driver. I knew there and then that I couldn't trust Ash. He'd tried to keep Janet a secret from me, and he'd very nearly succeeded. I couldn't make excuses this time; I'd seen the proof of his deceit in a court of law.

I put my hand protectively on my stomach and then I looked Ash, shook my head and walked out of the courtroom. I didn't want to be Ash's girlfriend any more. He could see the baby but not me. He'd blown it once and for all.

Chapter 27
'If I can't see you, then I won't see him'

Ash was taken straight from court back to Doncaster Prison. I had a meeting with Social Services around this time, and I was warned that I had to keep myself out of trouble, or I would risk having the baby taken off me when he was born.

I'd been for a lot of antenatal scans by now – Ash had taken me to nearly all of them for months – and at this point I knew I was having a boy. I was very happy about this, and Ash had seemed delighted when he'd heard the news too. My parents were not pleased at all. They were scared that Ash might be more interested in having a son than a daughter, although now he was locked away they were desperately hoping I'd never see him again.

I absolutely didn't want to see Ash but I didn't want to cut him off from his son, and I needed to know if he was going to provide for the baby as he'd promised. Ash was ringing me from prison, begging me to get back with him, and I was saying no, absolutely not. 'You can see your son but not me,' I told him repeatedly, but I wasn't getting through to him.

I decided to go and visit Ash, to make it clear where we stood.

One of Ash's sisters was also visiting him in prison and we arranged to travel together. I'd met her many times by now, and she'd always been all right with me. On the journey she told me that Ash was still with his wife – they never had divorced as he told me – and she also said, 'Isn't it funny that you're both pregnant at the same time, and both expecting a boy?' I don't think she realised the effect this would have. I felt like I'd been kicked in the gut.

When I arrived at the prison I was still reeling from what Ash's sister had said. In the end I didn't even see him as the prison staff wouldn't allow me in because I was a child without a legal guardian.

I was so upset and confused. I was seven months pregnant and feeling incredibly protective towards my unborn baby. I felt very strongly that my son deserved a better life than the one I was leading. I didn't want him to come to any harm, or go through any of the pain and heartbreak I had in the last two years.

I needed help and support from my family, and I needed stability and normality too. I didn't care any more if my family would say 'I told you so'. Providing a good home for my baby was the priority.

I began to think about leaving Sue's and moving back with my mum and dad. When I spoke to my parents about it they were so relieved, and they wanted me home as soon as possible. Their past worries about me running away and getting myself into trouble and danger were irrelevant now. I'd done it all, and Ash was locked up.

I started staying with my parents a lot, even though I was still officially in care with Sue.

Ash was still not accepting the fact I didn't want to be with him any longer. He was phoning me about three times a day from prison, telling me he wanted me when he got out, and asking how the pregnancy was going.

I repeated that I didn't want to be with him any more, but he begged me for a second chance. He also got his cellmate Tommy to call me, telling me how it was tough for him and his girlfriend too, but that me and Ash would get through this bad patch.

I kept saying no, I didn't want to get back together, but Ash wouldn't give up. Tommy arranged for his girlfriend to deliver about £250 cash to me so I could get some bits for the baby. I took the money for the baby but didn't want a penny for myself. Then, when Tommy was released from prison, he turned up at my parents' house with a big bunch of flowers, saying they were from Ash. My sister Lisa came to the door and told Tommy to get away from the house, and as soon as he'd gone I went outside and put the flowers in the bin. Dad had the house phones cut off after that, although Ash still called me on my mobile.

I only spoke to him because I was still hoping he might help me with the baby, and I wanted him to share parental responsibility. Ash was such a good dad with his other kids and I wanted our child to know his father and benefit in the same way.

On the day I went into labour I was at home. Nanan was there and Mum was at work.

'Oh my God, it's coming out!' Nanan shouted when my contractions started. I was lying on the settee and she said she'd better have a look and opened my legs.

'Oh, it's OK! It's not coming yet!' she said.

Even in the circumstances I managed a smile because this was typical of Nanan: our nickname for her is 'Nutty Nanan'.

She phoned Lisa's partner and he drove us straight to Rotherham Hospital. I called the prison to tell Ash I was in labour and he rang me on the hospital phone. He was thrilled and thought it was the best thing ever.

'Na then, you motherfuckers, my girl is having the baby!' he shouted excitedly to his prison mates. 'My boy's nearly here!'

Ash reminded me to take deep breaths, like I'd been shown on the pregnancy videos. 'You're gonna be fine, Sam,' he said, coaching me through it. 'I love you. I'm so proud of you.' I swore back at him, because I was in absolute agony with the contractions.

Mum arrived on the labour ward. I heard her before I saw her, as she ran down the corridor shouting: 'Let me through, me babby's having a babby!'

I had gas and air and an epidural. Lisa and my mum were with me, and Mum held my legs up. 'Mrs Woodhouse, be careful! You're going to break her legs!' a midwife said, as Mum was pulling them up so high.

There were all kinds of complications that I was oblivious to at the time, and then I threw up, and the baby shot out.

I'll never forget holding James for the first time. He was slimy and slow-moving and quite puffy, but I thought he was a little angel in my arms. He cried and I was so happy. He was 8lb 7oz; a right healthy weight considering I was only nine stone and a size ten at the end of the pregnancy.

Ash's two sisters came to the hospital with balloons. My family weren't happy about this at all. They couldn't understand, and didn't want to accept, a culture where a married man's sisters would come and visit a 16-year-old girl when she'd just given birth to his child. Though I didn't agree with it, I understood the Pakistani way of life a lot more than I did at the start, and I said to let the sisters come in for a bit. It seemed only fair.

I took James home, and I can remember thinking how much I wanted to protect him from all the violence and danger I'd been around. He was so precious and innocent, and he deserved so much better.

I was completely unprepared for how expensive it was to raise a baby. All the supplies I'd got before James was born were running out, and when Ash called from prison I explained this to him. Ash's response was that if we didn't get back together, he wasn't giving me any financial support for James. Then he went one step further: 'If I can't see you, then I won't see him.'

I reiterated what I'd said countless times before. We were not getting back together, but I wanted Ash to have a relationship with his son, for both their sakes. I'd thought about the practicalities of this. I knew Ash would get back in my head if I saw him again, and I didn't want this to happen. I needed to focus on being a mother. I told Ash I wanted him to have supervised contact with James, arranged through Social Services. Ash refused this offer point-blank, and as far as I was concerned that was the end: Ash was out of our lives.

I got a new mobile and started making plans to move into a flat that my dad was buying for me and James. I intended to keep the phone number and address secret from Ash, but I was anxious he would find me and cause trouble when he came out of jail.

Social Services were worried too. In October, a strategy meeting was held on the subject of young people at risk of sexual exploitation. At the meeting concerns were raised to discuss 'possible intimidation and harassment by Ash towards Sam and baby' when he was released from prison. The possible need for safe housing, or conditions on Ash's licence when he was free, were also talked about. My social worker Margaret made a referral to Risky Business, which was a project set up to look out for vulnerable girls, so they could consider if I needed support when Ash was free. In November, there was a Public Protection Case Conference at which it was asked if an injunction could be sought by Social Services to protect me, prior to Ash's release. I didn't know about this because it didn't happen, but it's all on my file. There is another entry saying a researcher who had been investigating child sexual exploitation in Rotherham on behalf of the Home Office felt it would provoke Ash if I got an injunction.

* * *

I spent a really good few months with my family. My sister's baby was nearly a year old and was thrilled to have a little cousin, and me and our Lisa spent a lot of time together, chilling and enjoying being mums. I was convinced James was an angel given to me to save me, because cutting Ash out of my life was exactly what I needed to do.

Parenting was tougher than I imagined and I couldn't have managed without my family. When I look back at pictures of me holding James as a newborn I look a lot younger than 16, and I certainly felt like a little girl. I'd imagined it would be like playing dolls, only with a real baby, and I was utterly unprepared for the sleepless nights and endless rounds of feeding and nappy changes. I thought I'd be able to put James down for a sleep when I wanted, but of course he was awake when I was trying to sleep and I was exhausted all the time.

I can remember Lisa offering to have him overnight one time, to give me a break. Then she fetched him back half an hour later, saying: 'Here, you can have him back!' It was hard work every day. Lots of people said he was a difficult baby, but seeing James gurgle and smile was amazing. I loved him so much it was untrue.

Nobody spoke about Ash. His name wasn't mentioned at all. My family wanted to forget him completely. and move on.

Sadly, Mum and Dad hadn't managed to solve their marital problems, and they had decided to live apart and sell the family home to Lisa. Dad was buying a new place not far away, and Mum was renting a bedsit. Unbelievably, the place she found was opposite where Ash's family lived, and I went mad with her about that.

'He doesn't bloody scare me,' she said.

Ash was history and it was a fresh start for everyone. I couldn't wait to move into my own place. It would be me and James and I could devote all my time to him.

Chapter 28

'What are you playing at, Sam?'

When James was a few months old I took him out shopping with me in Rotherham town centre one day. It was December and James was tucked up against the cold in his turquoise pram. I was strolling along happily, looking at the Christmas decorations in the shops when all of a sudden, I spotted Ash walking towards me. He was with Bono and a friend of theirs.

My heart tightened in my chest. I hadn't expected to see Ash; I didn't know he was out of prison. I tried to walk away but Ash was having none of it, and he swaggered up to me.

'What are you playing at, Sam?' he shouted. 'Let me say hello to my son.' He leaned over the pushchair and pulled funny faces at James. James gurgled and smiled. 'See, he likes me!'

'I'd laugh too if you stood in front of me with that face,' I retorted bitchily. 'You've seen him now, so piss off, Ash.'

I marched off towards the inside market, hoping he'd leave me alone, but Ash followed, shouting at me to stop. I started walking faster, telling him I wasn't interested.

I stopped at a card shop in the market and bought a card saying, 'To my boyfriend'. Naïvely, I thought this might make Ash realise I wasn't interested in him any more and that I'd moved on with someone else. Of course, I wasn't with anyone, I just wanted to piss Ash off, but this backfired on me badly. He looked really angry and started making a massive scene, refusing to leave me alone. I felt scared, and I couldn't get rid of him.

'You need to fuck off right now or I'm ringing the police,' I threatened.

Ash didn't listen and I kept walking away from him as quickly as I could.

I'd reached the top-floor balcony and was standing by the lifts but I still couldn't shake him off.

'I'll have you done for this,' I said. 'Now fuck off!'

'Fucking bitch,' Ash said.

We then started trading insults and arguing really loudly. He wanted to get me as mad as possible, because one of the things he said was that he had slept with Emily, and that she was better in bed than I was. This was a stab to the heart, as it was the first time he had actually admitted sleeping with her, but I didn't show him how I felt.

'Fuck off, I'm not fucking interested,' I said.

Ash then lunged at me and grabbed me by the throat. We were standing next to the balcony, and he lifted me up by my neck and hung the top half of my body over the edge. The drop was really steep, down on to concrete below, and I was terrified he was going to throw me over.

I tried to kick and was grabbing on to him so I wouldn't go over the edge. I couldn't scream for help as his hands were so tightly around my throat, but people were watching and pointing.

Bono and their friend stepped in and dragged Ash off me. To my absolute disgust and horror, Ash then stormed up to the push-chair and kicked it over, with James inside.

'I'm gonna set you on fire and watch that black bastard burn,' he snarled.

I picked up the pushchair, made sure James was all right and ran for my life around the back of the market, pushing James as fast as I could. I kept looking over my shoulder and Ash was chasing me and screaming. I spotted a phone box and pushed James inside first to make sure he was safe, then grabbed the receiver. I started dialling and Ash was right in my face, throwing insults at me.

'You've fucked it!' I shouted. 'I'm gonna have you done for this.'

Our argument continued until Bono and their friend pulled Ash away again.

'Ash, leave it,' Bono said, pulling Ash's arm. 'Everyone's looking. The cops are gonna be here any minute, just leave it.'

They all started to walk down near the bus station in the opposite direction to me, with Ash still shouting abuse at the top of his voice.

I have no memory of how I got home or who I called from the phone box, but I know now that the number I dialled was my sister Lisa's because she told me later that she heard everything.

I was shaking like a leaf and crying hysterically. I told my family what had happened and my dad said I should contact the police. For the first time ever I agreed to make a complaint about Ash. Though my dad was absolutely furious about what Ash had done, he was delighted I was going to phone the police. We both hoped that with the help of CCTV footage from the market Ash could be prosecuted.

An officer called PC Dawson came to the house, and after I'd finished telling him exactly what happened he said, 'What do you expect? He's got every right. You've stopped him from seeing his son.'

My dad went mental. He had been trying to get me to speak to the police and make a complaint about Ash for more than two years. Now I'd finally done it, this officer had more or less told me it was my own fault I'd been hung over a top-floor balcony by my throat, and my baby had been kicked over in his pushchair.

Dad exploded. 'We've had this for two years, and you lot don't ever do fuck all about it. I want an officer who knows what they're doing.'

Dad then went into all the details of everything Ash had done, but nothing happened and Ash was never even questioned. After that I went to a solicitor's in town and asked them how I could apply for a court order to prevent Ash from coming near me. I wanted a quiet, safe life for me and James and I thought this was the best way forward.

* * *

When I finally moved into my own flat, I hoped it would be the fresh start I needed, but it wasn't to be.

One day my wheelie bin was set on fire. The bin was stored in an inside wall right up against my flat. I strongly suspected Ash had something to do with it, or had sent someone to do it, because of the vicious threat he'd made in the shopping centre, about burning me and James. Thankfully someone spotted the fire and it was put out before it spread out of the bin, but this really frightened me, because it could have escalated into a really big blaze.

A string of other incidents occurred too, which I was certain Ash was behind, though I had no proof.

My mum's car got trashed, and then Nanan's house was targeted, with people peeing on her windows and door, making noise outside and intimidating her and her friends. After that Dad bought Nanan a little flat close to the family to make sure she was safe. Very alarmingly, my sister and my cousin both had random cars driving straight at them, like they were trying to run them over.

The court order I'd applied for finally came through, and it meant if Ash came near me he would be arrested. This was a huge relief, although it didn't stop the harassment.

I started to notice Ash sitting outside my flat in his car at all different times of the day and night. I tried to ignore him but he came back all the time, playing loud music and sending people up to the door to knock and harass me. Sometimes they shouted that they had presents for the baby and could I open up the door, but I never did. Eventually there was someone sitting outside my flat in a car 24 hours a day. Whenever Ash was there he'd shout things out of the car window, like 'Sammy, you're a fucking slag.'

I called the police and reported him several times, and a female officer came to visit me. While she was in the flat Ash was sitting outside with his music on full blast, but the officer said there was nothing she could do, as Ash was sitting on a main road.

'Surely you can arrest him for breaching his injunction?' I asked. 'You do know the court order is one with a "power of arrest"?'

'No,' she said. 'Because you live on a main road there is nothing we can do.'

One time I decided to speak to Ash, to try to talk some sense into him. He said he wanted to see his son, and that he had every right to see him. I told him once again that the only way that could happen was if he had supervised access visits, which could be arranged by Social Services.

'If I can't see you I'm not interested,' he snarled.

Chapter 29
'Don't you remember all the bad stuff?'

In January 2002, when I was 16 and a half, Social Services closed my file. A note was written advising that further information about Ash could be obtained from the member of staff in charge of 'procedures for young people at risk of sexual exploitation'.

Around this time, my mum and dad got back together, having worked hard to repair their relationship. I decided to move back in and live with them in the house Dad had bought, because I didn't feel safe on my own in the flat.

I was scared of Ash and what he was capable of, and my priority was to keep James out of danger. Our fears were very real, as several more unsettling things happened. My sister Lisa had spotted Ash driving up and down her road, and I was questioned about a crime I had absolutely nothing to do with. Apparently, a woman had picked my picture out at the police station, saying I'd assaulted and robbed her. I was able to prove that at the time of the alleged attack I had been heavily pregnant and therefore didn't match the description of the very slim girl she had described to police. I strongly suspect this was Ash's doing, as I knew he had set people up before. I was sure he was trying to get me in trouble because he was so pissed off that I wanted no contact with him.

Terrifyingly, I started to hear a rumour that Ash was going around saying he was planning to kidnap James, and take him to Pakistan. I had no idea if there was any truth in this but I certainly wasn't taking any chances. The only time James was out of my sight or not being looked after by a member of my close family was when he was at the nursery school he had started attending, and so I decided I should give the school a photo of Ash, so they could be on their guard. I didn't have a picture of Ash, because I'd torn them all up when our relationship was disintegrating. I knew the police had to have one, so I phoned the station, got a number for PC Sadat and asked if he could get a photo for me. The fact he was friendly with Ash didn't worry me; this was a child's safety we were dealing with, and PC Sadat was a police officer first and foremost.

'Ey up, Sam, nice to hear from you,' PC Sadat said. 'I can pull a picture off his records seeing as it's you, but don't tell anyone or I'll lose my job.'

'Of course I won't. Thank you so much.'

PC Sadat brought the photo round to the house and we had a friendly chat about something and nothing, like we always used to. As he was walking away down the drive, PC Sadat turned and said something about the fact I was now single, and then he asked me if I fancied going on a date.

'No,' I stuttered. I was completely taken aback. I didn't look at PC Sadat in that way at all. It seemed so wrong and strange that he should even ask me this; I tried to put it out of my mind. I later discovered PC Sadat had been given a misconduct warning before for accessing information from the police database.

I felt more comfortable living with my parents than on my own in the flat, but I was afraid to go out, so much so that I developed agoraphobia and started refusing to leave the house at all. This was stressful for all of us. In normal circumstances, someone with agoraphobia would be gently encouraged by their family to venture outside, but Mum and Dad were scared of what might happen to me, and for a while they let me be, staying in the house, out of harm's way, looking after James and focusing on being a mum.

In time, Mum began talking to me about what I was going to do next in my life. She wanted me to have dreams again, like I did before I met Ash.

I'd not passed my Maths and English GCSEs, I had no other qualifications and I had a criminal record. For years, the only job I had ever really wanted to do was be a dancer, but I hadn't danced for so many years that I didn't think I could get back into that, at least not without a lot of training and dedication. The only other job I was interested in was modelling. Mum had told me all my life that I had the looks for it, and Sue had tried to get me involved in modelling when I lived with her, but Ash wouldn't allow it. Now it seemed like a good time to give it a try; I didn't have a better idea, and it still appealed to me.

The only problem was, since having James my body had changed a lot and I was really self-conscious. I wanted to have cosmetic surgery to improve my bust, but Mum wasn't sure. She said I was beautiful as I was, but I became adamant and I wouldn't stop going on about it. Eventually, she paid for the operation, for my 18th birthday. This really boosted my confidence, and by now I was over the agoraphobia. Time had been my healer: the more time that went by without me seeing Ash, the better I felt.

My family were there for me every day, encouraging me and looking out for me, but it was James who was my real inspiration.

I wanted to give him the world, and I wanted to be the best mum ever. I loved the days we spent in the garden, or going to the park and feeding the ducks and being with my sister and her little one. James reminded me of Ash when he was first born, but, as he got older, his skin went paler, his hair lightened to a mousy brown and his eyes turned the brightest blue. He was like a little boy version of me.

I'd occasionally find myself reminiscing about the good times me and Ash had together, particularly at the start of our relationship. I thought how Ash was the love of my life and how we'd lost our way, but then I'd pull myself up. 'Sammy, don't go there,' I'd tell myself. 'Don't you remember all the bad stuff?' I did, but my heart got the better of me sometimes. It never took long for me to put the wall up though, and shut off my feelings once more.

I entered a modelling competition and did well, and from that I was offered a lot of work. Then I got some modelling shots taken, and to my surprise I started getting loads more work, really quickly. Most of it was glamour modelling and topless modelling for magazines and newspapers.

I found it came quite naturally to me to pose for the camera, and I could feel my confidence steadily growing. I think this had a lot to do with the fact I felt like another person in front of the camera. I wasn't Ash's girlfriend; I wasn't Samantha Woodhouse either: I was somebody completely different, and I was glad of that.

One modelling assignment was in a strip club, and when I was there, I was asked if I fancied working as a lap dancer in a club in Sheffield. I really wasn't sure at first, but I auditioned and got the job.

I hated it to begin with. I remember my first dance. I was shaking as I stripped for three minutes, and as soon as it was over

I rushed to the toilet and was sick. The managers and all the girls were really supportive and welcoming and told me things would get easier the more I did it. A glass of wine would settle my nerves beforehand, they said.

It did get easier. It helped that all the girls and bosses were lovely in this club, and most of the clients were decent. There was the odd occasion, in the beginning, when someone would assault you, but it was accepted that a customer would grope you once in a while. I would not put up with that now, but back then I just got on with it. In fact, once I'd settled in, I felt right at home in the club.

Chapter 30
'We're getting help. It'll be all right'

I was at my parents' home, in March 2005, sitting in the conservatory, when our Lisa suddenly dashed in.

'I've got summat to tell ya!' she shouted.

'What?'

'It's Ash. He's dead.'

Mum and Dad were there and they started jumping up and down.

'The bastard's dead!' my mum yelled, punching the air. 'The bastard's dead!'

Lisa had heard from her partner that Ash had been involved in a gangland war over drugs, and he'd been shot.

Mum started cheering and saying she was going to have a party, and she really meant it. She actually started planning it there and then, but I couldn't join in any celebrations. I felt like I'd had a physical blow to my body.

I couldn't tell my family what I was feeling inside. I was still in love with Ash, that's what I felt, very powerfully. We'd never had closure. Our relationship had fizzled out and we'd never even had a final goodbye. Also, whatever had gone on between us, Ash was James's dad. My little boy had lost his father.

I sat there for I don't know how long, shocked and dazed. I was trying not to let my family see how I was grieving, and trying not to look at James and sob.

My head was filled with memories of me and Ash together, when we were happy. I thought about how he was almost exactly ten years older than me, so that meant he was only 29 years old, which was no age at all. James was three and a half, and he'd never known his dad.

Lisa's voice cut through my thoughts.

'Ash isn't dead,' I heard her say.

My jaw dropped. 'What the fuck is going on?'

'He was on life support, but he's pulled through.'

I didn't know what to say or how I really felt, and I sat there staring, trying to take it in. I'd become so used to hiding things from my family, and switching off my feelings when Ash beat me and made me do things I didn't want to do, that I found it easy to shut down. It was a way of protecting myself. If anyone had walked in the room and seen me in that moment they would never have imagined what was going through my mind. I looked composed, robotic even, but my head was in turmoil. I loved Ash, but I hated him. I wanted to see him, but I really didn't want him back in my life, or in James's life.

* * *

It was the Easter holidays, two days after Ash was shot, and Mum and Dad had Nanan over. Me and Lisa were there with the kids and it was good to be together, enjoying time with the family. I hadn't heard any more news about Ash, though there were rumours going around that he'd been shot in the stomach. It sounded like he was going to be OK. I tried not to think about what might happen in the future. It was all too much to take in.

Me and Lisa were talking about buying Easter eggs for the kids and planning what to do on Easter Sunday, which was a few days away. My family were all rallying around, trying to keep me busy and keep my mind off Ash. Nanan was making me laugh as she always did with her nutty ways, Dad was pottering around doing a few jobs as usual and James was sitting in a chair next to my mum, chatting away. He always called her 'Mama'.

Mum had been complaining of having a headache for a few weeks but she'd brushed it off, as she always did when she felt unwell. She hated going to the doctor, and nobody nagged her to go. It was hardly surprising that her head hurt after the emotional upheaval we'd all been through.

Mum went into the kitchen to put the kettle on, and while it was boiling, she went to the toilet. I was in the front room, sat in a chair watching TV, and Dad suddenly shouted, 'Samantha, get in here!'

'In a minute!' I called, not picking up on the urgency in his voice.

'No, now! Get in here now!' He repeated this but even then I didn't react the way he wanted me to.

'Oh, for God's sake, Dad, what is it? I'm watching TV.'

'GET HERE NOW!'

My heart leapt and I dashed to the downstairs toilet, where I saw my mum collapsed on the floor, barely conscious. She had fallen and hit her face on the marble flooring. Her face was a mess. Her teeth had been knocked through her lip and it was bleeding and badly swollen.

Dad said he thought she might be having a stroke and I got her in my arms and held her head while he phoned for an ambulance. Our Lisa appeared and started screaming. I can remember her putting her hands on her head and slipping down the wall.

Nanan got the kids away. It seemed that my little niece had followed Mum to the toilet and may well have seen her collapse, but she was too little to realise what was happening and said nothing. Then my dad went to check what was going on, because Mum had been gone a bit too long.

Mum started moaning as I held her tight in my arms. I knew I had to keep her talking to keep her awake.

'Mum, can you hear me? You need to stay awake. You can't go to sleep.'

'Babby, me head hurts.'

'It's all right, Mum. We're getting help. It'll be all right.'

At that moment Mum's eyes closed.

I continued talking to her in case she could still hear me. I was asking her questions, trying to get her to answer. She didn't. I started to talk to her about her favourite music, like Diana Ross, Elvis and Def Leppard. I asked her to sing to me, but she didn't sing either.

I started to sing quietly to her as I continued to hold her in my arms. I rocked from side to side as if I was cradling a baby to sleep. I'm not sure why I sang this song, but it just came out.

'Twinkle, twinkle little star, how I wonder what you are. Up above the world so high, like a diamond in the sky. Twinkle, twinkle little star, how I wonder what you are.'

I asked someone to fetch a blanket and wrapped it around her legs, to cover her up. I was on autopilot. My heart was beating really fast but I was focused on doing all I could for my mum. The paramedics put Mum in a wheelchair and took her out of the house as her grandchildren rushed to the front window and saw her being taken away.

Dad went in the ambulance and I followed in my car. When I arrived, me and Dad were taken into a quiet room. I knew it was bad news; the worst news.

Mum had had a brain haemorrhage. I heard the words 'brain dead' and then my dad burst into tears. I sat there, stiff as a board. Dad threw his arms around me. He isn't a hugger, and this was the first time he had hugged me like this since I was a little kid. He was crying uncontrollably, holding on to me.

All the family and friends were informed, and everyone who wanted to came to the hospital to say their goodbyes to Mum. She was one month short of her 47th birthday.

The immediate family gathered around the bed, crying and saying their last words. I did what I'd learned to do when I was with Ash: I blocked myself off behind my imaginary wall. I wouldn't show my grief in front of anyone, and I only ever shed tears for my mum when I was alone.

They switched off Mum's machine on the Easter Monday. It was 28th March, less than a week since Ash had been shot.

I wanted to keep my mind off it. Me and dad had recently bought a beauty salon together, which I ran, and I went straight back to work. It's not that I wasn't hurting. I'd become extremely close to Mum. She was my best friend and I kept telling myself that any minute now she would walk through the door, but she didn't.

The fact is I don't like people to see me hurting as it makes me feel weak and vulnerable, and when you're weak and vulnerable, that's when people take advantage.

Everybody in the family was grieving in their own way, and several people asked, 'How can he live and she die?' That's what they were all saying, one way or another. They couldn't take in the fact that Ash had pulled through – in the same hospital too – and my mum was dead.

Mum was going to be cremated, as this is something she always said she wanted. She hated spiders and bugs and said she didn't want to be buried with the 'creepy crawlies', as she called them.

Me, Lisa and Kate were asked if we wanted to go and visit Mum at the Chapel of Rest. We agreed to go together, taking with us some pictures of all the family and the kids to place in the coffin, along with some special possessions.

I was expecting to see my beautiful mum laid there, peaceful like Sleeping Beauty, in her favourite green dress we'd chosen for her to wear, which was one she got from Ireland when we'd attended a family wedding.

Me and my sisters walked into the small, cold room and saw the coffin. The atmosphere was very uneasy, and when I saw Mum it absolutely terrified me. She was cold and a funny colour, and I felt really scared. This wasn't my mum and this wasn't how she made me feel.

I quickly left, regretting I'd ever gone. I wanted to remember my mum laughing and smiling, and all the good memories we had.

The funeral took place at the crematorium. It was packed with family and friends and when Dad got up to speak about Mum, as others did, he broke down sobbing in front of everyone. Kate and Lisa rushed straight to him and hugged him. I sat like a statue in my seat and didn't flinch or show any emotion whatsoever.

Afterwards everyone gathered at a pub down the road from where I grew up. Me and Dad showed our faces, were polite, then left. I went to work at the beauty salon straight afterwards. Nothing about the funeral felt right.

It was difficult to go on living in the house where Mum died. The atmosphere wasn't the same. The house was at the top of a hill in a small cul-de-sac, with a really steep drive leading up to it. Every time I came home I'd look up at Mum's bedroom window, expecting her to be stood there. Then I'd walk through the back door and pass the downstairs bathroom where she collapsed, and I'd have an awful, empty feeling inside. It wasn't home any more and I started to refer to it as the 'haunted house on the hill'. I said it was cursed, and that bad things happened there. I wanted to move out, as soon as I possibly could.

Inevitably, I thought about the hell I'd put Mum through. I'd seen her change from a bright, sunny person to an anxiety-ridden wreck. Mum had always loved a drink, and she had become a full-blown alcoholic. My involvement with Ash, as well as her dad's death, fuelled her problem. Later, she did a six-month detox all on her own and had been controlling her addiction well for years. Life wasn't fair.

Chapter 31
'Sammy, I think you'd better sit down'

Before Mum died I'd met a musician in one of the clubs I worked at. Matthew was a good-looking guy and I thought he was right nice, though lots of people warned me that he was a 'player' and wouldn't treat me well. I thought I knew better and began dating him, and in the aftermath of Mum's death we started living together. Matthew moving in with me was a terrible decision. Our relationship was volatile and violent and I was soon very unhappy. My family didn't like him, and I fell out with my dad and both my sisters.

Towards the end of 2005 I discovered I was pregnant. Matthew was pleased and asked me to marry him but I said no, and we split up. I'd become completely estranged from my family by now: we'd fallen out over something else, not just the fact they didn't like Matthew. I decided to move out of Rotherham and asked the council to house me in a refuge for women fleeing domestic violence. I wanted to be in a 'safe house' where I could feel protected and start over. Matthew finally disappeared off the scene the day Reece was born, and a few days after I'd given birth I left the safe house.

I felt very low. I was really struggling on my own with my two boys, and I began to suffer from severe depression. I felt suicidal some days, and made some half-hearted attempt to kill myself, thinking everyone would be better off without me. I drank some bleach, but not enough to do real damage. I also tried hanging myself but that didn't work either. Then I crushed up paracetamol tablets and tried to swallow them with vodka, but I gagged and was sick. Next I got a knife and slit the skin on my wrists. I wrote letters to all my loved ones, explaining my reasons for ending my life. It shocks me to the core to think about this now, but truth was I was mentally ill and I needed help.

James was five years old by this time and he adored his new baby brother. He became a great little helper, although his behaviour generally wasn't good. He was becoming more challenging the older he got, and when he was difficult I'd often find myself wondering if he'd benefit from having his dad in his life. I didn't want Ash back in *my* life, but was this what James needed? I thought about this a lot, because I wasn't coping at all well.

I'd left my dad with the beauty salon when I moved out of Rotherham and I went back to lap dancing as soon as I could after having Reece, though I'd started to detest it. The girls I made friends with through work kept me going. We'd have a little drink and a laugh together before we started a shift; you had to have a drink to face the job, it was that bad.

In hindsight I can see how Ash's treatment of me had taken its toll. I'd listened to him telling me I was beautiful and amazing one minute, then calling me a whore and a slag and treating me like shit the next. I thought by taking my clothes off and working as a lap dancer I was empowering myself. I was the one in control and calling the shots, but I know now that I wasn't. It was another form of exploitation, because I was there for men's sexual gratification.

I now despised the clients and the bosses I was working for. The bosses were nothing but pimps in suits who saw us as worthless sex objects. A lot of the girls didn't declare they worked in the clubs and so the bosses ripped us off all the time. I was working a few nights a week and doing everything by the book – including paying for the best childcare – but there were loads of times when I was ripped off too.

In the depths of my despair I decided that I would contact Ash, to see if he could help with James. I needed help from someone. I was absolutely desperate.

I'd heard that Ash had ended up in a wheelchair after the shooting. If he was unable to walk there was no way he could be violent towards me, was there? I wasn't getting back in a relationship with him, so he couldn't cheat on me and hurt me in that way, like he did before. I also thought there was no way he would still be involved in crime after what happened to him. Years had passed. Maybe it was time for him to get to know his son?

I decided to get in touch with Ash through his relative Jahangir Akhtar, the man who had got involved that time when I was handed over to police at the petrol station. Akhtar had become a councillor on Rotherham Borough Council and he was quite a high-profile character in the community. I thought it would be better to try him than to attempt to contact any of Ash's friends or more immediate family who may bear a grudge against me.

I phoned Akhtar. Straight away he said: 'Oh yes, I remember you. You were Ash's girlfriend.'

'I didn't think you would remember me.'

'Of course I do. You're Peck's daughter.'

Akhtar asked me how the family was and if I knew about Ash's accident. I said I did and asked if he could help put me in touch with him.

'I will pass your message on,' he said, 'but I only see him at weddings and funerals.'

That didn't sound hopeful, so I decided to call PC Sadat. I was a bit wary of him since he'd asked me on a date, but at the end of the day he was a police officer. He'd been a friend to Ash and to me in the past and I thought he would be able to help.

'Sorry, Sam, not seen him for a while,' he told me. 'Can't help.'

I left it after that. Perhaps it wasn't meant to be.

* * *

When Reece was about one and a half I started dating a guy I met in one of the strip clubs. Simon wasn't a client, he was connected to someone in the business, and he was friendly and charming. He told me right at the start that he'd not long since come out of prison for a minor crime, related to drugs. I accepted this and didn't judge. It was a world Ash had somehow sanitised, and one I, naïvely, wasn't too worried about.

We began spending a lot of time together. Simon eventually met the boys and was really good with them. He'd play football with James and talk to him about sport and boy stuff that I couldn't relate to, and it was really helpful to have another pair of hands, as I'd been so used to doing everything on my own.

We'd been together for about six months and things were going well. Then one night we had a row because I didn't want to go out to the pub with him. Simon turned right nasty and grabbed me by the throat, so I punched him, splitting his lip. Then I told him it was over.

'You've got three seconds to get the fuck out of my home or I'll stab you,' I shouted.

One of the girls I worked with knew what had happened, and she asked me afterwards if I knew Simon had been in prison.

'Ye, he told me all about it when we first met.'

'What did he tell you?'

'It was a drugs bust, wasn't it?'

The girl's face fell.

'Sammy,' she said. 'I think you'd better sit down.'

The girl, who had known Simon for many years, told me that he had been in prison for a shocking rape. I felt sick to the pit of my stomach.

I could handle him having a criminal record, because it was what I knew from Ash and I even had one myself, but not this. It was completely off the scale of what was acceptable. Even Ash would never in a million years have done anything like that, I thought.

* * *

I wanted to be on my own after Simon, but I wasn't in a good place at all. It was very tough being a single mum and I was getting a lot of threats from Simon and his friends, due to ending the relationship. I was still estranged from my family and my only friends were the girls I worked with, though I was only really close to a couple of them.

I decided a fresh start was what me and the boys needed, and I moved to Nottingham.

I was so lonely, and I was struggling to cope as a single mum. James was particularly challenging. I was constantly ringing Social Services to ask for support but they weren't interested.

I thought again about asking Ash to help with James, and one night when I was working in the club, I saw a friend of Bash. This set me thinking, and the next time I saw the friend I asked him for Bash's number.

Bash was surprised but pleased to hear my voice, and he asked if we could meet face-to-face. I agreed, even though I didn't think this was necessary, and we met in a pub about ten minutes from my home. I was cautious and not sure what to expect but Bash was really nice. He told me Ash had been looking for me for years and that he wanted to get to know his son, but he also said Ash was really ill, so he wasn't going to tell him just yet that I'd been in touch, as the timing wasn't good.

This was frustrating, but I accepted what Bash said and I met him several more times over the next few months, so he could let me know when the time was right to contact Ash. Then one day Bash suddenly announced he wasn't going to put me in touch with Ash after all.

'Don't do it, Sammy,' he said. 'Stay away from Ash.'

'I'm not trying to get back with him or owt like that. It's for our son.'

'I don't care. If you've got any sense you'll stay away from him. Ash won't be able to handle seeing you. He's not like the Ash you used to know, he's in a really bad way. I gave you advice years ago about staying away from Ash and you didn't listen, so you need to listen now.'

I was shocked and confused by this, but did I listen? Did I hell! I was Little Miss Know-it-all, thinking I was in control of every-thing and that I could handle it. After what Bash said I became even more determined to get back in touch with Ash: since I first met him it was like I'd had some kind of device implanted in my brain that made me do the opposite of what I was told.

I continued to keep in touch with Bash, hoping he'd change his mind, but then he started being really slimy towards me and trying it on. I wanted to speak with Ash, not put up with this crap, so I cut contact.

In the meantime, I told Social Services about my mental state and how badly I was struggling with the boys. I said that I'd contemplated killing myself because I felt so low, but I was told I wasn't a severe enough case for them to get involved and provide family support.

By now James's behaviour at school was completely out of control, and thankfully a support worker there, Marie, recognised that he had ADHD. Marie helped me to get James diagnosed and began to sort out some extra educational support for him. This helped, but now I had another concern, one that was really playing on my mind. All the stress I was under had led to me developing a stomach ulcer. I ended up being rushed to hospital for emergency tests and there was a lot of panic about how dangerous this was, and even some talk about it being life-threatening. My condition was very serious, but thankfully I didn't need an operation, and I went home.

After this scare I felt even more worried and vulnerable, thinking about how I was going to cope with caring for the boys on my own, especially if my health deteriorated.

I discussed this with Marie and she talked to me about the boys' fathers, and where things stood with them. I had no idea where Matthew was, and I explained that I hadn't spoken to Ash since James was a baby.

'Do you think Ash could help with James?' I asked Marie.

I'd never discussed this with a professional before, but I felt comfortable with Marie. I knew she had my best interests at heart and I valued her opinion, so I told her about my relationship with Ash.

Marie said she would do some background checks, and quite quickly she came back to me with the news that Ash hadn't been in trouble with the law since he was shot more than five years previously. She said it would therefore be OK to contact him and see what he said. I was so pleased. It sounded like the shooting had changed Ash for the better, and I felt a surge of hope for the future.

I can't lie. I still had feelings for Ash, even after all these years. He had been the love of my life and I thought he always would be. He'd had such a massive influence on me and was the father of my oldest child. This was most definitely not about us though; it never had been in all the time I'd been thinking about contacting him. I still hadn't forgiven him for how he'd treated me, and I was only prepared to contact him because I felt James needed the support of his father, and I had nowhere else to turn.

Ash had never paid a penny in child maintenance, but it turned out the Child Support Agency had his details. They contacted him and Ash asked if they could pass on his phone number to me. I agreed.

I sat in my kitchen in Nottingham, staring at the number. It was the end of 2010, and I'd been thinking about this moment on and off for years.

Should I, shouldn't I? What do I say? Am I ready to deal with our unfinished business?

I decided to text first, as I was so nervous.

Ash texted straight back, saying something like 'Is this really you, Sammy?'

'Yes. If it's really you, tell me who my favourite singer is,' I replied, because I needed to be sure this really was Ash.

My phone beeped again.

'Craig David.'

As soon as I read the message I gasped. *Oh my God, it's really him.* I started pacing up and down my kitchen. My head was all over the place. I walked upstairs and sat on the bed and it felt like there was a whirlwind rushing through my body. I took a deep breath, bit the bullet and dialled his number.

As soon as Ash picked up I began struggling with my breathing.

'Sam, I can't believe it's you. How are ye?'

Hearing his voice after all this time was so strange. It was like being in a different dimension. I was 25 years old but I felt like a teenager again. It had been nine years since I'd last seen Ash, but it could have been yesterday.

I told him why I was phoning and Ash took my breath away even more by saying, 'I've always loved you.'

I couldn't speak.

'Why did you do it?' he asked.

'Do what?'

'Leave me.'

I was totally thrown by this. This was the boyfriend who had battered me and cheated on me.

'I've been looking for you for years,' he went on.

I reminded him that this was all about James, not us. I needed help with our son, and that was the purpose of this call. I told Ash that James was having behavioural difficulties at school, and that I thought he would benefit from having his father in his life, to keep him focused and on track.

Ash sounded happy to have been asked, and said that of course he would help me.

'What about you, Sammy? What's going on with you?'

I gave away a little bit about my life, telling Ash I had another son, and that I was on my own and not working as I'd temporarily given up dancing because of my health problems.

'I could look after you all. We could get back together. I could buy you a house and a car and pay off your debts,' he said.

'No,' I said firmly. 'That's absolutely not why I am ringing you. I need help with James, that's all. He's not doing good. I wouldn't be ringing if it wasn't for him.'

I think Ash was surprised at how forceful I was, and then he started telling me he'd sorted himself out, and that he was different now. I asked him about his injury and he told me that when he was shot through the stomach his spine was hit, which was why he was paralysed and in a wheelchair. He was hoping to get a specially adapted car soon, so he could drive again. He also told me his wife had left him after he was shot, and he was living in a house in the countryside in Goole, about 40 miles outside of Rotherham. The bungalow had been specially adapted for his wheelchair.

'Think about it, Sammy. You could move down to Goole. I could help you. You could help me. It'd be good for James. I'd help with Reece too … I could adopt him and raise him too.'

'Wow, Ash, you need to slow down! You're getting way too ahead of yourself.'

It was typical of Ash to rush ahead like this. He still sounded full of energy and his mind was buzzing with plans and schemes, just as it always did.

I found myself asking Ash about the times he cheated on me, because I'd never had closure, and I needed it, even after all this time. He'd only ever admitted to me that he'd slept with Emily behind my back, but I wanted to know about all the other girls he was rumoured to have slept with. I'd tortured myself about it for years, and now I wanted the truth.

'The only time I cheated on you was with Emily, and it was the biggest mistake of my life,' Ash said.

'What about your wife?' I asked.

'That doesn't count.'

The more Ash spoke about the past, the more uncomfortable it was to hear. I was starting to experience all those feelings I always avoided and didn't deal with, the pain and anxiety and fear I'd lived through as a teenager. I told Ash I didn't want to talk about it any more. My protective wall was firmly back in place.

We arranged to talk again and that night I couldn't sleep at all. My whole world was thrown upside down. I couldn't stop thinking about our conversation, and in the end I reached for my phone and texted Ash in the middle of the night.

'I can't sleep.'

'Me neither,' came his reply, straight away.

Ash rang me and I broke down crying, telling him I couldn't get him and Emily out of my head. I still couldn't get over it, all these years on. It had cut me so deeply.

'Look, Sam, it was the worst mistake of my life. That's all you need to know. You need to forget about what happened and then we can move on. We can do this for James. Do it for James.'

I needed time, but Ash began constantly ringing and messaging me. We spoke on the phone loads of times for weeks after that, chatting and reminiscing, and gradually he apologised for everything that went on in the past.

We talked about everything that had happened when we were together. We laughed about how he taught me to drive, the armed robbery that never was, how he used to sing to me, and even some of the stupid fights we had. Memories of him hitting me flashed in my mind, though I tried to push them out. I didn't like that he'd hit me, but I still thought it was what happened between boyfriends and girlfriends, especially when you were fiery like we were. We had a passionate relationship, and that was why we had so many bust-ups and so many mad moments; that's how I chose to remember what went on.

Ash kept taking me back to the good times we had, and after each call I was left feeling more positive about allowing him back into my life. He spoke again about officially adopting Reece, so he could help me raise both boys.

'No,' I said firmly. 'I haven't got back in touch for us to be together as a family.'

'I've always wanted a little girl with you,' he then said, which of course raised memories for me, of the baby I didn't have, who Ash always believed was a girl.

'Well, I'm not having any more kids,' I said, feeling uncomfortable. 'I've got my boys and that's enough.'

Ash then told me he hadn't had sex since the shooting, through choice, not because he couldn't. He also said all his friends had left him after he was shot, and that his family had had enough of him and his life had been really difficult.

The more I spoke to Ash, the more I felt sympathy for him. He started asking to meet me. I didn't want to rush into anything, but what did I have to lose? James could gain a father, and that was a chance I couldn't waste.

I eventually let James talk to Ash on the phone, which went really well. Ash was interested in everything James was doing and said he would love to meet him. Once James heard that he started nagging me to meet his father. I said I wanted to meet Ash on my own first to be sure it was the right thing, and then James wanted to know what happened in the past to break us up. I told him that me and his daddy were in love when we had him, but things didn't work out. Understandably, James didn't get why I was being cautious. He was only nine and he was getting excited every time Ash phoned. Then he started to resent me for not fixing up a meeting, so in the end I agreed that we would all meet together.

I told my support worker Marie everything about how me and Ash had talked, and with her blessing I arranged for Ash to come to my house. I was now living in a newly built three-bedroom house in a quiet cul-de-sac in Nottingham, and Ash said he'd come with his brother Siggi, who was also his carer.

Me and James sat waiting in our front room. I felt anxious, but James was so excited he started jumping on all the furniture.

'Is he here yet? Is he here yet?' he kept asking.

A black car pulled up outside and I opened the front door. James rushed straight past me and dashed outside.

I got butterflies in my stomach when I saw Ash's face, like I used to as a teenager. Then Siggi began to lift him out of the car. My stomach dropped and the smile slid off my face. Ash was so different it took my breath away. He looked thin and drawn in his wheelchair, and vulnerable too. I was used to seeing him looking lively, energetic and invincible, and my heart went out to him. This wasn't the Mad Ash I knew. He had warned me beforehand that he looked different to how he used to, but I wasn't prepared for this. I tried hiding how shocked I felt, as I didn't want to upset him.

'You're right skinny, Sam,' Ash said, as soon as he saw me. Even now it seemed he was worrying about me getting enough to eat. I found that quite nice.

James was buzzing and he and Ash looked so happy to meet each other. Once we were all in the house James hugged Ash and sat on his knee. My little boy was all smiles and I reminded myself that this was what it was about: James's happiness. I had to focus on James's happiness. That was why I was doing this.

Ash was right good with James. I couldn't believe this was the same man who kicked over James's buggy when he was a baby; it was like that horrible incident happened in another lifetime, and I had buried the memory very deep, as it was so disturbing. Also, I'm a naturally forgiving person, and I chose to look to the future, not the past. Ash could be good for James now, and James needed help. I had to put him first and I didn't want grudges from the past jeopardising my son's future.

Me and the boys had a holiday to Ibiza booked, and Ash asked if he could have James over for a weekend visit after we got back. I said I'd think about it. Marie popped in by chance when Ash was there, which was reassuring, as she seemed to think the meeting went well. When I said goodbye to Ash I felt optimistic; this had been a positive step forward, I was sure.

* * *

James talked to Ash several times on the phone before and after our holiday. I felt better in myself after having a break in the sun and, as soon as we got home, James was asking all the time if he could go and stay with his dad. I finally agreed, and we made plans for him to stay overnight at Ash's place in Goole, where he lived with several of his other children and various relatives. Despite the fact Ash had told me his family had had enough of him, they never turned their back on him. It was true he'd lost his friends, but the family never left him.

James couldn't wait for the visit, and he loved it from the moment he arrived. He was so excited to meet Ash's family, and Ash immediately started telling him, 'Anything you want, James, it's yours.' James was in paradise.

My relationship with Ash was friendly and civilised, and we made the arrangements with no problems at all. The idea me and Ash could get back together wasn't on the agenda at all, which put my mind at rest. Despite the fact I still cared for him, I'd made it crystal clear there was no way I wanted to have a relationship with him again. In any case, by now Ash had told me he was having another arranged marriage. He said he didn't want to go through with it and he'd rather be with me, but I told him that was simply not happening.

We were done with talking about the past now, although at one point I mentioned to Ash that I'd tried to track him down through Jahangir Akhtar several years before. It turned out that Ash saw him quite often, and not just at weddings and funerals as Akhtar had told me. I thought this was a bit odd but then didn't think much more of it. Akhtar must have forgotten to tell Ash I'd been trying to find him.

I missed James like hell when he stayed with Ash. I hated not having him around, and so did Reece. *Be strong*, I told myself. *This could be the making of James.* Having got to know Ash again over a few months I had no fear whatsoever about letting James go to stay, or I never would have let him.

Ash seemed to have mellowed. He was gentle and kind and funny with James, and I could see from the way Ash looked at him that he was proud to have James as his son. The farmhouse Ash lived in was well kept, and he had the support of lots of family members, some of whom ran a farm and business from the home, supplying food to supermarkets.

'My dad is so sound!' James said when he came home. He was buzzing. Ash had spoilt him rotten and he'd loved running around the fields on the farm. He immediately asked me when he could go and stay again.

I felt a pang of jealousy. It was like Ash had swanned in and instantly become the best dad in the world. James was going on about the things Ash had promised. He was getting him a games console and some new clothes and trainers, and James said Ash's house was better than ours, because it was bigger and there was loads of space to play.

I was torn. It was a kick in the teeth to have him talk like this after the way I'd struggled for years on my own. However, I had to admit that it was also exactly what I wanted. James looked happier than he had in ages. He was engaged and interested, and he clearly idolised Ash. I hoped this would be the turning point James needed, and that his challenging behaviour would improve and he'd start doing better at school.

Eventually I agreed that James could stay for several nights with Ash, rather than just one night.

'Don't worry about James,' Ash said. 'He can stay as long as he likes. He loves it here.'

'Are you sure it's OK with you?'

'Course I'm sure. He's a cracking lad. I love having him here. Don't you worry about a thing, Sam. It's the least I can do.'

Chapter 32

'Come on, we're leaving'

The downside of James going to stay with Ash was that when he was at home with me he rebelled and his behaviour was worse than ever. It was the same at school; he was giving his teachers a terrible time and Ash seemed to be the only one who could control James and bring out the best in him.

My stomach problem hadn't gone away and I was very ill again, and when Ash offered to have James for a whole week I agreed. He loved it, and so we set up another week, and another. Very quickly, James began to say he didn't want to come home at the end of his visits because he was so happy there with Ash. Reece and I missed James like mad when he was away but we visited frequently. It seemed to be working out well for everyone.

'I could look into getting him a place at the local school,' Ash suggested.

'I'm not sure about that. I need to talk to James.'

James was ecstatic at the suggestion, which stirred up another load of mixed feelings. I wanted him home. I missed him, and so did his little brother, but I had to put James first. It seemed like he was flourishing in Ash's care. He'd been given some jobs on the farm, which he loved, and I'd never seen him looking so enthusiastic and willing to please.

James was failing badly at the school he was at and so, for his sake, after a lot of thought, I decided it was a chance I couldn't afford to pass up. There was a place available for James at a school in Goole. We could at least try it for a term and see how it went; it seemed there was nothing to lose.

James punched the air in delight. Ash had taken him for a really short haircut and he looked like his dad. I had a slightly uneasy feeling about this; I should have listened to my gut.

Ash arranged absolutely everything, as I was still poorly and I needed to be at home for Reece. It all went so smoothly and I told myself it was meant to be.

While these plans were being made, James asked if he could take Ash's surname. This threw me. I thought it was a step too far and was way too soon, but I tried to look on the positive side. At least this showed how happy James was to be part of his dad's life. It was difficult to argue against, because I had decided to change my own name to something completely different.

This all seems strange to me now, but I think it shows how mixed up my feelings were at the time. When I got back in contact with Ash it brought back memories of the past and was a very unsettling period for me. I'm not sure I knew who I was; I didn't know who Samantha Woodhouse was any more and I thought changing my name would help me make a fresh start. I called myself Charlie and picked a new surname.

James didn't stop asking to take Ash's name and wouldn't let it drop, so in the end I compromised and made a double-barrelled surname for him from the new surname I was using, plus Hussain. I made the changes to both our names by deed poll at the same time.

James loved his new school from day one and started doing really well; so well that I wanted him to stay there. As soon as my health improved I made the decision to move into a rented farm near the school, so that James could live with me full-time again and still see his dad. It seemed like a good idea, because James's education was the most important thing in the world, and Reece could go to the same school, as he was due to start later that year.

Ash and I were getting on well. I felt like we'd become friends again, although he still asked if we could get back together. I kept telling him to forget that, it was never going to happen.

I settled into my new place, but Ash immediately started to change. He would have preferred James to live with him full-time, but I reassured him he could see as much of his son as he wanted.

James's behaviour and attitude at school were excellent, but unfortunately, when he was at home with me, he was still a real handful, worse than he had ever been. I wondered if he was playing me and Ash off against one another, as he'd say, 'Dad lets me do that' or 'Dad buys me that'. It was nothing major to begin with, but it was starting to become more and more noticeable and I was keeping an eye on it.

One day Ash started to tell me that he wasn't well at all, and that in fact he had cancer and didn't have long to live. When I was younger, he could have told me that the sky had fallen down and I would have believed him. It wasn't like that now, but it never occurred to me that anybody could claim they had cancer when they didn't.

I broke the news to James and we both sat sobbing on the settee. 'Don't worry, James, we will look after your dad and make sure his last days are the best he's had,' I said. We started to arrange a little holiday for a few days all together, at Butlins. I told Ash I would help him as much as I could, and we even talked about him moving into my place when his health declined, so I could look after him.

While I was still coming to terms with Ash's cancer, lots of other things started to go wrong, in quick succession.

Out of the blue James told me Ash had said he wasn't allowed to eat pork. I told him he could eat what he liked, and told Ash very clearly that I didn't want James to be Muslim. Ash obviously didn't take any notice of me, because then I heard that the family was planning to have James circumcised. I wasn't having that and I argued with Ash about it, telling him that if a doctor went anywhere near James, I would take legal action. James sided with his dad whenever we argued. I was also having trouble with some members of Ash's family by this point, and my instincts were telling me things were going very badly wrong.

Next, James told me Ash was planning an arranged marriage for him when he was 12, to one of his cousins. James seemed thrilled at the idea and announced: 'I'm going to have my own wife and love her and have lots of babies, and I'll be the best dad in the world.'

I hit the roof: it was like my son had been brainwashed.

I phoned the school to arrange an urgent meeting. I wanted to make it clear that James wasn't Muslim and that all decisions must be run past me. To my horror, I was told that the school had been informed that there was a court order against me, preventing me from having contact with James. I told them this was untrue and I would bring the proof, and then I rang the council and the doctors and they told me the same thing. My blood ran cold.

James was at Ash's house when I heard this, and I went straight round to pick him up. Ash's mum was on the driveway and she started speaking to me. It was hard to understand what she was saying as she didn't speak English well, but she told me, 'I know Ash done bad things in past but he a good boy now.'

I was polite and nodded and said, 'OK.'

James came out, and I wasn't happy to see he was talking to his uncle, Siggi. I'd had a really big bust-up with Siggi not long before this, as he was always ringing me and coming to my house, suggesting we should have sex and be in a relationship together.

'You're not a bad-looking girl, Sammy,' he'd said, the last time I saw him. 'And you've got sexual needs, so I'm going to be the one to sort you out, love. I've spoken to Ash about it and it's been agreed, but let's not mention this conversation to him.'

'I'd rather commit suicide, Siggi,' I'd replied, laughing at him and rolling my eyes, which he took extreme offence at.

After his insulting proposition, I'd told Ash to make sure Siggi didn't come near me again. It was inappropriate, and his ridiculous suggestions made my skin crawl.

'James, come on, we're leaving,' I said as soon as I clocked Siggi.

James got in the car, and as I was driving down the road he said that Siggi had asked him to tell me something.

'What?'

'Tell that white fucking slag to get the fuck off my drive,' he said.

I was shocked and furious. This was my young son talking, on the instruction of his uncle. I pulled the car over immediately. Then I rang Ash and told him there would be no more contact.

'If he's not Muslim, he's not welcome here,' Ash shouted. He screamed so loudly that James heard him down the phone, and he got right upset.

Me and Ash then argued about other stuff too, including the fact James had broken a window, which I had no money to pay for. Ash exploded, and then he issued a threat, saying that if I didn't fuck off, he'd have me shot.

I realised then I'd been a fool. Ash hadn't changed at all.

I called the police to report the threat, and they came out to see me. As the officers left I received a text message from Ash. He was watching my house from a distance and he said he knew I would call the cops.

I tried to carry on as normal for about a week after all this, but I was receiving threatening phone calls from Siggi, and he was parking outside my house every night in the early hours of the morning.

I was back in touch with my sisters. We first started talking again around the time I made contact with Ash; the family arguments we'd had were water under the bridge by now and we were getting close again, especially me and Kate. She'd been to stay in Goole with me, and she'd shared some concerns with me, especially about Siggi, as he was always so slimy. I packed my stuff up and phoned Kate in desperation. I couldn't get out of Goole quick enough, and me and the boys loaded the car and went to stay with our Kate back in Rotherham.

The whole unsettling experience of being back in contact with Ash had lasted six months: six months too long.

I felt right bad for putting James through the upheaval, and having Ash speak like that in front of him. James was very forgiving and still wanted to see his dad, but I explained it might be difficult now, and we'd have to wait and see. As for the cancer story, it turned out to be a cruel pack of lies.

I started to rebuild my life in Rotherham. It was good to stay with Kate for a while. In time I got a place of my own, the boys settled into two different schools which suited their needs, and life was just about getting back on an even keel. I felt I'd had a lucky escape, and I never, ever wanted to see or hear from Ash again.

Chapter 33
'It didn't happen to me'

I took a call from our Lisa one night, in September 2012, asking if I remembered a youth worker who knew me when I was involved with Ash. The name didn't mean a thing to me, and my gut reaction was that I didn't want to have this conversation. I was trying to move forward with my life, not look back.

'No. I've got no memory of that person at all.'

Lisa said she'd been taking her son to football training when this youth worker introduced herself, asking if she had seen the recent newspaper reports about grooming.

'No,' Lisa replied. 'What's this about?'

'I remember your sister from when she was a kid. One of my former colleagues has been wanting her to come forward. Your Sammy's is one of the worst cases of grooming we've seen.'

The more my sister relayed the conversation, the more I didn't want to listen. I didn't like the suggestion that I'd been some kind of victim, because I hadn't. I'd put my family through hell fighting to be with Ash. He had been my boyfriend, albeit a very bad one who was violent and cheated on me. I'd made terrible decisions because I was way too young to know better, but I hadn't been 'groomed', whatever that was.

'That's a total load of rubbish,' I snapped.

'Please hear me out, Sammy. I know you're going to say you don't want to know and you don't want to talk about it any more, but please listen before you dismiss this. I think you should talk to someone.'

My sister had waited a couple of days to pass on this news, because it was Monday now and I knew football training was on Saturday. She had clearly thought long and hard about what she was going to say to try to get through to me, but I was having none of it.

'No,' I replied stonily. 'I don't want any part of it. It didn't happen to me. I was in a relationship with Ash, a two-year relationship. It was different. I wasn't groomed.'

Lisa said she was going to get me some books that had been published about child sexual exploitation and she talked about how girls had been groomed for prostitution, trafficked around the north of England for sex and repeatedly raped by pimps.

'Don't bother, I won't read them,' I said.

These were concepts I couldn't identify with. While I was with him, I had only had sex with Ash. I hadn't been trafficked or prostituted out, and I had never dealt with pimps. Lisa still wasn't letting this drop. She was begging me to listen and at least read something about it, but I told her I wasn't changing my mind, so she shouldn't waste any more time trying to persuade me.

I put the phone down and tried to push it out of my head. I was annoyed at Lisa for ringing me like that, and I wanted to forget all about it.

A few weeks later I went to a petrol station to fill up my car. There was a queue to pay and as I was waiting I started to read a report on the front page of a local newspaper. It mentioned grooming and referred to a group of three Asian brothers who abused girls from 1999 to 2001. This caught my attention, because that was exactly the time when I was with Ash. I scanned the page for more information, eating up the words as quickly as I could. I started to feel sick as I realised the three Asian brothers had to be Ash, Bash and Bono. They weren't named, and there were no other details, but I was certain it was them.

I will never forget that moment.

My stomach dropped to the floor. The report said that a total of 54 girls had thought one of these three men was her boyfriend. Eighteen underage girls thought they were the girlfriend of one abuser in particular – the ringleader of the brothers. I knew that this person was Ash.

Lisa's phone call filled my head all over again. I'd argued with my sister that Ash was my boyfriend, not someone who'd groomed me, but now, after all these years, the penny had dropped. I wasn't the only girl who thought Ash was her boyfriend. I didn't recognise myself as a victim, but I couldn't argue with the facts set out in a newspaper, in black and white. Ash was, what? An abuser? That's exactly what he was. Ash groomed at least 18 girls, and I was one of them.

My head was reeling. I grabbed the paper, paid for my petrol and drove home with my heart pounding and my stomach in knots.

I phoned my sister as soon as I got in.

'It's them!' I screamed. 'It's them!'

Lisa didn't have a clue what I was talking about. She'd been drinking and I was in such a state I got mad at her and hung up. Then I went to the corner shop, bought four cans of Carling and sat in my kitchen alone, crying and drinking lager.

My whole relationship with Ash raced through my head. I thought I was special to him, because that's what he made me believe. I know he beat me and cheated on me, but crazy and exciting boyfriends like Ash did that, didn't they? Everybody knew me as Ash's girlfriend. That's who I'd been, that's who I was, wasn't it? I was his number one girl, the one he wanted to marry. The only reason things hadn't worked out was because he went to prison, we had problems and we drifted apart. Wasn't that the truth of it? When I reached 16, things started to go wrong.

Sixteen. Once I was 16, things went wrong. This thought made me feel nauseous. Even though he tried to get back with me when I was older, he had been the most involved with me, the most interested in me, when I was underage.

I couldn't, wouldn't accept this. I had too much evidence screaming against this. I thought of how Ash told me he loved me, and about the framed picture we got of the two of us with the hearts all around it. I thought of how Ash promised me the world and wanted to marry me, how we talked about raising a family together and growing old together. I had his child, for God's sake. If Ash was a – what? – a paedophile, then why did he get so involved with me? How could he be a paedophile? He didn't look like a paedophile. I'd known since I was a school kid that a paedophile was a fat old man who pervs on kids out the window, or pulls up in his van and offers you sweets then grabs you off the street.

Surely the authorities would have stopped me approaching Ash for help with James if he was a child abuser? My support worker had checked him out, and there was nothing on his records to show he was a danger to children.

I read the newspaper report again. It had to be true. I had to face it. It was there, staring me in the face and I couldn't deny it any longer. Everything had been a complete lie.

I fell to the floor, crying hysterically, curled up in a ball.

I was 27 years old, and the past 13 years of my life had been a big, fat lie.

I felt right dirty and disgusting. I'd been a fool. This was all my fault. Why had I been so stupid? I'd caused so much hurt and pain. I felt like a freak, someone who was beneath society.

When the boys were in bed I sat alone for hours, thinking and crying, trying to pick my way through the years. I couldn't get over the fact that Ash exploited me so thoroughly and so intensely it had taken me well over a decade to finally see through him, to see him for what he was and what he did to me.

I felt like I'd fallen into a big black hole I would never be able to climb out of.

I couldn't sleep, and over the next few days I started to feel terrified. How do you move on when such a large part of your past has been a lie? I didn't know who I was any more. And what about James? For his whole life I'd thought he was my ex-boyfriend's child, but now what? Who and exactly what was Ash?

The scale of what he'd done was very hard to take in. I started to see how Ash had carried on grooming me for years and years, long after I stopped seeing him. I doggedly believed what he wanted me to believe: that we had been boyfriend and girlfriend, that we had issues and we split up, like countless other couples. The way he turned from a gentle, charming person into someone so violent had shocked me when we were together, but now I was beginning to recognise that he'd treated me far worse than I ever could have imagined.

Ash was never my boyfriend at all. He was a paedophile who abused and exploited me when I was just a child. Horrifically, I'd let him turn the charm on James too. Ash had swanned in and became the best dad ever, and then when James was captivated he turned right nasty, just as he had with me. Thank God I had got James away from him when I did.

I didn't know how I was going to carry on.

I started to dwell on the darkest times with Ash. The beatings, the sex that hurt me, the cheating, the verbal abuse.

I could think of nothing but the pain and misery Ash put me through. I couldn't get the bad thoughts out of my head, and when I was asleep I had nightmares that woke me up in a sweat, crying and screaming, seeing Ash's face in my mind's eye. In those dreams he'd always be bad Ash, the Ash with mad, bulging eyes, the vein pulsating on his neck and the vile comments spitting from his mouth.

I couldn't come to terms with the fact he had destroyed my life when I was a child, and now he was destroying it all over again. It was like he was haunting me. I couldn't face another day, because how could I go on now my whole life was a lie? How I lived and the way I acted was starting to make sense now. How I'd struggled with relationships. How I became a topless model and lap dancer so effortlessly, so robotically. Why I couldn't deal with my emotions and built a wall around myself.

Chapter 34

'How old did you say they were?'

A researcher who had investigated CSE in Rotherham on behalf of the Home Office when I was a child had passed on a message to speak to me, so I tentatively agreed. She explained she was also a solicitor and knew a journalist from *The Times*, Andrew Norfolk, who was investigating child sexual exploitation in Rotherham.

'I could give you his number,' she said. 'I think he'd be interested in talking to you.'

'No. I'm not talking to any journalists. If anyone finds out, Ash and his brothers will kill me.'

I needed time to absorb my new knowledge. Some days I did nothing but cry hysterically, all day long.

I started not eating properly. I was already very small and I became really skinny. I think it was a way of punishing myself, for what I'd done to my family, and to myself. Ash was always wanting to feed me and make sure I had enough to eat, and I think not eating was a way of detaching myself from him. I would skip meals, sometimes hardly eating for days.

I cut myself too, on the wrists, and then, just as I had after Matthew I thought about committing suicide and wondered how. There were no tears. I was zoned out, my feelings side-lined so I could plan my escape without my emotions getting in the way.

I had suicidal thoughts the moment I opened my eyes. I could put a pipe in the car and poison myself. I could drive off a bridge. I could slit my throat. I could try to hang myself again, and do it properly this time. The kids would be better off without me, I thought, but then I'd look at them and realise it was the kids who were stopping me killing myself.

One day my brain was so full of these thoughts that I picked up a teacup and hit myself on the head with it over and over again, and then I cried uncontrollably. I knew I needed professional help, and I eventually managed to drag myself into an NHS medical centre, one that specialised in mental health. I had the kids with me, and I told a worker there that I felt suicidal.

'I'm ringing Social Services,' she said, picking up the phone.

'Thank God. Thank you so much,' I said, relieved I was going to get some help.

The worker looked at me in disgust. 'I'm reporting you,' she said. 'It's unacceptable to say that in front of the children.'

Social Services said I wasn't a severe enough case for them and put me in touch with a family support service. From this point on I was passed around just about every support service in Rotherham, but most didn't have a clue how to deal with my case. Eventually, Social Services did get involved, but I felt like I was going round in circles, having loads of meetings and appointments for hours on end, repeating myself and getting nowhere. I noticed that when I spoke about my life I'd get to the age of 16 and I'd be asked to stop. Then I would get a new worker. Nobody was geared up to help a grooming victim like me.

* * *

By the start of 2013 I was struggling to get out of bed in the morning. I was barely eating and painfully thin, I was doing the bare minimum with the kids and I was drinking to get myself to sleep at night. I was still dragging myself to loads of different support services, and continued to do so for months, but nothing was helping.

Every day, memories came back to haunt me. I could see Ash being right nice to me, and the nicer he was the more I could see how hard he was trying to groom me. It turned my stomach. I thought about my long-term foster carer and my social worker, torturing myself with the 'what ifs'. What if they had kept me away from Ash? He had fooled them as much as he fooled me, but how had that happened when they were adults, trained in caring for and protecting children?

I was so angry it hurt inside. What if the police had prosecuted Ash for having underage sex with me the first time I got pregnant? Or what if he'd been prosecuted for girls he abused before me? I wasn't his first victim so I'd never even have met him if the police had got him earlier. I couldn't get the thought out of my head.

I picked over my life since Ash again and again, and started to see how I went on to choose men who were bad for me, and how I let men use me. The glamour modelling and lap dancing were all a part of Ash's legacy. He had brainwashed me to think that it was normal to be treated like nothing more than a sex object, there for the gratification of men. I had no self-respect, no self-esteem. He took those things away from me and left me an empty shell of a person.

To make matters worse, Ash started to make threats to me. He'd been calling on and off for a long time, since I left Goole and tried to cut contact. It started when James took my mobile phone and rang his dad without my permission. After that Ash kept ringing and messaging. I should have ignored him but I didn't. I argued with Ash and called him a paedophile, and he started to tell me he was going to have me killed.

I reported Ash's threat to the police and they said the dispute between us was classed as a 'domestic' and that I should ignore it.

I felt abandoned and betrayed by everyone in authority. I'd been let down by Social Services and now the police were leaving me at Ash's mercy yet again. It felt like nobody was answering my cries for help, and I was too weak and broken to keep on crying.

I told my sister Kate I'd had a breakdown and wanted to kill myself, and she got an emergency social worker and two mental health workers to come out and assess me, and discuss the help I clearly needed. Two male mental health workers and woman called Nikki Ledingham came to see me. They knew nothing about my history and Nikki asked me if the children could go to their father, to give me a break and help me to cope.

'Absolutely not,' I said. I explained that I wasn't in touch with Reece's dad and added, 'James's father is a paedophile. He abused me. Under no circumstances can James go to him.' I was sitting on a big spinning chair in my living room and I started crying. It was a watershed moment. It was the first time I'd accused Ash of being a paedophile to anyone in authority like this and that word hung in the air.

'I want to kill myself,' I cried. 'It's the only way I can be at peace.'

Kate was there too and she now started crying with me, and we hugged.

'Don't cry,' I told her. 'I'll be happy when I'm at rest. You should be happy for me.'

* * *

After that I was diagnosed with major depression and prescribed antidepressants. It was decided I should stay with Kate for the weekend, and I didn't argue. I was glad decisions were being made for me, as I couldn't make my own.

Nikki Ledingham then said she would start to put together a timeline of what had happened to me.

Over the next few weeks I slowly began telling my story. Nikki listened patiently and encouraged me to talk about all the happy memories I had of my childhood, including my dancing, the holidays and happy times I shared with my family, leading up to my early teens.

When I got to the point where I described going out with boys, and in particular the two older boys I dated as a young teen, Nikki paused.

'How old did you say they were?'

'Both about 18.'

'And you were 13 when you were with them, and you had sex?'

'Yes. But that was just the way it was. All my friends had older boyfriends and everybody was having sex …'

Nikki went on to establish that my 'boyfriends' Phillip and Richard both knew Ash and worked for him and Bash, selling drugs. I could see she was getting really concerned.

'I think the grooming started earlier than you thought,' she said.

My heart nearly stopped. I immediately understood what she was saying. They had been adults too, and I was a child. Phillip and Richard had also abused me, just as Ash had. Richard was the one who was 'friends' with Ash, when I first met him. Had he deliberately gained the trust of me and my friends and then introduced some of us to Ash and his brothers and associates?

This was getting worse and worse. I really didn't know who I was any more because even more of my life had been a lie. Then Nikki said something to me that nobody had ever said before, and it made a little light go on at the end of the tunnel.

'I think the authorities have failed you,' she said. 'I think you were a victim of grooming over many years. It's time this was handled professionally.'

It took me a minute to take in what she had said.

'I don't like the word victim,' I stuttered, stalling for time. 'I would prefer not to use that word. It makes me feel weak, being called a victim.'

'I understand,' Nikki said. 'And you're right. You were a victim, but now you are a survivor.'

Another shard of light broke through, and when she asked me if I would be willing to talk to the police I actually smiled.

'Yes,' I said. 'I really would like to speak to the police.'

* * *

From that day I started to feel more positive about the future, because I felt that the chance to put right the wrongs of the past was now within my grasp.

The antidepressants helped get me back on an even keel mentally and I was coping with the kids much better and looking forward to a better life.

I wanted Ash to pay for what he'd done to me, and I wanted him jailed so he couldn't harm anybody else.

Chapter 35

'Opinions have changed now'

The police arranged for a female officer to come to my house and I was feeling hopeful and brave just before she arrived. This was a huge step for me to take.

Unfortunately, when I saw who the officer was, my mood immediately plummeted. I knew PC Diane Garner of old, and she remembered me too, from when I was a teenager. She always saw me as Ash's willing girlfriend, and I didn't expect this view would have changed.

I welcomed her into my home nonetheless, and we began to talk. Years previously I had spoken to PC Garner regarding a different incident, which she had dealt with really badly. Now she told me I would never be a reliable witness because of my criminal involvement with Ash's gang. I was going to the police *because* of my involvement with him, so this really annoyed me.

I wasn't going to let her put me off this easily. I asked about evidence the police may have about me being groomed, in terms of old records of all the occasions I'd been seen with Ash. PC Garner didn't sound optimistic, but she said she would look to see if there was any evidence in the files to support me, and then get back to me. Then she warned that if there wasn't any evidence, it would be my word against Ash's.

I was getting really irritated, but I'd come this far and I certainly wasn't giving up now. I was also thinking to myself that if pursuing this further meant I would have to face charges about any of the criminal activities Ash got me involved in, then I would.

I made an appointment for PC Garner and her male colleague, DC Lee Robinson, to come out to my sister Lisa's house to speak to me again a few days later, but before they turned up I felt really pessimistic. I felt sure they weren't going to take me seriously and my gut instinct was that I didn't trust PC Garner, so I decided to secretly record the meeting, on my sister's mobile phone.

I'm very glad I did. The officers asked Lisa to leave the room in case she was a witness in any future case, and what followed was astonishing.

Both officers were very laid-back in their manner. I was told the police were understaffed and that they were not sure how long an investigation might take or what Ash could be charged with. The officers said the only evidence they had managed to find was a missing person's report, and I told them I knew for a fact my dad had given the police an 11-page statement when I was 14 and first started going missing, and that he had also handed in my teenage diary to the police, which detailed my relationship with Ash. We had never got the diary back, but it now seemed to have disappeared without any trace whatsoever, along with my dad's statement.

We discussed the fact Ash was James's biological father, and that I was 15 when I became pregnant. The officers said DNA evidence could be used, but added that in order to take a sample it would have to be explained to James why he was being tested, and that it was inappropriate to tell a boy his age that his father was a suspected paedophile.

I asked whether police officers involved with my case in the past would have to make statements if I provided their names, explaining that I could give details of officers who Ash used to get calls from when we were together. DC Robinson told me he couldn't guarantee that.

I was getting increasingly frustrated. I fetched up the time when me and Ash were caught by the police having sex when I was 15 and I hid under the bed then got done for having a baton in my bag. DC Robinson's reply was that if the police saw that and didn't do anything about it at the time, but made a statement now, 'They know full well they're going to get in the shit because why didn't they do something about that?'

I couldn't believe my ears, and then PC Garner chipped in with her opinion on this, agreeing that she didn't think some officers would wish to give evidence. 'They know I know stuff about them what they could get sacked for,' were her exact words.

DC Robinson went on. 'It may be that if we went to speak to that person, they might turn around and say, "I didn't see anything like that." I can't force them to write something if they say, "I never saw that."'

He added: 'Opinions have changed now. Now we identify that as child abuse. Before they'd see it as sort of a lovesick teenager who keeps going back to this fella.'

The officers asked me if I wanted to take things further and I said no, not at the minute.

PC Garner told me to get back in touch if I changed my mind, but I decided there and then that relying on the police to help me was the last thing I was going to do. I didn't feel supported in any way, and I was scared that if I did press charges then Ash would get let off.

I thought long and hard about what to do next. First I contacted a solicitor so I had some legal protection, and then I put a call in to the police to request to see my files before anything else disappeared. It transpired that the researcher who had contacted me had been sent to Rotherham's Risky Business project in 2000 – the year I twice fell pregnant by Ash – after the Home Office commissioned research into child sexual exploitation in various locations around the UK. She spent a year going through the project's files and compiled ten profiles of victims and six suspected abusers in Rotherham, or 'child prostitutes' and 'pimps', as they were called then. The aim was that the information could be passed to the police so they could investigate the perpetrators and secure the appropriate convictions. Unbeknown to me, I was one of those ten victims, and Ash was one of the named abusers. A whole chapter of the report was devoted to detailing everything the authorities knew about Ash. The information had been obtained from different agencies' records and was based on sightings, or obtained directly from girls being exploited. I had spoken to the female researcher when she was compiling her report, though I can hardly remember it.

Her report was written up in 2001. Ash was referred to as a 'suspected pimp and drug dealer'. The authorities knew his full name and nickname of Mad Ash. They knew two of his family's addresses and had details of his relatives and the fact his brothers Bash and Bono were also suspected pimps and drug dealers. They knew Ash had a criminal record with convictions for various violent crimes, including wounding, stabbings, assault, affray, robbery, arson, burglary, kidnapping and false imprisonment. They had a list of all the cars he had access to, complete with registration details, including the Subaru with the G8ASH number plate. They knew which hotels and takeaways he used, which schools he was sighted outside, and they had a long list of taxi firms he was linked to that were also suspected of being involved in the exploitation of children. The authorities also had a list of places where Ash had been sighted dealing drugs or handing over exploited children, and the details of a mobile phone shop where he got doctored mobile phones that were untraceable. Councillor Akhtar was identified as a possible relative, and Karen MacGregor as someone who was suspected of being seriously involved in the sexual exploitation of young women, and who harboured young people for Ash. A woman called Shelley Davies was also listed as one of Ash's many known associates, and so was the woman I knew as Sarah, whose house I had stayed in, where Ash had sex with me all day and night long. Sarah was on the list as Sarah Iqbal, though it was noted she used various false names, such as Assia, Kim and Sarah Walsh. Like Karen MacGregor, Sarah was marked out as a person who harboured young people for Ash and was believed to be seriously involved in the sexual exploitation of young women.

The researcher had been astonished by the scale of abuse she found, and she wrote a ten-page interim report that criticised Rotherham's council leaders and the police for failing to act on the information others in authority had been feeding them since 1999.

She sent this report to South Yorkshire's chief constable and to the University of Luton, which was processing data from around the UK for the Home Office. Then the shit really hit the fan. The researcher was given a roasting by senior members of Rotherham police. Records were allegedly tampered with and some information went missing from Rotherham Council. None of the researcher's work was ever published and the council closed the project due to bad practice.

Chapter 36

'If this doesn't expose it, then nothing will'

By the summer of 2013 I had another family support worker from Rotherham Council. She was called Natalie Enderby and was a breath of fresh air. Everything I discussed with her was met with a positive response. She truly wanted to help me, and she gave me a lot of confidence.

After an incident with Social Services I rang Natalie to let off steam.

'Maybe it's time to give Andrew Norfolk a ring,' she said.

'You're right. I've had enough.'

* * *

I knew now that Andrew was chief investigative reporter for *The Times*, and had been reporting on the problem of child sexual exploitation for a few years. He had done stories about cases in Rochdale and, in 2011, he'd started writing about Rotherham. All of this had passed me by; I don't think I had ever picked up a copy of *The Times* in my life. I was still a bit scared of talking to the media, because it was such a big step and I had never done anything like that before, but I'd come to the conclusion I had nothing to lose, and if I could at least help highlight the dangers of CSE it would be worth it.

I was right nervous. Months before I'd sent an email to *The Times'* general email address and got no reply, and I left it. Now I decided I'd phone Andrew's office in Leeds. There was no reply so I left a voicemail, and then Andrew called me back.

'I got your number from a solicitor,' I said quietly. 'She said you would know who I am. My name is Sammy Woodhouse.'

He said he was sorry, but he didn't know who I was.

My heart sank and I was about to bottle it and say 'Never mind' when Andrew asked me to give him some more information about myself.

'I've got a kid with Ash, from Rotherham.'

I could almost hear the light bulb go on in Andrew's brain.

'Oh, wait a minute,' he said. 'We should meet. Can we arrange to meet?'

Andrew came to my house on 25th June 2013, a few days after I turned 28. I was very nervous but I made us both a mug of tea and slowly started to tell him my story.

Andrew wasn't how I imagined an investigative reporter from *The Times* might be. He was a real gentleman and was patient and kind and let me take my time. It wasn't easy for me to describe what had happened to me over the years, but Andrew was very understanding and he made it as easy as he possibly could. I trusted him, and I told him he could do whatever he thought was best with the information I had given him.

We spoke on the phone loads of times after this initial visit, and I was learning more about the CSE problem in Rotherham all the time. Andrew had seen the evidence linking Ash to the 18 girls, including me, who thought he was their boyfriend, and the 54 victims who thought that either Ash, Bash or Bono was their boyfriend. The more I found out, the more I wanted justice for every victim, and jail for every child abuser.

Over the next few weeks Andrew met with my dad and my support worker Natalie. I gave him my Social Services file, which proved I was telling the truth. The evidence was staggering.

'If this doesn't expose it, Sam, then nothing will,' he commented.

Andrew was ready to publish my story in August 2013. He'd approached Ash to give him the right to reply, though I didn't find out about this until he had already bowled up to Ash's house in Goole, where he still lived with several members of his family.

'Shitting hell!' I said when Andrew told me what he'd done. 'You shouldn't have done that! You can't just walk up to the Hussains' house! You could have got shot.'

I couldn't get the image out of my head of Andrew – middle-aged, dressed in a smart suit and with his round spectacles on – walking up to Ash's house unprotected.

Andrew shrugged my fears off as he described what happened. He had an experienced photographer with him, who'd worked in war zones, and they drove up the long driveway to the family farmhouse. Andrew got out while the photographer positioned the car ready for a getaway.

Siggi came out first, and then Bash appeared. Andrew politely asked if he could talk to Ash, explaining what it was about and giving Bash his phone number.

'That were ages ago,' Bash said. 'It's all in the past.'

Bash told Andrew to get off their property and stood firm on the drive, staring and looking aggressive.

Andrew and the photographer decided to leave. They had another address for the Hussain family, also in Goole, so they drove there. The property was still being built, and there was a vicious-looking Alsatian dog chained up, barking loudly. Andrew and his colleague had a look around, and then Bash arrived in a car and threatened to set the dog on them if they didn't leave.

They left. Then Andrew got a call from Ash on his mobile, asking what was going on. When Andrew told him he was investigating claims of child sexual exploitation, Ash denied everything. Then Andrew said, 'OK, so what if I mention a girl called Samantha Woodhouse?'

There was a momentary pause and then Ash said, 'It's best if you speak to my solicitor' before putting the phone down. Ash's solicitor was still Wazir. He told Andrew that Ash couldn't speak to him 'due to ill health'.

I'd given Andrew everything, including photographs of me as a child. I knew now that Ash was suspected of grooming dozens of young teenagers to sell for sex, and it was very clear to me that the police and social services knew this but, inexplicably, still let him roam the streets of Rotherham.

A few days before Andrew's article was about to go to print he emailed South Yorkshire Police, giving them notice of what *The Times* intended to publish. The email was 4,000 words long and included quotes from the secret recording I'd made of my meeting with PC Garner and DC Robinson.

This sent the police into panic mode.

I got a call from a sergeant from Rotherham Police. He said he was stood outside my house, and that he wanted to meet with me urgently, but he couldn't tell me why over the phone. I was worried about my safety and arranged to meet him at my sister's house. He arrived with a social worker and said: 'I don't care if you are recording me.'

The officer wanted me to make a statement about Ash as soon as possible, but I was suspicious because I felt he was being pushy. I asked him if I could end up being done for my involvement in crimes with Ash when I was a kid and he reassured me that no, that wouldn't happen, as it was part of the grooming process. After that I agreed that I would go into the station and make a video statement the following day.

I called Andrew to tell him about this latest development. He had become my rock, and I found myself thinking many times that it wasn't the role of a journalist to support me, yet he was doing a far better job than the vast majority of the Social Services' specialists and health professionals I'd come across over the years.

Andrew explained that if I made the statement *The Times* wouldn't be able to print my story, as I would then be part of an on-going investigation. I asked him, honestly, what he thought I should do.

'It's entirely your choice,' he said, despite the fact he'd put so much time and effort into the article. He added that it was good if I wanted to come forward to the police, as the police needed to investigate my case.

When I'd asked the police officer his opinion he'd told me: 'You can't do both. Do you want people to know your story or do you want Ash locked up?'

My decision wasn't difficult: I trusted Andrew, I wanted the story out there, and I had faith that it would prompt, not hinder, the criminal investigation that Ash deserved to face.

I called the police and postponed making my video statement until the day of publication. I also warned Social Services the article was coming out. I asked the police for two conditions if I was to go ahead and make my statement. Firstly, I wanted a new team of police officers fetched in to investigate my case, with no officers from Rotherham involved, as I didn't trust some of them. It was important to me to be in control. Secondly, I wanted safety alarms fitted in the house.

I was absolutely terrified of what Ash might do. I was scared of being attacked or even killed. I really thought he could be capable of murder.

I discussed my will with a solicitor and put details on an app on my phone of who should have custody of my children, and how they should be educated, if I was no longer here.

I also wrote a letter for the family, put it in an envelope and told my sister Lisa where to find it if I died.

It was neatly written and covered four sides of A4 paper. I didn't cry as I wrote. I had to shut off my emotions, because facing them was too hard.

I still have the letter, and here are some extracts:

I firstly want to apologise for all the hurt and suffering that has happened because of me due to Ash and his family. If I could go back in time I would but I can't, but at the same time I wouldn't because he gave me my son and throughout the heartache and pain my children are the greatest thing in my life and I wouldn't change them for the world. They make me complete. I remember when James was born my mum and dad tried everything to protect me but even though their baby was having a baby, he was an angel sent to me from God to guide me and keep me safe, as if it wasn't for him I would be dead or in prison …

There are so many good memories from my childhood. The pool hall, dancing to Bob Marley in the function room, at Christmas buying a Cabbage Patch doll even when you couldn't afford it …

Lisa, I want to thank you for being strong. I have so many great memories I don't even know where to start. I could sit here forever but I don't need to as I know you know what they are and they will be kept forever. Thank you for all your support through everything we have been through as a family …

To Nanan, the one and only Nutty Nanan. You never fail to make me laugh and I want to thank you. You made me strong enough to get through the things I have. I'll never forget the memories of Cleethorpes. I remember being Little Miss Princess and you taking me to a dress shop and buying me a white silk dress…

I wrote reams to my boys, telling them how much I loved them and how proud I was of both of them. I talked about how James was my willing little helper when Reece arrived, and how Reece was always such a positive and smiley little boy. I told them both to learn from my mistakes and said:

I want you both to have the most amazing life possible and to do this you need to have your education. Stay away from DRUGS, ALCOHOL, SMOKING AND THE STREETS. It might seem cool at first and everyone is doing it, but trust me, it's not. Your life will be ruined. I want you both to stay strong and stay on the right path… you're both amazing and can do anything you want to do. Surround yourselves with positive people and stay away from negative people, they will only bring you down. STAY WITH POSITIVE PEOPLE!!!

I ended the note by telling the boys I would always be with them: '*Mummy will always be your angel, looking over you.*'

My story was published in *The Times* on 23rd August 2013. I first saw it appear on their website late the night before. I was at our Lisa's and I felt panicky. Seeing my story in black and white, with colour photographs of me with my face obscured, sent shivers down my spine. I went by the pseudonym Jessica, to protect my identity.

Reading my story like this, I could finally see very clearly through Ash's lies, and I could also see what an absolute, total and utter fool I'd been. Andrew had done a thorough and brilliant job, but I was still expecting to be absolutely slated. Even though I'd been a trusting child when Ash groomed me I didn't expect much sympathy; I'd been gullible beyond belief, even as an adult, and I was still carrying self-blame.

The opening paragraph of Andrew's article read: 'It is the story of a man who stole childhoods, and a town whose care authorities wrote detailed reports about what he was doing, then sat back and let him get on with it.'

Ash was publicly named and shamed as my abuser for the first time ever, which was a very brave move by the newspaper. Nothing had been proven in a court of law, but I'd given Andrew my Social Services file, and he had seen so much evidence of Ash's guilt that he had the confidence to go to print without holding back. My story was spread across four pages.

'It is evident that some police officers and social workers grew deeply concerned about Jessica's welfare,' Andrew wrote. 'However, their efforts to protect the child from Hussain foundered in a swamp of corporate incompetence, complacency and confusion, characterised by a lack of leadership and poor inter-agency communication.'

He also explained in the article how, in 2012, *The Times* had revealed a decade of 'institutional failings' in Rotherham that allowed offender networks in the town to 'target, pimp and traffic young girls with virtual impunity'. Despite this, Rotherham Council didn't investigate the failings, and nobody was held to account. He reported that the police had asked the newspaper not to publish my story for fear of prejudicing their inquiries but pointed out that they had had 'more than a dozen years' to investigate the crimes against me.

I spooled down to the comments at the bottom of the online article to see what the reaction from the public was, and I couldn't have been more surprised and relieved. People from all over the world were praising me and saying how strong I was for coming forward. This gave me a huge confidence boost, and when I spoke to Andrew he was really pleased too; the response had been overwhelmingly positive and supportive of what we were both trying to achieve.

Ultimately, we hoped that now I had told my story the people in power would finally sit up and listen, and take action to protect other kids. We also hoped Ash and his associates would finally be brought to justice. However, I don't think either of us bargained for just how much impact the story would make.

When my story hit the newsstands and wires the next morning, the reaction struck me like a hurricane. Reporters from all over the UK, Europe and America wanted to speak to me. I gave loads of interviews for days, telling every journalist I spoke to that the reason I was doing this was to encourage other survivors to come forward, so we could get as many abusers as possible behind bars.

Martin Kimber, the chief executive of Rotherham Council, issued a lengthy statement, apologising to the young people who had been 'let down' and admitting that the town's 'services to safeguard young people prior to 2009 were simply not good enough'.

He later told the Select Committee he had acted following the report in *The Times* on 23rd August 2013 'relating to the experiences of a young female who had suffered child sexual exploitation in Rotherham [...] and who had been let down by services at that time.' He added, 'There had also been previous articles on a similar subject. The article of 23rd of August was fundamentally different. It contained inferences that a then senior politician might have had some knowledge of these historic matters. I was shocked at this inference and had never heard or suspected this might be the case. This was a significant moment. I felt there were issues associated with the history of the town that were not fully known to me, and that other officers and members were not aware of. I was uncertain how this should be tackled but ultimately advised that an independent examination of historic cases was needed.'

Jahangir Akhtar was named in *The Times* for his involvement in my 'no prosecution' handover deal to police at the petrol station when I was 14. Not only was he now deputy leader of Rotherham Council, he was also vice-chairman of the Police and Crime panel, which scrutinises the local force. He denied any wrongdoing but stepped down from both roles on the day my story was printed.

As I'd planned, I gave my first ever formal police interview about Ash on publication day. I did this at Rotherham Hospital and I remember it vividly. The police officer asked me, 'Do you feel guilty, Sam?'

'No, why would I?'

'Well, because a lot of good professionals are going to lose their jobs.'

'Well, if they did their jobs right in the first place this wouldn't be happening, would it?'

Not long afterwards that officer was removed from the case.

My interview became the starting point for Operation Clover, the name given to the long-running police investigation into Ash and his brothers and associates. It had triggered the opening of every non-recent case in South Yorkshire regarding CSE; I couldn't have felt prouder. I was going to have to do separate interviews about the police officers and the criminal activity I was involved in.

'You're looking at 102 years in prison, don't do it,' my solicitor advised after looking at my criminal record.

'You'll be killed if you talk,' said the solicitor who did the Home Office research.

I decided to carry on regardless, but every time I heard a knock at the door I was petrified. Would I be arrested? In the end, the CPS rightfully decided not to prosecute me.

Two days after I gave my initial interview James said he saw Ash at the side of our house in a black car, which scared the life out of me. I knew full well the violence he was capable of, and despite the fact he was in a wheelchair I now became terrified he would harm my kids.

I called the police, and I think that's when I really started to see how much Andrew's report had changed my life. I was listened to, I was taken seriously, and I was given an incident number and advice about what to do should Ash reappear.

The days of being viewed as a stupid little girl who got what she deserved, or a 'white slag' who was willingly prostituting herself, had finally ended. It had taken the best part of 14 years.

Chapter 37
'I'll support you on everything'

Not only did Rotherham Council ask the police to investigate all non-recent cases of CSE on the back of my story appearing in *The Times,* but the council was shamed into ordering an independent inquiry into how the sexual exploitation of children had been handled by the authorities. This was good news, but the fact the council had ordered the inquiry itself didn't inspire confidence. The word was that the council leader was hoping that as well as investigating the problems of the past, the investigation would ultimately show how much things had improved in recent years.

I was anxious every day, wondering what the outcome of the inquiry would be, and hoping and praying that it wouldn't be a cover-up.

Thankfully, Professor Alexis Jay, a social work expert, was brought in to lead the inquiry.

Professor Jay published her report on 26th August 2014, a year after my story had first been printed. I was at home, having just finished recording an interview with a reporter when the news broke. The Jay Report had found that at least 1,400 children were subjected to sexual exploitation in Rotherham between 1997 and 2013. 'It is hard to describe the appalling nature of the abuse the child victims suffered,' Professor Jay told a packed press conference. Her report found children as young as 11 were raped by multiple abusers, abducted, trafficked to other cities in England, beaten and intimidated.

It was horrible to hear that so many kids had been exploited, but knowing the problem had been officially recognised like this was a huge relief and filled me with confidence. *This is it*, I thought. *Now they'll have to believe us. Things will actually get done.*

The first person I spoke to was Andrew Norfolk. Even he was gobsmacked by the scale of the abuse uncovered.

Rotherham Council and the police knew about the level of CSE in the town but didn't do anything about it; the Jay Report had found police had treated victims with 'contempt', there had been 'blatant' failures in council leadership and, horrifically, the abuse was continuing to the present day. Council staff had reported that they were afraid of being labelled racist if they mentioned the fact most victims were describing their abusers as 'Asian' men. This last point seemed to be the only tiny shred of explanation anybody had come up with for the collective failure of so many people in authority who could have, and should have, exposed the scandal many years before I did.

Journalists from all over the world were ringing me and I ended up giving interviews until the early hours of the morning. I thought this level of interest would only last a day or two, but reporters and television and radio crews began to descend on Rotherham. Many asked me to speak on camera, which I did, with my identity hidden. My story made headlines from China to Australia and South America.

It was impossible to keep all this from my boys, and a lot of people who knew me from school and when I was growing up had worked out that I was the girl in Andrew's report, and the girl with her face turned away from the camera on the TV. Ash's abuse of me had clearly been obvious to many of my peers, but not to me.

'Why are you on the news?' Reece asked one day.

'Something bad happened when Mummy was little, and I'm speaking out to help other people come forward.'

He accepted this. He was seven now, and more interested in the fact I was on TV than what had happened to me; he gave me a big smile and told me I was a very important person, and he felt right proud of me.

James was 12, and he understood a lot more. 'I'll support you on everything,' he said. That kept me strong, although I hit a low point when he later told me that a friend of his had said, 'Your dad's a paedophile.'

I was heartbroken, and I sat James down and told him in simple terms that his dad had been too old to be with me when I was a teenager, and there was going to be a police investigation into what had gone on. I told him if anyone asked questions he was to say he didn't know anything, and I showed him how to respond to an emergency at home, as I still had serious concerns for our safety, with very good reason.

One day a woman came to my house asking questions. I was trying to help her as she had been abused by the Hussains, but she had clearly not come to terms with it yet, as I found out Ash had sent her, and she was secretly recording me. When I found this out I confronted her, and she apologised and eventually pressed charges against one of Ash's brothers.

There was massive political fallout from the Jay Report. Rotherham's council leader, Roger Stone, the chief executive, Martin

Kimber, and the director of children's services, Joyce Thacker, all quit their jobs. The South Yorkshire Police and crime commissioner, Shaun Wright, tried to cling on but eventually stepped down after several weeks of pressure. He had been a Rotherham councillor overseeing children's services between 2005 and 2010.

I was ecstatic when they had all gone, but outraged as they all had a big pay-out. It looked to me like they'd been paid for failing to stop children from being abused.

I told myself the most important thing was that more victims now started to come forward, and I believed Ash and other abusers would soon be convicted. Then something else happened that really stunned and upset me: Rotherham Council started trying to discredit the findings of the Jay Report. They even spent £20,000 attempting to find out who leaked some of the information to Andrew Norfolk that enabled him to write his newspaper reports.

I was gutted, and wondered if I would ever live to see justice. Rotherham Council needed to put their energies into helping the police lock up the abusers, not into covering up their mistakes and trying to protect their reputation. I was determined this couldn't be the end.

Having more victims come forward all the time was the only thing that kept me going. I took a lot of strength and encouragement from that, and every morning when I opened my eyes I told myself that we can do it, we won't be beaten any more.

Thankfully, within weeks, it was announced that an independent inquiry to inspect Rotherham Council was being commissioned by central government. Surely this would be a turning point? I dared to hope that it might, but after all that had gone on I was wary.

The inquiry was to be led by Louise Casey, the government's lead official on troubled families, and when she came to Rotherham she asked to meet me.

I was right nervous, but as it turned out I needn't have worried. Louise Casey was down-to-earth and I immediately felt comfortable talking to her. I told her my story, and I even relaxed enough to tell her that the hotel where we were sitting drinking tea was one where Ash used to take me to have sex. She shook her head in sadness and disgust.

Louise clearly wanted her inquiry to get to the truth, and she seemed bold and brave. If she couldn't help get justice for victims, I didn't know who could.

In November 2014 I was in the offices of the *Rotherham Advertiser* with our local MP and a group that included a girl who had been abused when she was very young when my mobile rang. It was the police with big news: Ash had been arrested for multiple child sexual exploitation offences along with his brothers Basharat and Bannaras, aka Bash and Bono.

I felt a shot of adrenaline rush through me, but I didn't jump up and down or celebrate. It was a breakthrough, but there was still a long way to go. I couldn't let myself get too optimistic. I'd had too many disappointments in the past.

Ash, Bash and Bono were bailed, which really annoyed me as I thought they should have been remanded in custody, but at least the wheels were in motion. I was told it could take months and months for charges to be brought as Operation Clover was on-going.

* * *

Some members of my family helped me stay strong and optimistic. Christmas was coming, and for the first time since my mum had died we decided to spend it together. During all the years I was denying Ash had exploited me this had been impossible, as there was so much bad feeling, frustration and conflict within the family. Now, even members of my extended family who I'd become estranged from had started accepting me back into their lives.

After a massive Christmas dinner we all went back to Lisa's house. We wore matching Christmas jumpers, had a few drinks and really chilled out. Nobody talked about the past and it felt good to be surrounded by family and to have some normality for the boys.

Thanks to a local journalist called Chris Burn I started my first campaign, calling for better counselling to be available to victims. I'd been on a long waiting list for counselling ever since I first recognised I was abused, and I wanted other victims to get the help they needed much quicker.

I really enjoyed the campaign work. I had some focus, and at least this was something that I could control and push forward myself at my own pace. The campaign was successful and funding was given, which enabled myself and other survivors in Rotherham to get help.

In 2015 I started voluntary work at a small charity managed by the person who previously ran Risky Business. The charity supported other survivors and family members and helped to secure a lot of funding. At first, I spent most days there, but things went wrong and I left in May 2016. In my opinion, the problem was that the manager and some members of staff were sharing confidential information about survivors to others, lying about us and turning us against each other. I reported the manager and charity for bad practice and several investigations started, which made headline news in Rotherham. I felt the way the charity was being run, and the way we were being used, was wreaking havoc with me and other survivors, because the professionals who were meant to be helping us were creating more stress for us, not less.

The manager told lies about me and my family, saying bad things about what happened to me as a child. She and her family really turned against me for reporting her to the authorities and I believe they started to spread horrific lies about me on social media. For example, it was claimed online I had exploited a child and was having children gang-raped, and the posts even said I was passing on intelligence to ISIS and that the Army had witnessed me doing so and I was under investigation.

The manager and her son did indeed try to have me placed under investigation, reporting me to officials over what was said online. Of course, they failed to provide evidence to back up the allegations, as they were nothing but malicious nonsense. The manager also had me placed under investigation for harassment against her. I was cleared, because reporting a professional for bad practice and speaking publicly isn't harassment.

I provided the police with evidence proving that what the manager said about me was untrue. I also told them I was being stalked, as the manager and members of her family started to contact me and my son directly, and she came to my house. The manager asked a police officer to ring me and tell me that if I continued to speak out the survivors wouldn't receive compensation. I told the police officer the manager was absolutely deluded and explained the circumstances, stating, 'She's trying to silence me for reporting her for bad practice.'

The stalking continued and then fake accounts on social media started to appear, including pictures of me, my family and my children. There were also threats that our true identities would be revealed, as at that time I hadn't yet taken the decision to waive my anonymity.

I was placed back on medication for depression and had an alarm re-installed in my house for safety, although I wasn't happy with how the police handled the matter at all. It was appalling I had to go through all that.

The charity was eventually raided by officials and legal documents relating to me and my children that had been stored there were returned to me. I felt Rotherham and its CSE problem was becoming like a circus, and I am still waiting for the findings of an independent review of the charity and its staff to be made available to me.

* * *

Thankfully, the more I spoke out publicly as a survivor of CSE, the more victims continued to come forward. I felt proud of myself, because this was what I wanted and what mattered most. However, two social workers from Rotherham Council said I'd put my own children at risk by coming forward as a victim, and they put James and Reece on a protection plan for 'at risk' kids. I'd been asking for help for years with my sons and the council had never put them on a protection plan before. It felt like I was being blackmailed, to stop me encouraging other victims to come forward. It nearly worked. I considered stopping, but then I realised this was the very last thing I should do.

The resulting child protection report read, 'It is of heightening concern that Sammy has recently invited the media into the family home to discuss her childhood experiences of being sexually exploited, which has been televised. This is part of an on-going police investigation. While Sammy was disguised as a silhouette and the identities of James and Reece have been disguised, the family home was visible in its entirety. This has potential to place both James and Reece at risk of harm should their identities be revealed'.

What annoyed me about this was that at this point I'd never spoken about my children to the press, and the only thing you could see in my house was plain grey wallpaper and a shiny vase. Another said, 'Sammy does not appear to see herself as a victim of child sexual exploitation during her childhood. This raises concern about Sammy's understanding of the grooming process. James and Reece may be at risk of harm should their identities or their mother's identity be revealed as part of a police investigation regarding their mother and her childhood experiences.' *That's funny*, I thought, *how can I not recognise myself as a victim? It was me who spoke out saying I was a victim in the first place. Now I'm the one trying to tell the nation what grooming is.*

Not long afterwards, false accusations about me started going into Social Services reports too. For example, one said I had abandoned my children for two weeks to go to Ibiza. Fortunately, I could prove this was untrue: I had only ever been to Ibiza once, and both my boys were with me – we went to celebrate their birthdays. A Rotherham teacher also said she could confirm I allowed James to be part of a drug-dealing gang when he was six years old.

I was furious: I didn't even live in Rotherham when James was six and my son never got further than the back garden without me. As if I'd allow him out on his own at six, let alone into a gang! I knew I was going to get a hard time for speaking out but this was ridiculous. I needed to stay focused.

I was a survivor and a campaigner now, and I had to stand up for myself and others. I made a verbal complaint to Rotherham Council, explaining I felt I was being blackmailed into quitting by the remarks in the child protection report. Later, one of the social workers who commented in the report left the council and stopped working altogether as a trainee social worker. The other subsequently apologised to me and admitted she had made mistakes, but said she had learned a lot from my case and that she didn't understand CSE at the time. She was being given extra training in CSE and how to approach victims in due course, education I have since helped to compile and provide.

* * *

By now the Independent Police Complaints Commission (IPCC) was investigating complaints of police misconduct in relation to CSE in Rotherham, and PC Sadat was one of many officers under investigation. At the end of January 2017, he was put on restricted duties as a result of allegations made against him, and on the very same day he was hit by a car. The police described it as a tragic accident, and he died from head injuries nine days later. I was shaken when I heard the news: PC Sadat was only in his forties and I'd met him many times.

Unbelievably, some in his community and others blamed me, as I'd previously spoken out in the press about him and his conduct. Following the accident, the media republished my story and a hate campaign started against me and the reporter who wrote the story. I went to stay with family until everything settled down. A Facebook page had been set up for PC Sadat and Lisa was reading all the comments. His supporters not only said I was to blame for his death, they said I loved to be raped and was making it all up for money, even though I had never received any money. Lisa was devastated.

When I complained to the police they refused to act, telling me it was freedom of speech and that our country had fought long and hard for it. Then they went further still, announcing that South Yorkshire Police was putting in complaints about what I'd said in the media about PC Sadat, and saying how disrespectful to the officer it was. I was speechless, but I wasn't quitting.

Chapter 38
'Don't worry, I am not a serial killer!'

Louise Casey's findings were published in February 2015. I was at a children's home that day to discuss CSE training.

We put the TV on and sat in silence waiting for the news to come on. You could hear a pin drop as the headlines started. I held my breath as the newsreader said Louise Casey had concluded she had found a council that was 'not fit for purpose'.

Staff from the children's home all started cheering, and I started crying. It was the best news I could have heard. I knew it was true, but having an important government figure like Louise Casey spell it out like this to the whole country was fantastic.

Louise said she had found a council 'in denial'. Her investigation had uncovered an unhealthy council culture of 'bullying, sexism, suppression and misplaced "political correctness"', and her conclusion was that the council had at times 'taken more care of its reputation than it had of its most needy'. The Jay Report's estimate of 1,400 victims being affected by CSE was, in Louise Casey's opinion, a conservative one. She said the figure of 2,000 was probably more accurate.

Almost as soon as the report was published, the entire cabinet of Rotherham Council resigned. Then the council was taken under central government control. Things were really happening, at long last.

Through my campaign work I was invited to Downing Street to meet Prime Minister David Cameron, in March 2015. He was launching a summit on how to tackle 'industrial scale' child abuse in the UK, and five of us went along to discuss Rotherham. The group included Professor Alexis Jay and our local MP, who I travelled on the train to London with. I was feeling nervous, and when I walked in the famous front door of Number 10 I glanced around me and thought, *Is this really happening?* Then I took a quick selfie on my mobile phone.

'You can't do that, put it away quick,' said the security guard.

'Just one more,' I replied cheekily.

I stayed very calm when I was introduced to the Prime Minister. We chatted about how much work needed doing and how I thought the government should help improve services for victims, and introduce mandatory education about grooming in schools.

I also told Mr Cameron I wanted grooming victims to be given guarantees that if they came forward, they wouldn't face charges over any criminal activities they had been involved in through their abuse. I explained that I had asked a lawyer to look at my own criminal record, and this lawyer estimated that I could be sent to prison for 102 years for all the crimes I had committed when I was being abused by Ash. The Prime Minister nearly fell off his chair and I had to jokingly reassure him, 'Don't worry, I am not a serial killer!'

What I didn't tell Mr Cameron was that at one time on my criminal record, alongside firearms offences for the CS gas attack and carrying the baton, and the assault charges relating to fights, it also said that I had committed 'consensual rape'. It slipped my mind on the day but I think Mr Cameron really would have hit the floor if I'd remembered to tell him that. How can you have consensual rape when rape means you've said no? The term doesn't make any sense at all, and thankfully this no longer appears on my criminal record, though how and when it was taken off nobody has been able to explain to me.

We had a group photograph taken to mark the occasion, and when Mr Cameron left the room I allowed myself to relax for the first time all day. I started giggling and clapping and saying how well I thought the meeting had gone, and then suddenly the Prime Minister popped back in the room unexpectedly. I felt right embarrassed that he'd caught me celebrating like this. I laughed about it afterwards though. This was a day to remember. I wanted to be seen and heard by the people in power, and I wanted my voice to make a difference. The Independent Inquiry into Child Sexual Abuse (IICSA) – the largest public inquiry of its kind – was already underway, which Alexis Jay would later take over as the Chair.

Back in Rotherham, a teenage relative of Ash came up to me when I was in the car with my kids and really frightened me. He called my name and used James's name, and then started taking pictures of us on a mobile while he made a call on another phone. He started following us, and I was scared he was trying to call other people to come and join him. I was crying and shaking afterwards, but once I'd calmed down, I decided I wasn't going to let this beat me. I reported it to the police, telling them I was scared for my safety, and the safety of my kids. This was witness intimidation, and I wasn't putting up with this or any other crime against me, ever again.

The police began an investigation and I thought, *bring it on.* I was strong now. I was standing up for my rights and I wasn't going to be victimised any more.

I eventually found out the teenager's name was Kaleem Ali, and he was the 18-year-old son of Ash's uncle, Qurban Ali, who was a suspect in Operation Clover.

Ultimately, Kaleem Ali was found guilty of witness intimidation and was sentenced to a 12-month community order, tagged and given a restraining order against me for three years. James gave evidence, and I was so proud of him.

* * *

It was June 2015 when I got the news I'd been waiting for from Operation Clover.

A police officer who had been working on my case phoned and explained that Ash had finally been charged with multiple child sexual exploitation offences, as had Bash and Bono. The charges relating to Ash dated back to 1990 – nine years before I met him, when I would have been just five years old.

It was going to be a high-profile trial lasting about two months. Of the 54 victims the police identified as being linked to Ash and his brothers, 21 had testified and 12 were giving evidence in court. I was one of those 12, Holly was another. Eventually I found out there were five other defendants, all associates of Ash.

I could hardly believe that my speaking to Andrew Norfolk two years previously had ultimately triggered Operation Clover and fetched us to this point.

I was filled with emotion and started crying and thanked the officer for informing me. His name was Andy Stephanek. Apart from the odd occasion when I screamed down the phone if I wasn't happy – usually about something that happened on social media – we had built up a good relationship as he worked on my case. Andy always dealt with things well, and I was grateful to him.

The first person I called was Andrew Norfolk. I was still crying and struggling to get my words out. I eventually did, and he was thrilled as much as me.

It was daunting thinking of what lay ahead in court, but I also felt impatient and was thinking once again, *bring it on*. Justice was within touching distance.

* * *

The trial was set to start on 7th December 2015.

In addition to Ash, Bash and Bono – by now aged 40, 39 and 36 – three other men and two women were also in the dock for various child sexual exploitation offences. I only knew one of the other defendants – 58-year-old Karen MacGregor. She was the woman who was involved with the house Ash claimed he was getting for us to live in.

The build-up left me feeling stressed out before we even began. I'd been hoping to get it all out of the way before Christmas but that clearly wasn't going to happen. I'd also asked the police if I could go first giving my evidence, so I'd then be allowed to watch the rest of the trial, but I was told I was going to be one of the last girls to take the stand as witnesses were giving evidence in chronological order. I wouldn't give evidence until well into January, and the exact date changed seven times, due to various unavoidable delays.

I was trying to keep everything as normal as possible at home for the boys but I was in such a low state mentally, and James especially could see how I was suffering.

It was hard to think about anything but going to court. As it drew closer, I began feeling really on edge about my and the boys' safety, so I started to make plans to move house before I gave evidence. This put me under more pressure, and I also went to view the video statements I'd given the previous year, which added to my stress.

As soon as I sat down to watch them I felt anxious. I told the police officer I didn't want to see my face, and so she turned the computer round. The moment I heard my voice, going into detail about events from the past, I started to cry. I was as a little, 14-year-old girl again, feeling so vulnerable but with a wall around me, pretending I was OK.

After that I also had to give more statements to the police, as I began to have flashbacks of things Ash had done to me, and things he had told me that I hadn't remembered until now. I thought that at any time my head was going to explode, but I had to keep going, for my kids and for myself.

I was shown where I would stand in Sheffield Crown Court when I gave evidence, and it was explained that Ash would be visible to the judge on a video link, as he had claimed he was too ill to attend court and would be in bed at home. He wouldn't be able to see me and I wouldn't be able to see him, as I would be behind a screen. Lisa and my dad were also going to be witnesses, so we wouldn't be able to speak to one another until we had all finished giving evidence. I only knew one of the other victims – Holly – and I wouldn't be allowed to speak to her either. It was all getting very real, and I could feel the tension rising, minute by minute.

Throughout the trial, I would be referred to as Girl J.

Chapter 39
'He was an adult and I was a child'

It was here at last – the day the trial was finally starting. I woke up on the morning of 7th December feeling like Superwoman, ready to take on the whole world. I was brimming with strength and determination, and nothing was going to get in my way.

I had written a letter to the judge, Sarah Wright, which I asked Andrew Norfolk to hand in when he went to court. There had been talk of media restrictions, but I wanted as much detail publicised as possible. I explained to the judge that a media ban would make it feel like victims were giving evidence in secret while the authorities were protecting defendants.

'The people of Rotherham would think it's yet another cover-up over child sexual exploitation,' I wrote. 'Please let the public know the names of all those on trial. Please send out the message to victims that you can come forward and get justice, and a message saying that if you do hurt children you go to prison, no matter how long it takes.'

I got my wish, and almost every media restriction was lifted. I felt invincible. This was a great result and I was full of hope. I wished I could have been in court from day one. I was raring to go, longing to have my moment in the witness box.

This buzz lasted for several days, but once the victims started taking the stand my mood began to slip. I was listening to the news at home and hearing headlines about what was coming out. It was very disturbing, and when I was on my own fears started to creep in about how this was all going to end.

Some of the other victims had been subjected to types of abuse I'd never encountered. I became filled with doubt. What if the jury believes Ash, not me? What if they can't see through his lies to the gullible little girl I was when he exploited me?

My family were keeping a close eye on me and I had support from several other people, but at the end of every day I was on my own, with my kids, fretting and worrying and trying to put a brave face on for the boys.

The court heard that girls were 'targeted, sexualised and in some instances subjected to acts of a degrading and violent nature' when they were teenagers. One survivor told the jury how she was abused from the age of 11, and that Ash passed her on to his brother and friends, often as 'payment' for debts. She was beaten, had a cigarette stubbed out on her chest and was tied up and raped, often by numerous men, one after another, 'at the say-so of Arshid Hussain'.

One of my local papers ran a story about 'babies born to paedophiles' as it emerged that I wasn't the only victim who had become pregnant as a result of the abuse. I panicked and rang James's school, telling the teachers to keep him away from all newspapers and TV news.

The distressing stories kept coming. One survivor told how she thought she was going to die when her hands and feet were tied and she had petrol poured over her by her abusers. Another described how Bash took her to the Peak District and subjected her to two hours of physical and verbal abuse before knocking her to the ground, spitting on her and telling her to dig her own grave. I felt sick.

When my turn finally came to give evidence I went to court with two police officers who'd been assigned to look after me – Simon Taylor and Carly Booth – plus a social worker.

We all sat in a little room at the back of the court while I was waiting to be called in. I'd dressed in smart trousers and a polo neck jumper and jacket, and on the outside I looked calm and composed. Inside, my stomach was going crazy.

Suddenly I was being led down loads of corridors, past the judge and barristers and taking the stand in front of the jury, some of whom smiled at me, so I smiled back, instinctively.

When the questioning began from the defence barristers I remembered everything I had been told, and I began by sticking to yes and no answers and keeping my replies brief and to the point. I spoke about various events, including the time I was handed over to the police at the petrol station, and I described how I felt mesmerised by Ash.

'It was like he put a spell over me. He made me feel really good about myself.'

Ash's barrister suggested to me that I was Ash's equal, and at that point my blood rose and I decided I wasn't going to stick to a yes or no answer. I took a deep breath and said: 'He was an adult and I was a child. There's nothing equal about it, so no, I wouldn't say we were equal. It's only now I realise he wasn't my boyfriend. It was abuse.'

When we had a break at dinner time I felt so drained I lay down. My eyes were burning and it felt like I had a plank of wood across them. Once I was back in court I felt revived, and I rallied. As soon as I started speaking I zoned everything else out and concentrated fully on what I was saying.

I felt the barrister was trying to trick me at every opportunity, and he was patronising too, but I paid no notice to this. As much as I didn't like the fact, his job was to put his client back on the streets. I knew he was simply doing what he was employed to do, and this thought kept me calm and very focused.

I became bolder as the day went on. I didn't want to say, 'Yes, sir, no, sir, three bags full, sir'. This was my evidence, my life, and my justice. Once I started talking nobody could shut me up.

I was only meant to be in court for a few hours in total, but by the end of the day I hadn't finished giving my evidence. It was a Friday, and I would have to return on the Monday. That meant I wouldn't be able to speak to Lisa or my dad all over the weekend.

I went home feeling nervously exhausted. I couldn't eat or concentrate on anything. James was playing up really badly, so much so that I had to get a support worker to come round and take him out. I was still a mess. I felt like I was having a complete breakdown: my nerves were shredded and I was crying at everything and anything.

I didn't sleep a wink all Sunday night and when I woke up on Monday morning I wasn't fit to go to court. I texted Carly Booth. I've still got the message on my phone. Sent at 08:02 on 18th January 2016, it reads: 'I'm not going to court today I don't feel mentally strong enough after what happened at the weekend and I was in a mess early hours this morning and I haven't eaten since Saturday, I'm gonna get some rest today n go court tomorrow, I'm going back to sleep to get some rest, I'll speak to you later xx'

All hell broke loose when I sent that text. My phone started going mad with calls and messages, and Carly and her colleague Simon bolted up to my house with a support worker and started banging on my front and back door. I'd built up a really good relationship with the police officers. I called Carly the 'blonde bombshell' as she was so bubbly. She and Simon were very understanding and they always put a smile on my face, but now I thought, *Oh shit, they've found me!* My house was a new build and as I'd moved in so recently I'd naïvely hoped my address wouldn't be on the map yet and they wouldn't know where I lived.

'Can I come in for a wee?' Simon said in a text message.

'I'm not falling for that!' I messaged back. 'You can piss on the garden!'

I'd totally lost it. I was lying in my bed, refusing to budge even though the knocking on both doors was getting louder.

Lisa got wind of what was happening and sent a message to say she was coming round to kick the door down if I didn't get my arse into court. I was still having none of it, and then I received a message from a survivor, who had been abused when she was very young.

Before I read it, I went downstairs, as I knew if I didn't the door was going to get kicked in.

'Oh, thank God for that,' Simon said. 'Can I use the toilet please? I wasn't tricking you, I really do need to go!'

I sat on the kitchen floor.

'I'm not fucking going to court! You can't force me! I don't need complete strangers to tell me what Ash did was wrong. I know!'

Carly started telling me that I'd handled myself with such dignity so far and that this was the last hurdle and I needed to keep going, as I was nearly there.

'I'm not! I thought it would fix me but it's not.'

In desperation, Carly told me she could arrest me and force me to go to court that way. I still wasn't budging.

I began reading the text the young survivor had sent me. She said that victims like her looked up to me and were inspired by me. I knew that she had gone to court in a separate trial years earlier, when she was still a very young kid, and that she had been incredibly brave, giving evidence and being cross-examined for days.

It was only then that I started to see sense and, with the encouragement of Simon and Carly, who offered more words of wisdom, I agreed to go to court.

'You're right,' I told them. 'I'll regret this for the rest of my life if I don't go.'

I wasn't even dressed. I had a shower, threw up with nerves, and then put on a trackie top and scraped my hair back. I didn't give a shit what I looked like; all I cared about was getting this done.

I ran into court with moments to spare and took the stand. Once I started talking I was fine, and people even told me I looked incredibly dignified and composed, even though I didn't feel it.

I was so focused on what I was saying that I completely forgot Ash was on the video link, listening to everything I said. At one point Bash claimed that he had never met me in his life before. This gave me an extra shot of determination to prove the liars wrong.

The jury was read a transcript of the conversation I had with DC Lee Robinson, when he warned me that officers who knew what had happened to me as a child wouldn't give evidence that would get them 'in the shit'.

I was beginning to feel confident that things were going to go my way.

My evidence was completed that day, and I left the court feeling absolutely wretched and wrung out. Simon and Carly took me home. They were fantastic with me, and I told them that if I could make clones of them and scatter them around South Yorkshire as police officers I would. Simon had to pull over on the drive home as I was retching and threatening to vomit. My body was like a whirlpool, but I'd done it.

When it was my dad's turn to give evidence later that week he described how he called the police and drove round looking for me when I didn't come home, how he'd fought with Ash, how I'd skip school and run away, and how Ash would climb in my bedroom window.

Our Lisa took the stand and said my involvement with Ash had 'ripped apart' the family. 'My dad used to drive round every night, go to hotels giving her picture out, saying, had they seen her? He used to do it until the early hours while my mum were in bed crying. It was every night for two years.'

Lisa also told how she spoke to Bash on the phone one time when I was missing. 'I said if she weren't home in the next hour I was ringing the police and reporting Ash for kidnapping and rape. He said I was a little white slag. I said if she is not home in ten minutes, he is going to be done for rape. She was home in ten minutes.'

When I found out later what she had said I was shocked: I was hearing things I'd never heard before, because at the time of my abuse I was so disconnected from my family and I didn't listen to what they said.

Lisa also told how Ash controlled my actions. 'It were like a spell. I have never seen anything like it before.' That rang so true. She had seen very clearly what was going on.

Chapter 40
'My life starts now'

I was in bed at home when I got a text message from Andrew Norfolk, telling me the verdicts were in. He was in court so I couldn't phone him. I took a few minutes to mentally prepare myself before I texted him back.

'What is it?' I wrote, holding my breath and hiding under the duvet. I felt I had the whole world resting on my shoulders.

Ash faced five charges specifically relating to me: one of anal rape, three indecent assaults and one of child abduction. He had initially faced six charges but one count of child abduction was dropped halfway through the trial, due to the fact my foster carer Sue had allowed Ash to have access to me.

'Guilty. Guilty. Guilty. Guilty. Guilty,' Andrew texted.

I gasped and couldn't take it in. I quickly texted thanks and thought about how big this moment was for Andrew, and *The Times* too. By now he had devoted five years to his investigations into CSE. He had worked tirelessly to protect girls like me and jail monsters like Ash. We would never have reached this point without him and the newspaper, and I couldn't wait to talk to him and tell him how grateful I was, and how much I appreciated everything he had done.

I started to get ready to leave the house, because James was in lessons and I needed to tell him as soon as he came out of class, before anyone else did.

I was smiling to myself but I stayed calm as I got dressed. Then suddenly everybody was ringing and saying how happy they were, and our Lisa was screaming and having a total hysterical meltdown. It seemed like everybody was crying except me. The adrenaline started pumping as I spoke to my family and friends, and that's when the enormity of the news began to hit me.

On my way to collect James I slowly began to take it in. It felt like my entire life had been flipped upside down.

James had just finished his lessons when I arrived, and I walked across the car park. He'd been through so much and I wasn't sure what to say or how to tell him.

'Good news, he's been found guilty,' I said calmly, once I'd got James on his own.

'Good,' he replied. 'Can we go back to normal? Can I play out again?'

When I heard him say that it really got to me, and that's when I finally started to cry. It had been so tough on the kids, and normality was what I wanted more than anything. I wanted my boys to be happy and to be able to live a normal, safe life.

It was fantastic when I finally got to talk to Andrew Norfolk. I thanked him for everything he'd done, but in his typical way he didn't want praise. He was chuffed to bits, telling me I'd been amazing and he was proud of me and what I had achieved.

Later, he described the tension he felt when he was sitting in court, waiting for the verdicts.

The courtroom descended into silence, and Andrew said he was totally unprepared for his emotional reaction. He was trembling and on the verge of tears, and he was imagining what would happen if Ash and the others were found not guilty. It would undermine everything he and *The Times* had done for so many years to expose the scandal of CSE.

The court had to wait for what felt like an age for Ash's verdicts relating to me to be read out, as my name was near the end of the long charge sheet. Andrew's nerves were stretched to breaking point and tears pricked his eyes as the five guilty verdicts were returned.

In total, Ash had been found guilty of 23 serious child sexual exploitation crimes. Bash, Bono, their uncle, Qurban Ali, and the two women, Karen MacGregor and Shelley Davies, had also been found guilty.

Yet more victims came forward after the verdicts, which I was so pleased about, because this trial had only scratched the surface of the 1,400–2,000 estimated cases of CSE in Rotherham.

Two further Operation Clover trials would follow, as well as Operation Thunder, in regards to non-recent abuse. Eventually, a further 20 were convicted after 21 survivors gave evidence, sentencing criminals to 290 years and 6 months. Others were subsequently jailed, running to the final total of 360 years' imprisonment for multiple perpetrators. Ash's brother Siggi – aka Sageer Hussain – was jailed for 19 years in November 2016, when he was 30 years old. He was found guilty of four counts of rape and one of indecent assault: he had waged a 'campaign of violent rape' and intimidation against a girl who was only 13 at the time.

The National Crime Agency would investigate the rest, making this the biggest abuse investigation in history.

* * *

On the day of Ash's sentencing I went to court with my sister Lisa and Carly Booth. We drove round the back of the court and then sat in a room waiting to be called.

'I don't want to sit here and hide away,' I said, getting impatient. 'I want to go into the main court. I've got nothing to hide or be ashamed of. What do you guys think?' We all agreed, and headed out to sit in the public gallery.

I stared around me. You couldn't see the floor of the courtroom because it was so full of survivors and their families and supporters, plus loads of police and media.

I thought to myself: *Nobody can call me names any more. Nobody can call me a liar.* It was a fantastic feeling, but it didn't last long.

I didn't realise that before the sentences were passed, Ash's barrister, and others, would have the chance to plead their case again in their mitigation statements. To my dismay, Ash's barrister started to claim that Ash's abuse against me was 'consensual'.

I'd written a victim impact statement that Judge Sarah Wright had read previously, and she drew on this in her response to the barrister, addressing Ash directly.

'This wasn't a "relationship" as has been suggested by the defence,' the judge said. 'She was a child and you were an adult. She lost her education, her friends, her family as a result of your actions.'

The judge went on: 'She vividly describes her life as being shattered into a million pieces and she feels she is just held together by sticky tape. Despite the substantial hurdles she has encountered, your victim has shown considerable courage, tenacity and a steely determination in bringing these horrific crimes to the attention of the public.'

I gulped and my heart pounded. I felt proud and I began to quietly cry. Many people were in floods of tears; it was an incredibly intense emotional experience.

When the time came for the individual sentences to be read out we'd been in court for about three hours. Some of the other survivors were crying hysterically by now, having also had some of their victim statements read out and listened to re-caps of evidence, but I stayed calm, wiping my tears away as quickly as they came.

Ash was visible now on the video link, sat in his wheelchair in a prison room. For most of the time throughout the trial he had pretended to be asleep, but suddenly he was alert and wide awake. He appeared to be looking straight at me, though of course he couldn't see me and could only hear what was happening.

I felt no fear: he was a guilty man now. All Ash could do was wait to find out how many years he would be locked up for.

When the judge read out his sentence there were yells and shouts of 'yes' from the women I was sat with, and gasps from all around the courtroom. Lisa and the others all hugged me at the same time, but I sat there motionless. My eyes were drawn to Andrew Norfolk, who was directly in front of me, on the level downstairs.

I nodded my head with a big smile on my face. I was trying to keep calm and dignified even though there were fireworks going off in my stomach. I wanted to scream from the rooftops.

Ash was being sent down for 35 years. I could hardly take it in. *Thirty-five years.* This was a huge sentence, far bigger than I'd dared to hope for.

Thirty-five years was an amazing, fantastic result. Hopefully he would never come out of prison. Relief started to flood through my body.

Bash got 25 years and Bono, who had pleaded guilty to ten offences, got 19 years.

In all, the six guilty abusers received a total of 102 years in prison. This had turned into one of the biggest child abuse trials the country had ever seen.

I was told I could leave the court by a back entrance if I wanted to, but I chose to walk out the front, with my head held high. This was an important decision for me. I was proud of what I'd achieved, and I was going to enjoy and savour this moment of victory.

I spoke to reporters outside. I told them the news hadn't yet sunk in, but that I felt the result would give me closure at last.

'My life starts now,' I said.

And it did.

Epilogue

My childhood was stolen from me, and that's something I've had to learn to live with.

I can't turn back the clock and change the course of my life. If I could, I would tell the trusting little girl I was: 'He is not your boyfriend. This is not love, it is abuse. He is a paedophile who is grooming and abusing you, and being allowed to do so by the very agencies that are here to protect you. This is not normal or OK, this is grooming at its finest. You're not a slag, a criminal, his equal, his girlfriend or his mistress. You're just a child. You're a victim and you're not to blame.'

My abuser not only stole my childhood, he destroyed my mental health and stripped me of the chance of happiness in my twenties. I suffered from major depression, I was left with disengagement and emotional detachment issues and I developed an eating disorder that I only recently defeated. I lost precious years with my family and friends, and because of what he did with Emily I have major trust issues and have never been able to form new friendships. I also lost my education and gained a criminal record. I lost every last shred of my self-esteem, and I almost lost my children.

For more than a decade I failed to recognise my abuse, which led me to unhealthy relationships with others. I was brainwashed so thoroughly that even as an adult I thought it was normal to have abusive boyfriends and to put up with jobs I hated, where I was sexualised all over again, this time for the pleasure of strangers.

My abuser's final insult was to turn his charm on my son and attempt to absorb him into his world. The thought of it still makes me shudder. If only I knew then what I know now. It is something I will have to live with for the rest of my life.

I have been asked many times how I cope, now I know the truth? How am I not crippled by bitterness and regret? How did I find the courage to speak out in public when my whole world was shattered into a million pieces? How did I stand strong and confront my abuser in court, even when I felt like an empty shell of a person, broken and held together by sticky tape?

The answer is simple: I have forgiven him. Staying angry about the past would only make me and the people I love suffer. Only we would lose out, and we have already lost too much. If I don't move on and look to the future I will always be my abuser's victim, and I am not that vulnerable little child any more. I am not what he moulded me to be. I am my own person, and I can use my experiences in a positive way to help others, and to make changes for the better.

Five years ago, I couldn't sit in a room with a group of police officers, no way. I was angry and quite violent. And then I realised that by being constantly angry, the only person I was hurting was myself. It's like me drinking poison and expecting eveyone else to drop dead from it.

The moment I came to terms with myself as a survivor I knew I had to speak out, not only for my family and for myself but also for others who had been affected. We all deserve justice, and I am determined never to give up.

I feel empowered and motivated because I have realised there can be life after abuse, and it can be a great life that is fulfilling and helps others. I have a plan and a purpose: I feel I have the world at my feet.

My aim is to prevent future generations of children from having their lives devastated by child sexual exploitation, and I am working to improve the lives of children who have already been groomed, and to help get them the support and justice they deserve.

I was a founder member of the Rotherham Steering Group, which came together in the wake of the Rotherham abuse scandal and was a group of survivors and family members affected by CSE. I compiled a national plan to help educate professionals, including the National Crime Agency, on how to approach victims of abuse.

I started several campaigns. My education campaign meant I met with the Department of Education to discuss mandatory learning in schools, to ensure all children in the UK are educated around healthy relationships, friendships, grooming and abuse. This comes into effect in 2018.

I also started a licensing campaign asking for all taxis to be installed with CCTV and audio, among other things. Rotherham Council was the first to implement this and I've fed into the national licensing review to have these suggestions put into place nationally. This campaign also covers all areas of licensing including hotels, takeaways and limousines.

In addition I'm campaigning for Sammy's Law. This is a law I want put in place to ensure children can't be charged for committing certain crimes while being groomed. I want anyone who was groomed as a child to be cleared of crimes they committed under the direction of their abuser, on a case-by-case basis. Sammy's Law will help encourage more victims to come forward and will give survivors a much better chance of moving on with their lives, without the burden of a criminal record. This has had the support of chief constables, police crime commissioners, charities, MPs and officials around the UK.

In March 2017, I received a letter from the Criminal Injuries Compensation Authority (CICA) that blamed *me* for being abused. In my opinion, CICA wasn't fit for purpose. I spoke to others nationwide who believed they had been treated badly by CICA and as a result I started a campaign and met with government officials to call for an improvement in their service. I wanted to ensure victims aren't blamed, are compensated accordingly and that all staff are trained properly. Other charities and MPs are supporting me in this campaign and so far it has been successful: CICA has already started to change some of its policies.

There was some bad news in September 2017. A report into Rotherham Council's handling of CSE concluded that no legal or disciplinary proceedings should be brought against any current or former senior officers at the council. It concluded the scandal was 'more cock-up than conspiracy' and blamed 'multiple and systemic failures' rather than any individual. I was disgusted that not a single person involved with Rotherham Council's failings was being held to account. I'm not letting this go. I am fighting for victims to be adequately compensated and I am trying to change employment laws to allow professionals to be punished for failings: mandatory reporting of failings should be compulsory. I'm also striving to shape better services for children and families, working with Rotherham and other councils around the UK.

We have a mountain to climb, but I've already taken great steps. I've met with the Ministry of Justice and the Home Office to ensure those steps continue, which led to me being asked by the government to join a panel of inspiring woman for International Women's Day 2018, to share my work.

I've delivered CSE training to Tact, the UK's largest fostering and adoption charity, and to several police forces, including South Yorkshire and Bedfordshire Police, as well as the National Crime Agency. I've made a government training video on grooming, which is mandatory viewing for NHS professionals. Additionally, I have helped secure millions of pounds' worth of funding for charities, including £3.1 million for Barnado's to fund a team of specialists tackling child sex abuse in Rotherham. My campaign work for more funding for counselling and support services continues.

Most importantly, I have encouraged many other victims to come forward; either by working with them directly or through the hundreds of interviews I have given to the media to raise awareness. I have a website – sammywoodhouse.com – and I'm setting up a company to build on my media and campaign work and deliver motivational talks and consultation work to schools, councils and professionals working with children and vulnerable adults.

No child is immune from the risk of CSE. It doesn't matter what your family background is, what colour you are, how well you are doing at school, what religion you follow or even what sex you are: boys as well as girls are victims of grooming.

I tell other survivors that in coming forward they will not only help themselves, but others too. I had no idea when I told my story that I would be lifting the lid on industrial-scale child abuse in Rotherham, nor did I anticipate how many victims would step forward and give the evidence that is putting child abusers behind bars.

'If I can do it, anyone can,' I tell others, and this is the truth.

I've learned a lot in recent years. I recognise how I always see the best in people, and I've learned how a person can make a difference by having self-belief. I know how powerful words can be. I know there are good professionals as well as bad. I know I can achieve great things, and I know how important it is to surround myself with positive people in order to succeed.

Writing this book has been extremely hard. I have had to return to scary places in my mind in order to tell my story, and I have had to channel the feelings that I hide so deep and don't want to face. If it saves one child from becoming a victim it will have been worth it. If my book encourages one victim to come forward, it will have been worth it. If it educates someone on CSE and the effects it has, it will have been worth it.

CSE is something that's happening not just in Rotherham, but also in every town and city around the globe. It is up to all of us to challenge it, to make the world a safer place for our children, to prevent it from happening and to keep encouraging others to come forward and get justice.

If I could say one thing to every victim of CSE in the UK it would be this:

Believe in yourself. There is nothing more powerful in life than YOUR TRUTH and YOUR VOICE. You don't have to just survive … you can thrive!

I'm proud to say I am Sammy Woodhouse. Thank you for reading my story.

Acknowledgements

Thank you to Rachel Murphy for helping me write my book, for being patient, for understanding how difficult it was for me to write it, for encouraging me and keeping me going in the times I found it so difficult. Also, thanks to my literary agent Jonathan Conway, and Kelly Ellis, Beth Eynon, Lizzie Dorney-Kingdom and everyone else at Blink Publishing.

I'd like to thank the people who have supported me throughout my journey. Chief Constable Jon Boutcher and PCC Kathryn Holloway for being the first to publicly support Sammy's Law, Kylie Morris ISVA and Rape Crisis England and Wales, social worker Nikki Ledingham, family support worker Pat Hickling and the fabulous Natalie Enderby, my best friend Nina, family members Linda and Lisa.

Thank you to the Operation Clover team that investigated and helped bring my abuser to account. Detective Sergeant Steve Smith and Senior Investigating Officer and Detective Chief Inspector Martin Tate. Detective Constable and OIC Andy Stephanek, Detective Constable Carly Booth and Detective Constable Simon Taylor for supporting me through the lengthy investigation. You have all helped me change my life around; I put my trust in you all and I was right to do so. You didn't just help me on my journey, you were a part of it. You are exceptions to South Yorkshire Police. Congratulations on coming second at the national awards!

Thank you to all the members of the Rotherham Steering Group. We are no longer a group but I wish all of you the very best for the future. I will never forget the tears and laughter we shared. Jenny, I am proud of you and your girls. Thank you for being a friend.

I'd like to thank the people in the UK and around the world for all the love and best wishes you have shown me and my family. Your messages of support have been overwhelming but incredible, and we have taken great strength from them.

Andrew Norfolk, you entered my life as a reporter tackling issues others feared to confront. I know how difficult this has been for you but you never gave up despite the hurdles placed in front of you. You took great risks. You gave me a platform to speak so I could tell my truth and use my voice. You have been there for me every step of the way, never giving up hope, always believing in me even when, at times, I didn't believe in myself. You taught me I could be a better person and that there was a light at the end of the tunnel. It should never be a reporter's job to mentally support a survivor but you have. No matter what day or time I needed to talk to someone you were always there. I can't begin to put into words how much strength you have given me. From the day I first met you, you have been an absolute gentleman. I trusted you and I was right to do so. It's an absolute honour to not only know you but to call you a friend. Thank you for always being there, a true selfless hero.

Praise needs to be given to all the brave, courageous survivors and families that came forward to the authorities, having to relive their experiences as I did. Despite all the evidence, abusers wouldn't be jailed or charged without us coming forward. No sentence will ever compensate for what we have all been through, but it will help keep others safe and give us some closure. Our stories not only exposed Rotherham but also helped raise awareness in the UK and around the globe. Its impact shook the world. Not only did we expose CSE, we continued to speak out to help others. Some of our paths may never have crossed or may never do so, some still carry our differences, but together we stood tall, strong and united. We stood together and showed we won't be defeated. To do this it takes strength that only we will ever understand. Be proud. We made a difference. You're inspirational and don't ever let anyone tell you different.

The most important people in my life are, without doubt, my children. Together as a family we have experienced things no one should ever have to, and there have been many times when I didn't think we were going to make it. Despite all the difficulties, we have got through them together. We are now able to move forward and get our life back on track. James has not only had to come to terms with what happened to his mum but has had to deal with the fact his dad was the cause of it, as were his uncles. The mental effect this has had on him has been massive and he has struggled with many things, and for him every day is a battle. Throughout all his difficulties he has supported me every step of the way and encouraged me to keep going. I am extremely proud of both my boys for their strength and patience. I love them both more than life itself. They are my world. They are my heroes.

Child Sexual Exploitation (CSE)

In Rotherham alone, more than 1,500 children were victims of CSE between 1997 and 2013. It is a global problem and no child is immune from the risk of being affected.

What is Child Sexual Exploitation?

- A form of sexual abuse, where an individual or a gang, using money, power or affection, exploit children up to the age of eighteen. This abuse can also be committed online.
- Both males and females of all backgrounds, ethnicities and religious beliefs can be perpetrators.
- Children are often encouraged by the perpetrator/s to bring along friends and siblings of a similar age.
- Victims can be boys or girls from all backgrounds, ethnicities and religious beliefs. They are brainwashed (groomed) into believing they are special, loved and cared for by the perpetrator/s, or they can be exploited through threats and violence.

What are the signs?

- Mood swings: angry, emotional, withdrawn, suicide attempts, depression.
- Bruising and/or scarring on body.
- Receiving gifts.
- Staying out late or not returning home.
- Secretive and distant towards family and friends.
- Skipping education, grades dropping.
- Involved in criminal activity.
- Using alcohol or drugs.
- Eating disorders.
- Not sleeping, plus nightmares, anxiety and panic attacks.
- Violence or aggression towards parents, siblings or animals.
- Sexually transmitted infections.
- Pregnancy or miscarriage.

Why won't a victim come forward?

- Doesn't recognise it as abuse.
- Too difficult to talk about.
- Believes abuser is their boyfriend/ girlfriend, or thinks it's normal.
- Thinks the abuser will change.
- Embarrassed, ashamed, judged, worried will be blamed, rejected, isolated or called a liar.
- Emotionally attached to the abuser.
- Feels it will put them and their family at risk.
- Don't know who to tell or trust.
- Addicted to drugs or alcohol.
- Has committed criminal offences.

What can a parent or carer do?

Keep a diary and make sure everything you log is dated and timed. Share information with the relevant authorities and agencies: the police, medical professionals, Social Services, teachers.

What should you log?

- Dates and times.
- Names or nicknames, ages, physical descriptions, including those of any witnesses.
- Addresses and locations.
- Phone numbers.
- Messages.
- Social media content.
- Car registration numbers, plus the make, model and colour of vehicles.
- Your own activities that day, like what you were wearing and what the weather was like, to help you remember.

All this information could help prevent abuse now, or could be used to jail an abuser in the future. If a child discloses information to you, be as accurate as possible when logging it as you could be called as a witness.

Where can you get help?

See my website sammywoodhouse.com for more information, including advice on online safety and a list of useful organisations. Follow me on Twitter for up-to-date news and links @sammywoodhouse1.